Monotheism and Tolerance

Indiana Series in the
Philosophy of Religion
MEROLD WESTPHAL, EDITOR

Monotheism and Tolerance

Recovering a Religion of Reason

Robert Erlewine

Indiana University Press

BLOOMINGTON & INDIANAPOLIS

This book is a publication of

Indiana University Press

601 North Morton Street
Bloomington, IN 47404-3797 USA

www.iupress.indiana.edu

Telephone orders   800-842-6796
Fax orders   812-855-7931
Orders by e-mail   iuporder@indiana.edu

♾ *The paper used in this publication meets the minimum
requirements of the American National Standard for
Information Sciences—Permanence of Paper for Printed
Library Materials, ANSI Z39.48-1992.*

MANUFACTURED IN THE UNITED STATES OF AMERICA

Library of Congress Cataloging-in-Publication Data

Erlewine, Robert.
    Monotheism and tolerance : recovering a religion of
reason / Robert Erlewine.
        p. cm. — (Indiana series in the philosophy of
religion)
        Includes bibliographical references and index.
        ISBN 978-0-253-35419-8 (cloth : alk. paper) —
ISBN 978-0-253-22156-8 (pbk. : alk. paper) 1. Freedom of
religion. 2. Religious tolerance. 3. Abrahamic religions. 4.
Enlightenment. 5. Cohen, Hermann, 1842–1918. 6. Kant,
Immanuel, 1724–1804. 7. Mendelssohn, Moses, 1729–1786.
I. Title.
    BL640.E75 2010
    201'.5—dc22
                                             2009028609

1 2 3 4 5   15 14 13 12 11 10

For Molly,
I shudder to think where I would be
without you.

CONTENTS

ACKNOWLEDGMENTS

As this project comes to completion, I am struck by the good fortune I have enjoyed in the years I have been working on it. It is hard to express in a few paragraphs the debts I owe and the gratitude I feel toward so many, for their support, insight, and generosity. But I will try.

I would like to begin by thanking Edith Wyschogrod z"l, H. Tristram Engelhardt, and Kenneth Seeskin, who were instrumental in the development of this project in its earliest stages. I would like to thank Matthias Henze for not only introducing me to Jan Assmann's work, but more importantly for serving as a mentor during my time at Rice University and beyond. Gregory Kaplan deserves special mention. During a real time of need as a graduate student, Gregory, at no small cost to himself, stepped up to fill the breach. His wonderfully pugnacious style of pedagogy taught me more about what it means to think carefully and rigorously about a subject than perhaps any other teacher I have had.

I would like to thank Werner Kelber, Jeffrey Kripal, David Cook, Anthony Pinn, David Adcock, Claire Katz, Leah Hochmann, and Hartwig Wiedebach for helping me to develop this project in various capacities. Matt Schunke and Torin Alexander also deserve thanks for being valuable conversation partners during my time at Rice.

The final form of this book is indebted to three scholars in particular. Leora Batnitzky read an earlier version of the manuscript and her insights helped to contextualize my claims in regard to the history of Jewish philosophy, the Enlightenment, and the question of modernity. In addition to his generous responses to my numerous questions about the publishing process, Merold Westphal also provided instructive comments on an earlier version of the manuscript which helped me to avoid hyperbole and clarify my terminology. Finally, Susannah Heschel offered highly insightful suggestions for revision during the copyediting stage, during which she generously worked within my rather tight time constraints.

It is imperative to thank two individuals who have graciously taken me under their wings as a junior colleague. Randi Rashkover read part of the manuscript when it was in an early stage and has been a helpful interlocutor and friend ever since. Martin Kavka deserves special thanks. He has not only been an important interlocutor and editor—he has read and helpfully commented upon almost everything I have written—he also has often served as a mentor (if not a therapist) for me, helping me to navigate various perils of being a professor and scholar. I am very grateful to the two of them.

I would like also like to thank the Provost and Dean of Faculty at Illinois Wesleyan University, Beth Cunningham, for providing much-needed funds for this project. My colleagues in the Religion Department at Illinois Wesleyan University deserve special thanks for providing a lively and pleasant environment in which to work. I would like to thank my department chair, Brian Hatcher, for helping me to navigate the world of publishing. I would like to thank Andrew Pavelich, Carole Myscofski, and Jason Moralee for reading various parts of the project and discussing them with me. Kevin Sullivan deserves special thanks not only for reading and commenting upon various parts of this monograph, but also for his moral support and friendship from the beginning of my time at Illinois Wesleyan. Sonja Fritzsche deserves thanks for her frequent advice regarding the translation of often extremely difficult German prose. I would also like to thank Regina Linsalata for all of her help. I want to thank Andrew Smith for his comments on various chapters of this work, as well as for being an invaluable interlocutor especially in regard to political philosophy and the question of religion. I would furthermore like to thank my students, particularly Drew Snodgrass, Kari Irwin, and the members of my class on Religious Tolerance and Pluralism in the fall semester of 2007.

I would like to thank Dee Mortensen at Indiana University Press for making this publishing experience as pleasant as possible. I would also like to thank David L. Dusenbury at the University of Wales for his excellent copyediting and for the many important questions he raised which helped me to clarify my thinking.

Finally, I would like to thank my family. My family has been a wonderful source of support and encouragement throughout this whole process. My grandparents, Frieda Horowitz, and John and Millicent Erlewine deserve thanks for their generosity and unconditional love. I would like to thank Laura Robey, and the Robey family in general, for welcoming me into their home and for their warmth and love. David, Thuy, Thomas, and Emily Erlewine have been wonderful bastions of support and camaraderie. I would like to especially thank my parents, Christopher and Barbara Erlewine. Their support and enthusiasm for my pursuit of a rather impractical career has never wavered. I am truly lucky to have such a family.

Most importantly I would like to thank my wife, Molly. She is my spouse, my partner, my best friend, and my greatest critic. I could not imagine a life without her. But I cannot fail to also mention my dog, Sawyer, whose tireless disregard for my work has forced me to take myself less seriously.

Part One | Overcoming the Current Crisis

1 | Monotheism, Tolerance, and Pluralism

THE CURRENT IMPASSE

The contemporary values of tolerance and pluralism, so often the object of unhesitating praise, nevertheless pose significant challenges for religious life, at least as it is commonly understood by many major religious traditions. If the religious adherent cedes too much to these principles then she compromises the very foundations of the grand tradition she has inherited or adopted. Yet the dangers of not recognizing these principles, as the news daily attests, leads to endless violence and misery. The present world-historical situation suggests that this problem is particularly acute in regard to the Abrahamic-monotheistic religions, i.e., Judaism, Christianity, and Islam. The structural antagonism and hostility toward the Other[1] which thrives unrestrained in the more extreme strands of these traditions cannot stand unchallenged if we seek to live in peaceful societies. And yet, calls for tolerance and pluralism either go unheeded or only further exacerbate the situation, given that those who make them fail to take into account the contours of the symbolic or discursive structure shared by the Abrahamic religions.[2]

Indeed as the calls for tolerance and pluralism, usually made by secularists and religious liberals, grow stronger in the public arena, one cannot help but notice the growing backlash against them. While I certainly do not wish to claim that the dramatic surge in fundamentalist movements is solely a negative reaction to the increased prominence of the principles of tolerance and pluralism in public life, it is nevertheless no mere coincidence that this phenomenon is manifesting itself with such distressing intensity at the same time as these principles receive increasing emphasis in public life. There is clearly a link between the prominence of tolerance and pluralism in the public sphere and the strong reaffirmations, by more and more religious movements, of the truth and authority of accounts of revelation which seem inimical to these principles.

Are more conservative, traditionalistic conceptions of the monotheistic worldview simply incommensurable with the principles of tolerance and pluralism? When religious traditions find themselves in tension with these principles, to what degree, if at all, should they change in order to accommodate them? Indeed, is the discourse surrounding tolerance and pluralism adequately nuanced to address the complexities of religious life? Or does it possess blind spots and prejudices that make it problematic? These vitally important questions must be addressed. And while it would undoubtedly be beneficial, given our present world-historical situation, if monotheistic religions could find more fruitful ways of dealing with Others than hostility (whether implicit or explicit), which all too frequently emerges in situations involving diversity, this does not justify an unqualified celebration of the principles of tolerance or pluralism. Indeed, secularists and religious liberals haranguing fundamentalists and conservative traditionalists to adopt the principles of tolerance and pluralism, or chastising them for their failure to do so, will not accomplish the reforms they desire. If monotheistic religions are going to constructively deal with their predisposition to agonistic relationships with the Other, and thus to intolerance, then such measures must originate and find their basis within these traditions themselves.[3]

One attempt to ameliorate violent intolerance from within a specific monotheistic tradition—or rather, a particular religious-philosophical tradition of such attempts—can be found in the works of Moses Mendelssohn, Immanuel Kant, and Hermann Cohen. These figures attempt to reconfigure the moments of the discursive structure shared by the Abrahamic monotheisms, so as to ameliorate the monotheistic intolerance which is directed toward the Other without vitiating the monotheistic structure itself. Unlike so many of their contemporaries, and unlike so much secular philosophy and liberal theology (Jewish and Christian) at present, regarding religious tolerance and pluralism, these thinkers of what I call the 'religion of reason trajectory' preserve the basic structure of the monotheistic worldview, including such notions as election and world-historic mission, while still accounting for the social and political aspects—which necessarily involve living and interacting with the Other—of modern existence. As such, their efforts are not only strikingly different from alternative approaches to this vexing problem, but they are also more promising.

Ironically, while Kant—by far the most famous and influential of these three figures—is included in this study, he takes on a rather marginal status within the religion of reason trajectory. Kant is of course the only non-Jewish thinker in this trajectory, and his work is most important as a transition between Mendelssohn and Cohen, as well as for the ways in which it deviates from, and therefore highlights, the shared project of these other thinkers. The attempt to reconfigure and rationalize the basic structure of the monotheistic worldview is, at its core, a project of Diaspora Judaism. Mendelssohn and Cohen lived and worked out their philosophies of religion, of monotheism, as disenfranchised minorities—as Jews in Christian Germany. Both Mendelssohn and Cohen suffered significant discrimination as a result of their Jewish religious commitment and ethnicity. In the times and places in which they wrote, it was essentially taken as self-evident that Christianity was a religion of universality, while Judaism was a religion of sheer particularity.[4] Judaism was cast as a mere ethnicity and a body of laws, a 'religion' lacking spirit.

In this context, perhaps because of the need to defend Judaism and critique the self-satisfied Christian culture of their day, Mendelssohn and Cohen thought more deeply than their Christian peers about the dialectic between particularity and universality at the heart of the monotheistic religions. As a result, while their bodies of work are in constant conversation with, and deeply indebted to, Western (and therefore Christian) philosophy, they philosophize about religion differently than their Christian contemporaries. They recognize the particularity of the religious tradition out of which they philosophize but insist that, despite its particularity, it nevertheless maintains universal significance. In this manner, they are able to create a more nuanced, socially acceptable, and even productive form of religious intolerance—i.e., a way of life that refuses to compromise the truths central to one's religion, without doing violence to the Other on a physical or conceptual level.

To be sure, for many years, in part because of the nature of the situation in which Mendelssohn and Cohen wrote, their work has been dismissed by Jews and non-Jews as mere apologetics, as a failed attempt at dialogue with a German culture that would never accept them. However, I contend that this is not only a misunderstanding of their project, but also that perhaps it was their difficult social and political situations which made them particularly sensitive to the complexities of religious intolerance. Since even 'secularist' discussions in the Enlightenment tacitly presumed the universalism of Christianity, any Emancipation for the Jews required the forfeiture of their particularity. Yet, while both Mendelssohn and Cohen were very much public intellectuals, they refused to compromise their particularity—their Jewishness—even though this carried a cost in their personal lives. Both not only maintained their particularity, but both also insisted that this particularity held universal significance. As Jews in a Christian world, they did not have the luxury of dismissing those with whom they disagreed, even on ultimate matters. However, contrary to the Christian 'universalism' regnant in their respective times, neither Mendelssohn nor Cohen was willing to denigrate the Other even when the Other contended that their truths views were false, anachronistic, and even insidious. As such, their thought provides important resources for our own tumultuous time, when obligations to honor God and neighbor so often seem to be at cross purposes.

The works of the religion of reason trajectory are relevant beyond Judaism, or at least this is the wager of this book, because, as several scholarly works (which I will discuss shortly) argue, the Abrahamic monotheisms share certain basic features (what I call their 'discursive structure') which is itself grounded on a tense dialectic between particularity and universality. Violence that is associated with religious (or at least monotheistic) intolerance is bound up with this dialectic. This is not to suggest that all monotheistic communities are violent as a result of engaging in this dialectic, but rather, when monotheistic communities do embrace violence on religious grounds it tends to be rooted in this dialectic. What is of interest in this trajectory of thought that culminates in the work of Cohen, is that it translates this dialectic between particularity and universality into an ethical monotheism grounded in responsibility for Others. The strength of this strategy, especially as it unfolds in Cohen's work, is that it resists the liberal and secularist desire to undermine this dialectic in the name of tolerance and pluralism, while simultaneously privileging ethical responsibility for the Other. For this reason, Cohen's conception of monotheism provides a responsible foundation for modern Jewish thought. But no less importantly, it deserves the attention of Christian and Islamic philosophers and theologians, in that it offers powerful resources for mitigating the violence that can arise from monotheistic intolerance without forfeiting the very structures constitutive of the monotheistic worldview. That being said, while the religion of reason trajectory engages with the discursive structure shared by the three Abrahamic monotheisms, it is nevertheless deeply rooted in European philosophy and the European Enlightenment. Thus the extent to which it might translate to Islam, if at all, is beyond my scholarly capacities to assess.

In this chapter, I will address the context in which I seek to incorporate or resuscitate the thinkers of the religion of reason trajectory. I will begin the discussion by providing rudimentary definitions of the principles of tolerance and pluralism which are drawn from recent philosophical discussions. Next, I will uncover the structural moments constitutive of the monotheistic worldview, laying bear its inherent agonism with the Other and hence its tension with the principles of tolerance and pluralism. I will then discuss the work of John Hick and Jürgen Habermas, two prominent contemporary thinkers who represent significantly different but highly influential approaches to ameliorating the tension between monotheism and tolerance and/or pluralism. The failure of these thinkers to adequately address this problem, despite their rigorous attempts, will further illuminate the nature of the tension between monotheism and the principles of tolerance and pluralism. By highlighting this impasse, I hope to establish that we have much to learn from this strand of thinkers coming out of the German-Jewish Enlightenment—namely, that they offer alternative ways of thinking about monotheism that remain distinctly modern. Such pioneering efforts cannot be ignored in this time of crisis, when monotheistic intolerance and violence are rampant.

TOLERANCE AND PLURALISM

Though the principles of tolerance and pluralism, as I have noted, receive high praise in the current intellectual climate, what they actually entail, and especially their costs, are often not considered in much depth. Indeed, religiously liberal and secular-minded theorists have been too quick to champion these values without critically thinking through their costs. In order to genuinely appreciate why tolerance and pluralism are problematic for the Abrahamic monotheisms, it is important to consider these principles with some care, rather than offer glib trivializations. Fortunately, tolerance (or toleration)[5] and pluralism have become significant objects of philosophical inquiry in the past few decades. This scholarship will help to clarify the implications of these principles.

Philosophers often define 'tolerance' as a principle which claims that more good arises on a societal or even a moral level in not acting rather than acting on one's moral disapproval regarding the actions,[6] beliefs, and practices of the Other, so long as the Other does not directly obstruct the well-being of oneself or other Others.[7] Thomas Scanlon explains, "Tolerance requires us to accept people and permit their practices even when we strongly disapprove of them. Tolerance thus involves an attitude that is intermediate between wholehearted acceptance and unrestrained opposition."[8] As philosophers such as Jay Newman, Nick Fotion, and Gerard Elfstrom elaborate, tolerance involves a hierarchy in beliefs, in that one considers one's own conceptions or practices to be more true, ethical, or valuable in some sense than those which are held or performed by the Other.[9] However, historian Perez Zagorin points out, philosophical definitions of tolerance such as these neglect not only the historical evolution of the word but also its most common usage, which not only pertains to religion but is essentially "equivalent to the condition of religious freedom."[10] Now, while Zagorin's point is well taken, for our purposes the two conceptions need not be in competition.

If we concede that religious tolerance entails religious freedom, we are nevertheless left with the question of how precisely tolerance relates to religious freedom.[11] Historically, where coexistence between monotheistic religious communities has been achieved prior to and for much of modernity—and indeed, it remains prominent today—it has most often been on the basis of tolerance-as-restraint. That is, one may very well have little or no respect for the beliefs and practices of the Other, in fact, one may find much that is wrong with them, but still refrain from actively inhibiting the Other's pursuit of what is entailed by her own conception of human flourishing. However, at least historically, there have been clear limits to this restraint which were often derived from theological and political concerns rather than philosophical ones. Monotheistic religions have shown themselves grudgingly amenable to tolerance-as-restraint in this vein, usually when there was one dominant monotheistic religion tolerating other, smaller monotheistic communities, and there was little danger of these smaller communities exerting significant influence in the public sphere.

It is important to clarify, however, that for tolerance-as-restraint to count as genuine tolerance, and not a mere concession to political necessity or pragmatic opportunism, one must not work for or intend to work for in some future, however distant, the eventual elimination of the otherness of the Other, simply seeing the Other qua Other as having a merely temporary existence. That is, even if one ascribes little to no worth to their beliefs and practices, one must not actively intend for her otherness to be eliminated.

However, with the rise of democracies, the privatization of religion in modernity and so on, tolerance has come to increasingly take on connotations of respect which is owed to the beliefs and practices of the Other even if one disagrees with her on doctrinal matters. This particularly modern form of tolerance, what I term tolerance-as-respect, demands that the Other be recognized as a fellow citizen whose beliefs and practices must be recognized as politically—if not epistemologically or metaphysically—worthwhile, or at least worthy of a fair hearing.[12]

'Pluralism' is a position which rejects the privileging of any one value or worldview over all others because it places inherent value in the diversity of perspectives. Pluralism goes further than tolerance in that it rejects the hierarchal privileging of one's own position over the Other's as morally and politically problematic. As David O. Wong points out, the pluralist fuses "moral relativism" with "one or more ethical premises."[13] Underlying this skeptical egalitarianism is the view that human beings are radically finite, historically and culturally situated beings who lack any capacity to climb above their own contingency in regard to truths and values. By forfeiting the accessibility of any comprehensive truth, pluralists, as their name suggests, place inherent value in the diversity of worldviews.[14]

Tolerance and pluralism, despite their differences, are both predicated upon a profound regard for the Other. They involve curtailing either the ramifications of one's beliefs (tolerance), or acknowledging the limits of one's entire worldview (pluralism), as an implication of the recognition of the Other. At their foundations then, both tolerance and pluralism privilege a symmetrical relationship between the self and Other and demand that her otherness not only be suffered, but respected as such (though there is some variance as to how much one must respect it). Intolerance, then, is the unwillingness to suffer the otherness of the Other, the unwillingness to limit the implications of one's worldview in order to make room for the Other and her worldview. And while 'intolerance' is often used as a pejorative term, it has no negative valence in this study. To be sure, there are problematic forms of intolerance, but that need not mean that all forms of intolerance are problematic as such. In fact, there are various forms of intolerance, and we have been too quick to paint all points of view which do not privilege the symmetrical relationship with the Other with the same tarnished brush.

Regardless of whether tolerance and pluralism are worthy of the praise they so often receive in our current political and intellectual climate, they are by no means easily achieved. As individuals enmeshed in disparate, incompatible, and often mutually antagonistic worldviews are regularly brought into contact with each other in an increasingly globalized world, tolerance and pluralism are frequently invoked as the solution to the tensions which inevitably arise. It is imperative to think carefully regarding what degree and in what capacity entrenched and intractable worldviews, like those of the Abrahamic monotheisms, which offer a comprehensive vision of the universe and human existence, can reconcile themselves with these principles, if at all.

MONOTHEISM

In recent years a variety of scholars have written about an agonism toward the Other that is inherent in the Abrahamic monotheisms.[15] Unfortunately, these scholars operate independently from one another and rarely refer to one another, much less make use of one another's work. In this section, I will bring together their disparate insights and synthesize them with each other and my own suggestions, in order to generate a more expansive understanding of this agonism and the structure that underlies it.[16] I will use Martin Jaffee's article, "One God, One Revelation, One People: On the Symbolic Structure of Elective Monotheism,"[17] particularly his account of the "discursive structure" common to the Abrahamic or what he terms "elective-monotheisms,"[18] as a framework by which to incorporate and synthesize these reflections. This structure is an attempt to elucidate the agonistic logic which underlies many if not most sects and groups within Judaism, Christianity, and Islam from which the tension with the modern values of tolerance and pluralism emerges. To be sure, this is an ahistorical and essentialist model—whose purity probably few if any empirical iterations have fully embodied—but I bring it forward for the purpose of highlighting the fundamental tension between the modern values of tolerance and pluralism and the logic underlying monotheistic religions. This will provide a framework in which to explore the innovations of the thinkers of the religion of reason trajectory: Mendelssohn, Kant, and Cohen.

For the purposes of this work, I take as axiomatic Jaffee's claim that "Judaism, Christianity, and Islam are equally rich, historical embodiments of a single structure of discourse that underlies the historically developed symbol systems specific to each community."[19] That is, while the Abrahamic monotheisms—i.e., Judaism, Christianity, and Islam—have different symbolic systems and historical traditions, they share a common discursive structure, one whose metaphysical underpinnings and structural moments manifest an agonism toward the Other, or at least the otherness of the Other. This discursive structure and its metaphysical underpinnings follow a logic that is rooted in a tense dynamic between particularity and universality, wherein a particular community is imbued with universal significance, and as a result is brought into conflict with all other particular communities, which lack this universal significance. I term this logic 'scriptural universalism.'[20]

According to Jaffee the discursive structure shared by Abrahamic monotheisms consists of four schematic points or moments.[21] The first moment occurs when the universal and transcendent Creator God makes itself manifest to a particular human community, what Jaffee terms the "Recipient Community," in an act of revelation. Second, this particular community which has been chosen or elected by God, in turn, gives itself over in obedience to the Creator's love and will. The Creator's love is bestowed at the price of a collective endeavor which God entrusts to the community, and which the community willingly agrees to undertake. The third moment constitutes the 'lived time' of history, the gap between the original revelatory event and the community's successful completion of the task for which God unified the community in the first place. And finally, there is the eschatological conclusion, when the community fulfills its mission, which brings about the "reconciliation of the human order with the divine love and will."[22]

In the moment of revelation, the universal God of creation becomes manifest to a particular community through an act of revelation. Though not discussed at length in Jaffee's essay, this is a significant moment for understanding the logic of scriptural universalism and its tension with the principles of pluralism and tolerance. Egyptologist and cultural historian Jan Assmann in particular has written extensively on the intolerant nature of revelation in monotheism. Assmann has famously characterized monotheistic religions as "counter-religions" (*Gegenreligionen*), in that simultaneous with their claims to truth, they reveal "a counterpart, that they oppose" (*ein Gegenüber, das sie bekämpfen*).[23] That is, monotheistic religions have "an emphatic concept of truth [*emphatischer Wahrheitsbegriff*]. They all rest on a distinction [*Unterscheidung*] between true and false religion, and proclaim on this basis a truth which is not compatible with other truths, but rather relegate all other traditional or concurring truths to the sphere of the false [*Bereich des Falschen*]."[24] Ultimately, Assmann claims that revelation is the source from which monotheistic religions draw this antagonistic energy.[25]

However, Assmann's insights leave some unanswered questions. What is the nature of this notion of 'truth' which is operative in revelation?[26] And why does the revelation of this truth in and of itself generate antagonistic energy? To be sure, the event of the universal God of creation becoming manifest in an act of self-revelation and giving information to a particular community would qualitatively distinguish and privilege this community above all others. But would this qualitative distinction, or election, by itself be sufficient to entail the violent antagonism of which Assmann speaks? Why would it not merely privilege the group in question? Why must it also entail hostility toward those who are outside the community? I mean to suggest that Assmann's account is not sufficiently foundational to understand the origins of this antagonism toward the Other. To understand this, we must go beyond the moments of the discursive structure shared by the Abrahamic monotheisms and approach the metaphysical foundation that underpins the monotheistic worldview as a whole.

The antagonistic energy that permeates revelation in the monotheistic worldview is ultimately rooted in a condition which is prior to revelation. This prior condition is, in fact, a metaphysical foundation, a conception of reality and human nature which anchors all the moments that comprise the discursive structure common to the Abrahamic monotheisms. It is this particular metaphysical conception of reality, this 'truth,' which is manifested in revelation but also makes revelation itself necessary, that is, requires the formation of a particular monotheistic community which sets itself in opposition to all Others. This foundation is also what necessitates the community's historical mission, which will conclude in the eschatological fulfillment of this mission. It is important to extend beyond the researches of both Jaffee and Assmann in order to explore the metaphysical paradigm which both situates the discursive structure of elective monotheisms, and serves as the ultimate ground of their antagonistic intolerance toward the Other. This foundational aspect of the monotheistic *Weltanschauung* has been carefully explored by Moshe Halbertal and Avishai Margalit in their book *Idolatry.*[27]

As Halbertal and Margalit point out, the metaphysical paradigm operative in the monotheistic worldview is fundamentally teleological: God created the world and everything in it, including human beings, with an express purpose in mind. In order to understand God's purpose for human beings, however, it is important to bear in mind that the word 'purpose' itself is significantly ambiguous when it comes to human existence. On the one hand, there are *defined* purposes, which correlate roughly to the roles a person might play in life, which are specific in nature and more or less assessable in terms of success or failure. An example of a defined purpose might be 'to become a practicing attorney in the state of Arizona.' There are fairly clear criteria by which one can assess whether someone has succeeded in this regard. On the other hand, there are undefined purposes, which pertain to that which underlies all the specific roles that a person might play, i.e., the attribute of the human as such. *Undefined* purposes involve issues of lifestyle, such as 'to live a good life,' where what constitutes success and failure is harder to ascertain than with defined ones, in that the criteria appear to be more relative. These are much harder to assess as they generally involve judgments of value where the criteria are more personally or culturally specific.[28]

Abrahamic monotheisms are premised upon the belief that the ultimate undefined purpose—the underlying attribute of the human as such—which is considered by monotheistic religions to be unquestionably more significant than defined purposes, is actually metaphysically or ontologically defined. By means of revelation—the giving of holy texts filled with laws, doctrines, and commandments—monotheistic religions seek to provide an account of the definitive, paradigmatic way that human beings ought to live their lives. That is, revelation discloses that this ultimate undefined purpose is in fact defined, and that it is to be fulfilled through following specific laws, rituals, norms, doctrines, etc. Monotheistic religions view revelation as the event of God providing the members of the community in question with the means by which to discern what this underlying, metaphysical account of the human as such is—or to use our own terms, the divinely ordained human *telos*—and more importantly, how to harmonize themselves with it. Those outside the community lack this vital knowledge, both of the specific nature of the undefined purpose which has been rendered defined, and how to go about realizing it.

While some antagonistic energy is generated in the distinction between the elected community and those outside of it as a result of revelation disclosing the universal human *telos*, i.e., that the ultimate undefined purpose is in fact defined and that the means of realizing it are quite specific, this energy grows more intense in the moment that follows revelation in the discursive structure of Abrahamic monotheisms. All human beings outside the elected community, i.e., those not privy to its revelation, lack access to what revelation discloses, namely, the prescribed beliefs, norms, laws, codes, etc., which render the undefined purpose determinate and defined. Thus, those outside of the elected community are now seen to be rooted in error, in a state of disharmony with the metaphysical order of the cosmos. The result of this is that the person living without revelation fails to live according to her own "dominant purpose," her own inherent *telos* as a human being.[29] While Halbertal and Margalit claim that all religions attempt to transform the ultimate undefined purpose into a defined one, the research of cultural historians such as Assmann and Jaffee suggests that this process carries a particularly antagonistic charge in monotheistic religions.

The antagonistic energy generated in revelation continues to foment in the transition from revelation to the next structural moment, the formation of the elected community by means of the mission entrusted to it by God. Bearing in mind the metaphysical doctrine of the universal human *telos* underlying the structural moments of monotheism, it is a mistake to think of the elected (monotheistic) community as either purely particularistic or purely universal. Literary critic Regina Schwartz highlights this ambiguity when she writes, "Monotheism is a myth that grounds particular identity in universal transcendence."[30] That is, the doctrine of the universal metaphysical *telos* of humanity has been disclosed to a particular community by the universal God in the form of revelation, and thus, only members of this specific community, as opposed to all others, can realize this *telos*. In scriptural universalism a dialectic of particularity and universality is in play whose importance cannot be overestimated.

Recent defenders of monotheism, such as Lenn Goodman,[31] Erich Zenger,[32] and Jürgen Werbick,[33] highlight the universality of the monotheistic God: The monotheistic God is the God of the universe and consequently of *all* human beings. However, they fail to take note of the important point which Jaffee makes: "Elective monotheism . . . is not primarily about God as he is in himself or in relationship to the created order of nature. It is much more about God as he is in relationship to historical human communities—a relationship characterized by the opposition of love and hate."[34] To be sure, the transcendent God as the creator of the universe is the God of all human beings, and as such is a universal figure. However, in and of itself, this does not entail that the principle of equality characterizes God's relationships with humanity. In fact, the identity that this God demands the elected community constitute is not inclusive in its universality but rather agonistic in its particularity.[35] While the mission which has been entrusted to the community by God carries universal significance—as the very fate of the world may hang in the balance—there is by no means an inclusive attitude toward those outside the community.[36] The mission entrusted to the community consists in restoring the human world to the way God wants it to be, i.e., life according to the laws and statutes in the revealed texts which alone bring one into accord with the universal human *telos*. Those who do not recognize the holy canon and live by its teachings, therefore, are not simply out of sync with the metaphysical order of the cosmos (i.e., in error), but are failing to live according to God's will (i.e., in sin). Since Abrahamic monotheisms link the metaphysical conception of the human *telos* with God's will, as Margalit points out, for these religions "error and evil should not be distinguished."[37] In short, the Other, she who stands outside the elected community, is not only alienated from her own *telos* but is also an obstruction to God's plan. She is God's enemy, worthy of hatred.[38]

Now that the community has been "galvanized" by its reception of revelation, it engages in a "redemptive historical career, a struggle to make manifest throughout the human world the reality of the Creator's self-disclosure and to transform the human order in correspondence to the Creator's love and will."[39] However, in order to bring about this eschatological redemption, as Assmann's research in particular has shown, all other conceptions of the human *telos*, the divine, and the nature of existence must be radically negated. That is, other cultures and religions and their attempts to render the undefined purpose of human existence determinate must be shown to consist of falsehood and lies, and thus to be negated and opposed. As a result the Abrahamic monotheisms, which are predicated upon this radical distinction between true and false religion, are permeated with moral and political significance. Or in the words of Assmann, "Monotheism is in its core political theology."[40]

History, the third moment of the discursive structure of Abrahamic monotheisms, is the 'lived time' in which members of the community actually encounter Others. It is the time in which this conflict with the Other is carried out. As Jaffee explicates:

History is the stage of the community's struggle to be worthy of its call. First, it struggles with its own internal resistance to the Creator's call, seeking to purge itself of flaws that it shares with humanity as a whole. This is the struggle to embody obedience and faith both individually and collectively. Second, but no less important, it struggles against the resistance to its mandate of the humanity beyond the community.[41]

This quote reveals that in the phase of history, the community's identity is constructed by the community defining itself against Others who stand both inside and outside of it. This struggle for identity has great importance for the Abrahamic-monotheistic worldview during the time in which the world remains unredeemed. It is this elected community alone that serves as the vital link between the human world and God, and thus, it is of the utmost importance that the community be worthy of its God-given task. Jaffee points out how the situation is made even more volatile because, "Within historical time, the Creator's presence and love are coterminous with the borders of the recipient community, nurturing it in its battle against the Other, the negation of the recipient community, and the enemy of the Creator."[42] In this passage, the word 'battle' can be a bit misleading, in that the mission of the elected community is to simultaneously preserve the purity of the divine message *against* the Other as well as to bring the message *to* the Other *for* the Other. However, 'battle' is ultimately appropriate, because according to the monotheistic worldview there will always be resistance to the message by the Other within history, and thus struggle with the Other in some form or other is inevitable.[43]

In order to understand the significance of the structural moment of history, the moment in which the actual mission or task of the elected community is carried out, the 'lived time' as it were, in which monotheistic communities encounter the Other, it is necessary to recapitulate the first three moments of the discursive structure of the Abrahamic monotheisms in terms of the dialectic of particularity and universality mentioned earlier. Monotheistic intolerance involves a tense and dynamic relationship between particularism and universalism. In revelation, the one true God of the universe, i.e., the *universal* God, reveals itself and a set of doctrines containing *universal* significance to a *particular* community. These doctrines contain universal significance in that they reveal the universal *telos* which is normative for all of humanity, and the particular ways in which human beings fulfill it. The implication of this act of revelation is that a particular community alone grasps, and thus can fulfill, the universal human *telos* ordained by the universal God. All other peoples and communities, as a result of their lack of access to this revealed knowledge, fail to live in accordance with this universal *telos*, and thus are estranged from the universal

God. That is, according to the Abrahamic monotheisms, a *particular* people is elected, and thus imbued with *universal* significance, through being entrusted with a task to bring to the rest of the world the knowledge of its *universal* significance that was revealed to it in its *particularity*. Until that happens, however, there is a tense relationship between those inside the elected community and those outside of it. Those outside the community are not simply those who need to receive the doctrine of revelation, but also those who oppose God by not living according to God's will.

The phase that Jaffee calls the "Historical Drama,"[44] namely, the struggle between the elected community and idolaters, reveals that the discursive structure of the elective monotheisms allows for a range of different modes of expressing their universally significant message. We know from history that Abrahamic monotheisms have embraced such modalities of promulgating their message as bearing witness, proselytizing, and forced conversion. And to be sure, Judaism, Christianity, and Islam are internally multifaceted and incredibly diverse, and each of these religious traditions has gone through many different stages of development. With this in mind, it is helpful to think of these modalities as a range of options that monotheistic religions have open to them that are commensurable with their discursive structures. Thus, even if certain traditions have historically tended to favor specific modalities over others, there is no necessary connection between a particular tradition and a particular modality that must be assumed at the outset.

All three modalities evince intolerance toward the Other, in that they are all rooted in overcoming the otherness of the Other. Bearing witness, or serving as a 'light to the nations' by means of the conduct and way of life of the members of a community, is the least intrusive and confrontational of the modalities of promulgation. While there are many forms of proselytizing, the forms under discussion here are the more aggressive sorts, which are bound up with power imbalances such that there are clear financial and political benefits for converting. This tactic involves a subtle, albeit very real, violence against the otherness of the Other, in that it presents coercive incentives for conversion that are rooted in disproportionate power.[45] Forced conversion, which often takes place alongside conquest or conflict, is more explicitly violent toward the Other. Thus, while all three are strictly speaking 'intolerant' insofar as all of them involve a community that works in some fashion to break down the otherness of the Other, it is important to point out that the latter two modalities involve violent forms of intolerance, whereas the bearing-witness modality is non-violent.

Given that I am privileging the work of two Jews who lived in the Diaspora and were themselves victims of aggressive proselytizing by Christians,[46] it should not be surprising that the method of promulgation I will champion here is that of bearing witness.[47] While Mendelssohn lived and wrote in the eighteenth century and Cohen in the late nineteenth and early twentieth centuries, both were very much shaped by the so-called 'Emancipation of the Jews.' While this historical situation is obviously unique, it is also clear that the emancipation process reveals social and political processes, as well as philosophical and theological challenges, that apply more broadly. I want to be quite explicit, however, that by no means do I want to suggest that only Judaism has the capacity to bear witness, while Christianity and Islam rely on violent forms of promulgation. Such a claim is not only false, but it undermines my own argument. It is the wager of this book that the strategy laid out by the religion of reason trajectory of thinkers should be accessible to, or open to appropriation by, the other Abrahamic monotheisms.

However, before we get to philosophical projects of Mendelssohn, Kant, and Cohen, it is important to realize that whether violent or not, there is a very real intolerance in the discursive structure shared by the Abrahamic monotheisms. Thus, we need to return to the model laid out by Jaffee and in particular its final moment, the *eschaton*. Here, the intolerant foundations of the monotheistic worldview can be seen with utmost clarity. The struggle between the elected human community and all other human communities ends, and the gap between human beings and God is healed. However, this reconciliation between God and humanity means one of two things, neither of which is savory from a tolerant or pluralist perspective. Either the Other is incorporated into the elected community, throwing off her old, corrupt and idolatrous ways, converting to the true way of life, and serving the universal God of creation properly, or the Other is simply annihilated physically and spiritually.[48] Either way, the Other as such ceases to exist.

HICK AND HABERMAS

John Hick and Jürgen Habermas, two preeminent thinkers regarding issues of intercultural and inter-religious discourse who nonetheless operate in significantly different philosophical idioms, both attempt to ameliorate the tension between Abrahamic monotheism and the principles of tolerance and pluralism. Whereas Hick attempts to provide a metaphysical account of religious pluralism, Habermas attempts to domesticate the violent and intolerant tendencies of monotheistic religions through recourse to his post-metaphysical account of communicative rationality and the epistemic processes of modernity. Despite the vast differences of approach between Hick and Habermas, both positions end up with remarkably similar results vis-à-vis the discursive structure shared by the elective monotheisms. Neither the philosophical-theological approach of Hick nor the secular, discourse-oriented approach of Habermas can envision a solution to the problem of monotheistic intolerance without repudiating the discursive structure of the elective monotheisms. Simply put, the solutions proffered by Hick and Habermas require nothing less than that monotheistic religions be stripped of their discursive structure.

Despite the fact that Hick and Habermas fail to present solutions that speak to the Abrahamic monotheisms qua elective monotheisms, it is nevertheless extremely useful to explore their approaches. Not only are their respective positions highly influential for many subsequent approaches—religious and secular—to the issue of religious tolerance and/or pluralism, but more importantly, their thought best illuminates the vexed nature of the problem of monotheistic intolerance where they fail to address this issue adequately. Ultimately, despite their significant differences, both thinkers prioritize the symmetrical relationship with the Other such that one's own beliefs and practices cannot take priority, at least not in any straightforward sense, over the beliefs and practices (i.e., the otherness) of the Other. Given that both Hick and Habermas demand equal regard for the beliefs and practices of the Other, they categorically reject any sort of unilateral vision that marginalizes the Other and her otherness. In contrast, on a foundational level the monotheistic religions are inherently bound up with an ambiguity often verging on agonism toward the Other herself, and which maintains a hostility (whether implicit or explicit) toward the otherness of the Other. As a result of this shared stress on symmetrical relations between the self and the Other, neither Hick nor Habermas is able to provide a framework in which the moments of the discursive structure of the elective monotheism can be sustained. This disconnect with the monotheistic worldview is illustrative of a certain foundational incommensurability between the modern principles of tolerance and pluralism and the discursive structure of the elective monotheisms.

Hick, who writes as a theologian within the Christian tradition as well as a philosopher of religion, thematizes the epistemic issues surrounding religious pluralism, providing a framework in which all religions are seen as possessing (at least potentially) equal value. Hick's project largely consists in working out a transcendental metaphysical scheme that seeks to elucidate the conditions under which religious diversity and equality between religious traditions regarding access to salvation and transcendence become plausible without impugning the realism of religious claims, at least not entirely, in the process.[49] That is, Hick attempts to provide the conditions for the intelligibility of religious diversity without reducing it to mere psychological projection or other naturalistic reductions. A main impetus for Hick's work is to undermine the agonism of competing religious claims for truth, including the agonism in the heart of the elective monotheisms. My concern is not with the philosophical tenability of Hick's attempt to provide an account of the conditions for the intelligibility of religious diversity without reductionism, a task which has already garnered a great deal of attention, much of it critical.[50] Rather, my concern lies with the relationship of Hick's thought to the discursive structure shared by the Abrahamic monotheisms.

Hick is clearly concerned with the agonistic tendency of the elective monotheistic religions, and indeed, his theology vigorously attempts to counteract the tendency of monotheistic religions to regard the beliefs, actions, and practices of the Other as inferior to their own. Without sacrificing the monotheistic idea that God deserves primary recognition,[51] Hick struggles to show how the otherness of the Other is also a form of recognition of God, and indeed an equally valid one. However, there are two ways Hick can pursue this agenda. As a Christian theologian he can work within the discursive structure of the elective monotheisms, or he can make a case that Christianity no longer needs this framework. Hick chooses the latter. My task here is not to impugn this choice on philosophical grounds but merely to show the implications of such a choice.

Hick, the philosopher *and* Christian, is willing to forsake the structural moments of election, history/historical mission, and *eschaton*—in addition to transfiguring revelation beyond recognition—for the sake of a symmetrical relationship with the Other. In order to do justice to the veridical capacities of the religious traditions of the Other and the experiences to which they attest, Hick devises his 'pluralist hypothesis.' According to this hypothesis God, or rather "The Eternal One"[52]—the pluralistic expression for the divine that Hick prefers—operates roughly along the lines of the Kantian categories of *Noumenon* and *Phenomenon*. That is, Hick distinguishes between the Eternal One as it exists in-itself and as it exists for-us. Thus, while the Eternal One (in-itself) genuinely exists, the particular shape or "the concrete form" in which the Eternal One (for-us) manifests itself to human consciousness, is shaped and determined "by cultural factors." Therefore, Hick claims, "different human awarenesses of the Eternal One represent different culturally conditioned perceptions of the same infinite divine reality."[53] This metaphysical 'hypothesis' about the divine and human perception of it, allows Hick to make the counter-intuitive claim that "Yahweh and Shiva are not rival gods, or rival claimants to be the one and only God, but rather two different concrete historical *personae* in terms of which the ultimate divine Reality is present and responded to by different large historical communities within different strands of the human story."[54]

Hick's philosophy of religious pluralism is predicated upon a notion

of religion and religiosity which eschews notions of revelation that privilege intellectual and doctrinal content, preferring more experiential ones
instead. Rather than the divine disclosing itself to one 'elected' community and providing it with laws, norms, and doctrines necessary for living
in accordance with the universal human *telos*, which engenders a world-
historical mission, Hick argues that contact with the divine is much more
universal. The divine manifests itself in religious experience, which has a
transformative effect on human beings, regardless of the religio-cultural
tradition through which this contact is mediated. Hick posits, "For our
human commerce with God does not consist only or even mainly in our
holding certain beliefs, but above all in experiencing the reality of God as
the lord in whose presence one is."[55] While there are numerous traditions
which differ widely regarding their conceptions of the divine and even differ about what this experience of the divine calls us as human beings to do,
Hick claims that there is an underlying continuity across religions and religious experience. This continuity or constant that Hick finds "manifestly
taking place—and taking place, so far as human observation can tell, to
much the same extent" across all the major extant religious traditions—is
"the transformation of human existence from self-centeredness to Reality-
centeredness."[56] As a result, different religious traditions are merely "alternative soteriological 'spaces,'" with no tradition possessing any inherent
superiority to any other.[57]

The religious pluralism of Hick's framework, which results not only in
the inability to find criteria to assess a particular religion but also in the in-
appropriateness of any endeavor to find such criteria, has ramifications that
transcend the epistemological/existential status of the divine vis-à-vis the
human. Hick's thought has significant implications for what Halbertal and
Margalit have termed the 'undefined purpose' of the human being, which
becomes the divinely ordained human *telos* in monotheistic religions. Hick
is attempting to undercut monotheistic intolerance at its root by removing
the agonistic elements from the divinely ordained human *telos*. To briefly
review, Halbertal and Margalit argue that all religions attempt to render
the undefined purpose of the human fixed and determinate through prescribed laws, beliefs, mores, and codes.[58] And I have extended this point
by claiming that cultural historians like Jaffee and Assmann have shown
that the rendering of the undefined purpose defined and determinate in
Abrahamic monotheistic religions is particularly antagonistic toward rival
understandings of the human *telos*, given that these religions understand
that their laws, beliefs, mores, and codes were disclosed by the universal
God to a particular community. As a result, monotheistic religions tend
to view the claims of other religions as not merely error, but as that which
leads one away from God, i.e., as sin. Hick tries to circumvent this agonism

by claiming that such an attitude toward the religion of the Other is un-warranted and erroneous. His argument rests on the premise that these different, apparently conflicting conceptions of the universal human *telos* are in fact not in competition with each other, but are rather equally viable alternatives for fostering "the transition from self-centeredness to Reality-Centeredness."[59] Hick's position implies that the doctrines of all religions (or at least what he will often vaguely refer to as all 'great religions') foster the fulfillment of a common universal human *telos,* which is certainly a claim that would be quite precarious to bear out through empirical and comparative research across traditions. As Keith Ward points out, Hick attempts to steer the reader away from such concerns about particular-ity through talk about religion and transcendence in only the vaguest and most abstract terms.[60]

While Hick argues that he has good theological grounds for his plural-ist hypothesis, given that all religious traditions account for the infinite or mysterious nature of God/the divine, which defies our finite attempts to grasp and understand it,[61] such a position does great violence to the discur-sive structure shared by the elective monotheisms. The pluralist hypothesis eradicates the tense dynamic between universality and particularity which is at the heart of scriptural universalism, the logic by which the structural moments of revelation, election, history/historical mission, and *eschaton* unfold. By rendering revelation universal, election and the world-historic mission become not only unnecessary but wrongheaded, and the notion of the *eschaton* becomes mere mythology. According to Hick, Christians "can revere Christ as the one through whom we have found salvation, with-out having to deny other points of reported saving contact between God and man. We can recommend the way of Christian faith without having to discommend other ways of faith."[62] It is imperative to notice that while ostensibly operating out of an explicitly Christian, and therefore mono-theistic framework, Hick has undermined or transfigured every moment constitutive of the basic structure shared by the Abrahamic monotheisms. Hick is able to reconcile Christianity with pluralism only by entirely shed-ding the discursive structure of the elective monotheisms, a move which he clearly does not view as problematic. Nevertheless, it should hardly be any surprise that Hick has raised the ire of many conservative Christian theologians, including Pope Benedict XVI, who are not as willing to part with the foundations and structure of the monotheistic worldview.[63]

Habermas, operating in a very different tradition and philosophical idiom from Hick, works to rehabilitate the notion of rationality for con-temporary thought after the attacks leveled at it by postmodernism. By grounding rationality in language—communicative rationality and lin-guistic competence—Habermas argues against notions of incommensurable worldviews and language games in endless conflict. Rather, he seeks to provide a social theory in which disputes can be worked out through rational discussion, through the reaching of non-coerced consensuses, and where a decentering of the self takes place so that that it can take into account the Other's point of view. Habermas brings this set of concerns to the problem of monotheistic intolerance, particularly in constitutional democracies, in order to work out the necessary conditions for religious tolerance and pluralism.

Habermas's social theory grounds reason in the rationality inherent in the processes of human communication, which he terms 'communicative rationality.' Communicative rationality develops teleologically toward a rationalizing of the lifeworld, toward a society driven more and more by rationally achieved consensus, by mutual understanding—agreement based on reasons—rather than various forms of coercion or unquestioned authority. However, this process of the teleological development of communicative rationality and its hold on human beings and society is a historical-developmental one. This process develops toward forms of society premised around achieving a consensus freely reached by all the members of society who participate equally in this process of mutual understanding.[64] Reasons must be given, and the participants must be free from coercion in their acceptance or rejection of these reasons. As Habermas puts it, "Every consensus rests on an intersubjective recognition of criticizable validity claims." That is, consensuses depend on the productive power of argumentation, of the giving of reasons, and of "*mutual criticism.*"[65] The consensus-reaching force of argumentation, of reason-giving, is not limited to people within a culture, but can, with great care and dedication, take place across cultures, fostering an international, inter-cultural community.[66]

Habermas propounds a "procedural notion of rationality,"[67] premised on the belief that there is the possibility for genuine dialogue across traditions and 'language games,' and that a mutually agreed upon 'truth' or understanding can be reached between very different parties. Habermas's social-political philosophy is predicated upon processes through which exclusionary traditions and narratives give way to the public sphere where everyone can participate in shaping the society. The public sphere is supposed to be a neutral territory where traditions and their hierarchies are systematically bracketed out, in order that, in the words of one critic, "all participants agree on *how* argumentation is to take place."[68]

Habermas's philosophical position is mostly in line with tolerance, albeit configured as tolerance-as-inclusion, whereby self and Other reach common ground and consensuses about such issues as community-formation by means of the giving of reasons and argument, in processes which are oriented by the rationality inherent in language. And yet, Habermas nevertheless maintains a complex relationship with pluralism. On the one hand, Habermas critiques the fundamental assumptions of pluralism for precluding the possibility of reaching any sort of consensus on an *a priori* basis, positing as it does an implicit metaphysical fissure between the self and Other.[69] On the other hand, despite Habermas's disputes with pluralists such as Jean-François Lyotard, he insists that there are occasions when this principle is essential. When it comes to views of the lifeworld as a whole, what he terms 'metaphysics,' Habermas is convinced that there is no possibility for rational consensus, and thus the adoption of the value of pluralism is necessary.[70] As a result, questions such as whether there is a divinely ordained human *telos* and what the nature of this *telos* might be, if it exists, are beyond the pale of rational discussion, without hope of reaching a consensus. In such instances, where discussion and deliberation are ruled out, tolerance and pluralism are essential. Thus matters of ultimate concern, i.e., those matters which are most important to Abrahamic monotheisms, Habermas insists must be bracketed and placed beyond the pale of public discourse. For this reason, Habermas has been widely critiqued as being insensitive to religious concerns.

While Habermas's social theory maintains a complex relationship with tolerance and pluralism, to the degree that these principles exist in his thought, they are grounded upon his belief in the possibility of a "non-coercively unifying, consensus-building force of a discourse in which the participants overcome their at first subjectively biased views in favor of a rationally motivated agreement."[71] Tolerance and pluralism are essential to the degree that traditions and their narratives, religious or otherwise, continue to play essential roles in the lives of human beings, particularly in regards to conceptions of the good, conceptions which the public sphere must exclude and which procedural philosophy cannot articulate.[72]

In the last few decades, Habermas has begun to take religion more seriously in his writings and thought, even acknowledging religion as an important aspect of contemporary existence. It can provide consolation in the face of the existential crises that regularly beset human beings and for which philosophy, now deprived of any metaphysical claims, can no longer serve as a surrogate.[73] In the wake of 11 September 2001, Habermas has been especially concerned with the possibility of religious tolerance within the context of liberal constitutional democracies.[74] The conditions for the possibility of religious tolerance are intimately bound up with what Habermas terms "the epistemic conditions of modernity," especially differentiation, reflexivity, and decentration.[75] Differentiation is the separating out of three distinct spheres of value, namely science, morality, and art, which are all fused together in traditional religious-metaphysical worldviews. With this separation, each sphere now develops freely according to its own inner logic, and each operates with its own special sort of validity claim (truth, rightness, and truthfulness). Reflexivity is the capacity to investigate validity claims without the coercion or constraints of dogmatism. And finally, decentration is a process of becoming less chauvinistic or self-centered in focus, by moving toward more universalistic and inclusivistic points of view. These conditions make possible a particular sort of self-critical posture in contemporary forms of religion, or what Habermas calls "modern faith." This posture allows these forms of religion to "stabilize the inclusive attitude that it assumes within a universe of discourse *delimited* by secular knowledge and *shared* with other religions."[76] In short, Habermas can only conceive of religions existing as productive members of modern, pluralist democratic societies if they severely curtail their prior exclusivist claims and dramatically revise their attitudes toward the Other. Habermas's so-called 'modern faiths' may claim descent from monotheistic traditions, but they no longer share the discursive structure of Abrahamic monotheisms—as this structure is incompatible with Habermas's epistemological conditions of modernity.

To see the degree to which these modern faiths are truncated and desiccated forms of elective monotheisms, one need only look to the 'religious-metaphysical worldview,' which Habermas largely equates with the pre-modern monotheisms.[77] In Habermas's paradigm of the evolution of communicative rationality, the religious-metaphysical worldview is an important midpoint between myth and modernity. While these monotheistic religions characterize a systematic advance over myth, for Habermas, they are deficient in all three of the epistemological conditions of modernity, in that their ultimate principles are not exposed to doubt or criticism,[78] they lack differentiation in regard to validity realms, and they are 'centered' vis-à-vis the Other as a result of being "immunized against dissonant experiences."[79] For our purposes, what is important is that they are utterly incommensurable with any sort of symmetrical relationship with the Other—the foundation of tolerance and pluralism—because, to use the language of our previous discussion of monotheism, they operate according to the logic of scriptural universalism.[80]

According to the overarching teleological scheme of Habermas's social thought, the historical stage of the 'religious-metaphysical worldview' is supposed to be sublated (*aufgehoben*, in a non-metaphysical sense) in modernity in a process that Habermas refers to as the "linguistification of the sacred." By this phrase Habermas means "the transfer of cultural reproduction, social integration, and socialization from sacred foundations over to linguistic communication and action oriented to mutual understanding."[81] In modernity, religions are supposed to lose their traditional power: "In modern societies these [traditional and religious] forms of life . . . have been subordinated to the universalism of law and morality."[82] The subordination of religion is possible, at least in part, because of what Habermas sees as the epoch-making collapse of metaphysics. The public, universal claims of religion are predicated upon theology, which is a metaphysical discourse that Habermas claims can no longer remain valid in this post-metaphysical era. As a result, religion is removed from the public sphere and limited to the private realm, given that it is rationally indefeasible in this post-metaphysical age.[83] However, given that the 'religious-metaphysical worldview' is dramatically reasserting itself against the demands of secular modernity, rather than quietly undergoing sublation, the tenability of Habermas's account is open to question. Obviously the accuracy of its descriptive level must now be seen as problematic. However, if the teleological movement he posits is coming undone, then one has very good reason to question the normative dimension of Habermas's thought at least regarding the domestication of religious authority, especially given that the conditions he considers to be necessary for a functional constitutional democratic society are being openly rejected by growing numbers of monotheists in such democratic societies. Since the descriptive level of Habermas's teleological account of societal development is bound up with the normative level of his argument, if the former fails so too the latter.[84]

In regard to the tension and hostility between monotheism and tolerance, neither the solution proffered by Hick nor by Habermas is suitable. Both thinkers require that Abrahamic-monotheistic religions denude themselves of their discursive structure. Yet without this structure, they are no longer Abrahamic monotheisms. Thus, their solution to monotheistic intolerance—to the agonism toward the Other in the heart of the monotheistic worldview—is to treat as valid religions that are monotheistic in name only, but whose content is something else.

Habermas, who explores the fundamentalist mindset in his recent writings, inadvertently provides us with a key for understanding why his and Hick's solutions were bound to be unsatisfactory or at least irrelevant to our current crisis. According to Habermas, fundamentalist movements arise in modernity, alongside modern forms of faith. In the face of the epistemic conditions of modernity, various forms of fundamentalism (of course, our concern is with monotheistic ones) attempt to reclaim the all-encompassing power of the religious-metaphysical worldview by simply ignoring those "modern conditions" whereby "an exclusive claim to truth by one faith can no longer be naively maintained."[85] As a result of its insufficient rigor, Habermas finds fundamentalism to constitute a "false answer" to the "epistemological situation" of the present, which calls for reflexivity and tolerance above all else.[86] That is, Habermas critiques the fundamentalist movements for their failure to embrace the linguistic-rational changes instituted with modernity, which subsequently results in their inability to recognize the value of the principles of tolerance and pluralism. Habermas simply accepts these characteristically modern principles as valid. However, if examined, the origin of these principles reveal a complex and problematic relationship with monotheism that renders their rejection by fundamentalists more complex.

The modern principle of tolerance emerges slowly in Western Europe out of the context of a series of brutal religious wars and persecutions following the Reformation.[87] The violence which emerged, in no small part because of the agonistic, often violent disposition of Abrahamic monotheisms (in this case, sects of Christianity) toward the Other, is therefore the explicit backdrop in the two most foundational accounts of tolerance in the Western philosophical tradition, those of Jean-Jacques Rousseau and John Locke. Without wishing to digress too far into the history of the principle of tolerance, it will nevertheless be quite helpful to briefly explore Rousseau and Locke's respective accounts of tolerance—accounts from which the contemporary principles of tolerance and pluralism derive in some form or another—in order to highlight the tendency of modern thought to explicitly reject the discursive structure of Abrahamic monotheisms.

In book 4, chapter 8 of *On the Social Contract*,[88] Rousseau elucidates his account of religious tolerance. Rousseau, long before Assmann, recognizes the political implications of the monotheistic worldview. With astonishing insight into the logic of the monotheistic worldview, he states, "Those who distinguish between civil and theological intolerance are mistaken, in my opinion. The two intolerances are inseparable. It is impossible to live in peace with people one believes to be damned; to love them would be to hate God who punishes them; one must absolutely bring them back [to the fold] or torment them."[89] In response to this difficulty, Rousseau turns the traditional paradigm, where theology dictates politics, on its head, such that now politics determines theology. Rousseau drains the monotheistic worldview of all antagonistic energy with the following axiom. "Everything which destroys social unity is worthless. All institutions which put man in contradiction with himself are worthless."[90] Any theological endorsement of religious intolerance, whatever its theological merit, is unacceptable for Rousseau because it is politically problematic. Since theology has been subordinated to politics, religious truth is no longer sufficient grounds for an agonistic relationship with the Other. Thus, Rousseau states, "whoever dares to say, *no Salvation outside the Church,* has to be driven out the State."[91] Theological intolerance, once seen as a virtue,[92] is now transformed into a political vice, as being 'unsociable,' and thus worthy of punishment. In such an environment, the discursive structure of Abrahamic monotheisms has not been refuted on rational grounds but quite literally rendered illegal.

Locke, the other foundational thinker of religious tolerance in the Enlightenment, develops his account of tolerance most thoroughly in "A Letter Concerning Toleration."[93] Whereas Rousseau brings about tolerance through subordinating theology to politics, Locke prefers to make subtle but nonetheless significant innovations in the actual discursive structure shared by monotheisms. That is, Locke inserts two profound changes into the foundational structure of elective monotheism, thus altering its basic logic. Locke introduces a split between the civil and religious spheres, and enacts a separation between the individual and the collective. These changes bring about tremendous ramifications regarding the notion of toleration.[94] These divisions, which are heterogeneous to the monotheistic worldview, enable Locke to break the iron grip of religious intolerance and violence.

Whereas Rousseau continues to maintain a state religion, albeit an extremely thin one (in the hopes of minimizing conflict), Locke completely fissures the spheres of government and religion.[95] Early in "A Letter Concerning Toleration," Locke states, "I esteem it above all things necessary to distinguish exactly the business of civil government from that of religion, and to settle the just bounds that lie between the one and the other."[96] In the discursive structure of the worldview of elective monotheisms, the boundary between the individual and the community as well as between the public and the private is quite blurry. Locke, however, now fortifies these divisions and makes them foundational in modern, liberal society. The government of a nation is concerned with the civil interest, i.e., the physical and material interest, of its people and nothing more. The religious sphere is exclusively limited to the "care of souls," which requires only "the inward and full persuasion of the mind."[97] As a result, government and religion are neatly cordoned off from one another. By means of this fissure between civil and religious society, Locke drains the intolerance inherent in monotheistic religions of political force. Locke seeks to achieve tolerance by depriving religious intolerance and disapproval of all physical, economic, and political power, because the realm of this intolerance is limited to principles which can only be legitimately disseminated through non-coercive persuasion. Government is likewise to have no say in the realm of religion, thus limiting its reach solely to the sphere of civil society. The government, now denuded of any religious affiliation, is to embrace strict neutrality regarding the religious lives of its citizens or subjects, and religion in turn is made apolitical.[98]

From its inception with Rousseau and Locke, it is striking that the modern notion of tolerance—from which the contemporary principles of tolerance and pluralism derive—is antithetical to, or at least in significant tension with, the discursive structure of the Abrahamic monotheisms. Neither foundational account of tolerance is willing to deal with the discursive structure of the Abrahamic monotheistic worldview on its own terms. While I do not wish to delve into questions of the ways in which, and the extent to which, Hick or Habermas is indebted to Rousseau or Locke, it is nevertheless instructive to see that the modern principles of tolerance and pluralism only emerged by means of their rejection of the discursive structure of Abrahamic monotheisms. I by no means wish to suggest that this is the *only* way to secure the conditions for tolerance and pluralism, but only that this is how these principles have been primarily secured in modernity.

While Habermas is certainly correct to critique fundamentalist movements for their shortcomings regarding communicative rationality, he nevertheless misses the larger point to which these movements, at least in part, seem to be responding. Since tolerance and pluralism are fundamentally modern values emerging with the Enlightenment—values which begin only where the discursive structure of Abrahamic monotheisms has been repudiated—solutions such as those of Hick and Habermas, which trade heavily on these principles, force religions *not* rooted in the values of the Enlightenment to face a terrible dilemma. Either the religious person can accept the principles of tolerance and/or pluralism which are incompatible with her religious tradition as it understands itself, but which the philosophy of religious pluralism or the epistemological conditions of modernity warrant; or the religious person can affirm a robust account of her religion, i.e., an account which preserves the discursive structure intact. There is no option to have both a robust account of faith and the acceptance of tolerance and/or pluralism. The thinkers of the religion of reason trajectory, i.e., Moses Mendelssohn, Immanuel Kant, and Hermann Cohen, however, propose an alternate approach to the problem of monotheistic intolerance, wherein the discursive structure shared by the Abrahamic monotheisms is not rejected but rather reconfigured to accord with tolerance and/or rigorous ethical responsibility for the Other. Notions such as election and the asymmetry of the monotheistic worldview are not rejected *tout court*, but rather are retrieved in Enlightenment and post-Enlightenment idioms. This occurs in such a way, in the philosophies of these thinkers, that the discursive structure of the monotheistic worldview and Enlightenment thinking are brought into contact with one another and mutually transformed. As a result, these thinkers avoid the dilemma plaguing contemporary thought on monotheistic intolerance.

2 | Learning from the Past

John Hick's and Jürgen Habermas's philosophical attempts to ground religious pluralism and/or tolerance, and thus to undercut monotheistic intolerance, are ultimately descended from the Enlightenment project of using reason to domesticate religion. Indeed, I will argue, both are very much descendants of Kant's own project of reconfiguring the nature of religion and of God in order to dissolve the force of particular religious traditions and privilege the universal human community. However, it is important to bear several points in mind. First, it must be acknowledged that the Enlightenment was not simply a process directed toward secularization, as is often presumed today. Against this contemporary prejudice, J. B. Schneewind writes, "the claim that the main effort of the moral philosophy of the eighteenth century was to secularize morality simply does not stand up to even the most cursory inspection." Moreover, Schneewind remarks that it is not "helpful to think in terms of a single movement of Enlightenment or *Aufklärung* or *Lumières.*"[1] I want to suggest, given that the Enlightenment was neither a univocal nor a uniformly 'secularist' phenomenon, that Mendelssohn and Cohen (as his inheritor) represent an alternate strand within the Enlightenment and modernity whose resources for our own time have yet to be sufficiently appreciated.[2] I also want to suggest that Kant's project of domesticating particular religious traditions in the name of the 'religion of reason' is itself ambivalent. It can lend itself to such thinkers as Hick and Habermas and the whole line of Kantian-proceduralists in philosophy departments today; but it is also rooted in a *Heilsgeschichte* of sorts involving the development of reason and the human species toward the ethical commonwealth, a process in which theological notions and tropes are by no means incidental.[3] As we will see, Kant's own religious and political writings thus represent a crossroads between the religion of reason trajectory and 'Kantians' such as Hick and Habermas.

If contemporary 'Kantians,' whether they be religious liberals like Hick or secularists like Habermas, attempt to undercut monotheistic intolerance by decisively subordinating the particular to the universal, and thus undermine the dialectic between particularity and universality at the core of the discursive structure of elective monotheisms, the religion of reason trajectory—Mendelssohn and Cohen in particular—take a very different approach. This project is no less a product of the Enlightenment, in that a notion of universal reason plays a decisive role. Reason is used to ease the tensions produced by this dialectic. Now to be sure, whereas Mendelssohn and Kant lived in the eighteenth century and were contemporaries and even knew one another, the founder of the Marburg school of Neo-Kantianism, Hermann Cohen, joins this group of thinkers with his work on Judaism and the 'religion of reason' developed around the turn of the twentieth century.[4] While Cohen repeatedly defended Kant's legacy in his works, I argue that, at least when it comes to the philosophy of religion, he and Mendelssohn are more closely allied in that they both preserve the dialectical core of the elective monotheisms intact. Cohen's thought, which is the consummation of the religion of reason trajectory, combines the most successful elements of Mendelssohn's and Kant's work, while adding profound and highly innovative insights of its own. Indeed it is Cohen who, recognizing the inherent asymmetrical foundations of the elective monotheisms, foregoes any attempt to reconcile monotheism and tolerance or pluralism, deciding instead to harness the ethical potentialities of monotheistic intolerance. It is this strategy, which not only divests monotheistic intolerance of all violence but also taps into its ethical dimensions, that makes this trajectory of thought relevant to us today. Where Hick and Habermas privilege universalism over particularism in the name of the values of tolerance and pluralism, Mendelssohn and Cohen not only preserve particularity and universality in dialectical tension, but also render any intolerance that arises as a result utterly free of violence toward the Other. Moreover, in Cohen's thought this intolerance is harnessed in an ethical direction. Mendelssohn and Cohen thus provide us with modern philosophies of religion—i.e., philosophies which grapple with epistemological challenges raised by modern existence—which nevertheless preserve the dynamic core of the discursive structure of elective monotheisms.

Unlike so many Enlightenment philosophies, then, those of Mendelssohn, Kant, and Cohen preserve key elements of the discursive structure of the monotheistic worldview and thus maintain a peculiar relation to standard accounts of modernity that has not been sufficiently appreciated. The ways in which their respective philosophies are refractory to conventional categories of 'modernity,' however refined and insightfully configured, can be seen if we turn to G. E. M. Anscombe's important and influential essay "Modern Moral Philosophy."[5] In this essay, Anscombe argues that the moral sense of 'ought' should be jettisoned from 'modern' philosophy, in that it is merely a survival from a divine command (i.e., monotheistic) conception of ethics, which is no longer recognized by philosophers.[6] Of particular importance for this discussion is Anscombe's claim, in terms reminiscent to those of Halbertal and Margalit, that in divine-command conceptions of ethics the 'ought' pertains to laws and commands, such that failure to meet them is a mark of being bad qua human being, rather than bad in a particular role.[7] Such a teleological view of the human being, Anscombe argues, has been abandoned by modern thought.

The profundity of Anscombe's insight is to recognize that by rejecting theocentrism and divine-law conceptions of morality—in that they entail some notion of a universal human *telos*—mainstream modern philosophy is left with only a plurality of local values and concerns, rather than a real basis for establishing good and bad in the human being as a whole.[8] Hick and Habermas are both responding to, and operating in accordance with, this story of modernity; the philosophies of both thinkers operate without any recourse to a universal human *telos*. Hick offers a hopelessly vague notion 'reality-centeredness' which sufficiently obscures any meaningful discussion of the universal human *telos*. Habermas is consciously modern in Anscombe's sense, in that he thinks any account of a human *telos* involves conceptions of the lifeworld as a whole. Since issues involving the lifeworld as a whole, what Habermas terms "metaphysics," are beyond any sort of argumentation, they are beyond the public sphere and even discussion, and hence are essentially non-philosophical.[9] And since both thinkers lack any viable notion of the universal human *telos*, they naturally reject the discursive structure shared by the elective monotheisms.

However, this is not the only story of modern philosophy. The thinkers of the religion of reason trajectory remain within the discursive structure of the elective monotheisms, even if they have to reconfigure this structure philosophically to fit with their modern sensibilities. As a result, Mendelssohn, Kant, and Cohen retain a notion of the universal *telos* of the human being, and thus they defy Anscombe's definition of the 'modern' thinker.[10] While some might be tempted to view this as a strike against them, it is rather precisely what makes them so important today. In contrast to Hick and Habermas, by retaining the notion of a universal human *telos,* the philosophies of these thinkers remain within the ambit of the discursive structure of the elective monotheisms.

The thinkers of the religion of reason trajectory preserve this 'pre-modern' notion of the universal human *telos* and yet remain distinctly modern in their philosophies by reconfiguring the moments of the discursive structure of the elective monotheisms. Their primary tool in this process of reconfiguration is rationalism. Like other modern rationalists, all three thinkers hold that reason presents a different sort of universalism than the scriptural universalism of the Abrahamic-monotheistic religions. For expediency, I will term the universalism rooted in reason 'rational universalism.'[11] A helpful example of rational universalism, one which is often used in Enlightenment accounts, is mathematics, since it not only claims certain things to be unequivocally true but can demonstrate the necessity for a particular ruling being as it is and no other way.[12] What is decisive about rational universalism is that it is a framework which possesses necessity (i.e., it can demonstrate why something has to be a certain way and cannot be otherwise) and universality in scope (i.e., its demonstrations are readily apparent to all 'right-thinking' human beings everywhere.) In short, rational universalism predicates its authority upon the fundamental capacity of reason in all human beings everywhere. Human reason is, generally speaking, everywhere capable of recognizing the basic truths of mathematics, in that they can be transmitted through argumentation and recourse to rules and axioms, whose necessity can be verified by virtually everyone: Human reason is sufficient for discerning their validity, merit, and usefulness. Similarly, in rational universalism, necessity and universality render any recourse to violent means of persuasion in regard to questions of 'truth' utterly unnecessary.

Whereas the logic of rational universalism is defined as possessing necessity, scriptural universalisms are characterized by being contingent. Scriptural universalisms are rooted in a set of holy texts believed to be revealed by the universal God to a particular community. These texts give the authoritative account of how all human beings are to live their lives if they want to live in accordance with God's will. They are universal in scope in that they claim to be applicable to, i.e., have relevance for, all human beings. However, scriptural universalisms fail to offer any rational necessity; they are not self-evident to human reason or penetrable in their foundations.

Instead they require the authority of God, the creator of the universe and humanity, to bestow universality and authority upon them. Without the sanction of the divine, the rulings of these texts are not recognizably authoritative; there is no readily identifiable reason one should follow them as opposed to some other system of belief and praxis. This does not mean there is no reason behind these rules, statutes, and norms, but if there is it is God's reason, which is qualitatively different from the reason of human beings.

Thus, it should not be surprising that in common forms of the Abrahamic monotheisms the radical dichotomy between God and human beings is stressed, such that God remains utterly unfathomable except for what is disclosed through revelation. Hence, for scriptural universalism rulings and teachings must be disclosed, at least in part, in a historical event rather than emerging entirely through a process of gradual discovery, like mathematics.[13] However, the authority ascribed to one tradition's founding events and 'revealed' scriptures can be contested, insofar as many traditions claim God's authority for their own specific teachings, and thus different scriptural universalisms clash with one another, in addition to clashing with communities that are not terribly preoccupied with universality. Hence these religions are often promulgated not through rational argumentation and scholarly interchange, but rather through persuasion, coercion, and violence.

Now we are in a position to appreciate a central feature that unites the work of the thinkers of the religion of reason trajectory, namely, to combine and integrate the order of rational universalism with that of scriptural universalism. By doing this, they hope to ameliorate the violence inherent in the intolerance of monotheistic religions. Mendelssohn, the last great advocate of Leibnizian natural theology, substitutes a more inclusive metaphysical paradigm for the metaphysical underpinnings of the monotheistic worldview in order to foster a less agonistic relation to the Other. While this new metaphysical paradigm does not fit seamlessly with scriptural universalism and the discursive structure of elective monotheisms, Mendelssohn fruitfully wrestles with the tensions that result. Kant stands at the margins of the religion of reason trajectory in that unlike Mendelssohn and Cohen, his solution to monotheistic intolerance is to radically subordinate the logic of scriptural universalism to rational universalism. Unlike Mendelssohn and Cohen, Kant's primary concern is not so much with monotheistic intolerance per se as with eradicating the conditions which produce intolerance in all religions, including monotheistic ones. Nevertheless, Kant finds certain aspects of scriptural universalism and the discursive structure of elective monotheisms to be necessary to this endeavor, if only in a somewhat enervated form. Cohen, unlike Mendelssohn and Kant, not only allows rational and scriptural universalism to coexist, but he renders their relationship productive. While Cohen ultimately privileges rational universalism, with the exception of its notion of an unfathomable God, he not only preserves the logic of scriptural universalism, but he brings it into a complementary relationship with rational universalism so that it serves as the vehicle through which rational universalism unfolds and establishes itself.

At this point, reservations are probably emerging in the reader's mind since to the degree that thinkers of the religion of reason trajectory take recourse to rational universalism, their positions seem hopelessly antiquated given the reputation of such an ideal in philosophy and the humanities at present. An obvious objection arises concerning the possible thickness of any such rational universalism, considering how Habermas has characterized, accurately I think, our present circumstances as a globalized, pluralistic world without any "substantive background consensus on the underlying moral norms."[14] This concern should be left aside for now, though as we will see, the loss of a shared world/moral order is not only a significant challenge that haunts the contemporary appropriation of the works of the thinkers of religion of reason trajectory, but also what makes their thought of vital importance today.

However, we can bracket the concern about rational universalism and discuss particular challenges as they arise for each respective thinker, but there is another challenge that concerns this endeavor itself and that cannot be put off. It is very popular in current philosophy of religion and theology to consider revelation and rationality as incommensurable, to stress the irreducibility of 'Athens' and 'Jerusalem.' If this prejudice is taken as axiomatic, then the very project of the religion of reason trajectory—especially the philosophies of Kant and Cohen, whose reconciliation of the divinely ordained human *telos* with autonomy involves the ultimate confluence of reason and revelation—is ruled out from the beginning.

Not surprisingly, then, these thinkers have met with serious criticism. Leo Strauss, one of the most acute critics of modern religious thought (particularly modern Jewish thought), argues that such a tactic indicates that even a modern liberal as serious about his religious commitments as Cohen, cannot take revelation seriously on its own terms, but rather operates on the basis of internalizing the radical Enlightenment's critiques of religion. Strauss insists that the attempt by post-Enlightenment thinkers to rationalize the foundational concepts of tradition "like creation, miracles, and revelation . . . differs from the disavowal of their meaning *only* in the well-intentioned, if not good, purpose, of its authors."[15] However, I contend that Cohen's ability to incorporate elements of the Enlightenment critique of religion while maintaining the discursive structure of elective Judaism intact is precisely what makes his philosophical reconstruction of Judaism so valuable to us today. That is, where Strauss and many others want to highlight the ultimate incompatibility of orthodoxy and modern philosophy, the ability of the thinkers of the religion of reason trajectory to not only hold these positions in tension, but to reconcile the discursive structure of elective monotheism with philosophical principles foundational to modernity, is precisely what demands our attention. What distinguishes these thinkers is their capacity to argue, in a critical and self-conscious way, for the universal significance of a particular community. The role of philosophical reason is essential in this project, as they refuse to begin with either dogmatic assumptions that are immune to criticism or with liberal ones which limit the values and worldviews of specific communities to mere particularity.

DIVERGENT REASONS

While Mendelssohn, Kant, and Cohen are all rationalists and all engaged in a similar project of 'rationalizing' the discursive structure of the elective monotheisms, it is important to remember that there are significant differences between these thinkers and their projects. That is, since these thinkers maintain very different conceptions of reason, not only do they maintain different understandings of what constitutes rational universalism, but they also hold widely divergent understandings of what it means to rationally transfigure the moments of the discursive structure of the elective monotheisms.

For Mendelssohn the cosmos itself is anchored in God's perfection, which entails such subsequent truths as the predominance of good over evil and the necessity of the afterlife. Reason, for Mendelssohn, is inseparable from this metaphysical order which is rooted in God's perfection; reason consists in the proper recognition of this order. While different cultures may represent these truths in different symbols, Mendelssohn is adamant that the "Supreme Being has . . . inscribed [these truths] in the soul with a script that is legible and comprehensible at all times and in all places."[16] In other words, reason for Mendelssohn is tantamount to a proper understanding of the metaphysical order of the universe, and rational universalism is rooted in the universal accessibility of this order.[17]

Kant marks a watershed moment in the history of philosophy, as his thought begins the undermining of the metaphysical endeavor of philosophy. Part and parcel of Kant's destruction of metaphysics is the transition that takes place in the conception of reason itself, the result of which is that reason ceases to be understood as a passive process of discovering eternal truths embedded or reflected in the cosmos. Instead, reason is an active, self-constructing process in which an ever-expanding community of participants deliberate together and in this process (re)form community, particularly its social institutions and ethical core. Given its emphasis on human agency, Kant's notion of reason is profoundly anthropocentric, in sharp contrast to the theocentric metaphysics that preceded it. Kant's notion of rational universalism is rooted in the reflexivity, decentration, and mutuality that arises as a result of the prioritization of the universal and necessary idea of God inherent in ethics, as opposed to the capricious and unfathomable anthropomorphic God of historical faiths. That is, by rendering God into a functionary of ethics and stressing the finitude of human agents, and thus their rootedness in radical evil, Kant's rational universalism consists in the *a priori* moral law and its outgrowth, the ethical commonwealth.

Cohen, writing in the wake of Hegel, has a more sophisticated notion of reason and its relationship to history than either Mendelssohn or Kant. While there are truths of reason that are discernible to all rational human beings, for Cohen, these truths are neither embodied in the universe and reflected in our consciousness (Mendelssohn), nor present in our reason on an *a priori* level and accessible through processes of discursive deliberation (Kant). Cohen goes even further than Kant in stressing the active nature of reason, in that it is the mind that quite literally 'creates'/'discovers' all truth. However, he nevertheless stresses that truth, even if it has universal validity, is 'discovered' in processes of hypothesis and verification. And once discovered, truth has to be further unpacked and deepened in a process of investigation and thinking through. In short, reason is the process of truth-seeking, and it is entirely active, a perpetual process of ongoing discovery. Thus, while all human beings have the capacity to recognize the universal truths of reason, such as universal morality, the difference between 'is' and 'ought,' these truths are by no means self-evident, but are literally produced in history understood as a process of reflecting upon questions. For Cohen the history of philosophy, or Judaism for that matter, is the process of thinking these truths through with increasing rigor and depth. Rational universalism, then, is an ideal that is to be realized in the future, when all people will participate in generating and recognizing the truth.

While their conceptions of reason differ, often significantly, one thing Mendelssohn, Kant, and Cohen share is recourse to the notion of a 'religion of reason.' Since these thinkers do not subscribe to a straightforward logic of scriptural universalism, they do not limit the capacity to fulfill the universal human *telos* to those within their respective religious traditions: Judaism for Mendelssohn and Cohen, and Christianity for Kant. For all three thinkers, the 'religion of reason' is something of an ideal which guides and orients (or should orient) other existing religions. And concomitantly, for each of these thinkers, there is a notion of a 'worse' sort of religion, what I will term 'idolatry.' These are religious sects or groups that have priorities and practices which conflict with, and actively inhibit, the development toward the 'religion of reason.' However, just as the specifics of what constitutes the 'religion of reason' varies with each respective thinker, so too does its counterpart, the notion of idolatry.

What unites Mendelssohn's, Kant's, and Cohen's respective accounts of the 'religion of reason' despite their many differences, is that since they maintain some notion of a determinate, universal human *telos*, their notions of the 'religion of reason' is partisan in its estimation of different religious traditions. To be sure, the universality of the 'religion of reason' serves to ameliorate the harshest intolerance of elective monotheisms toward the Other. Nevertheless, by stressing the notion of the universal human *telos* that is linked to the election of a particular community in some form, while nevertheless making use of reason to break the necessary connection between Other and idolater, these thinkers are able to navigate a course between the Scylla of violent intolerance and the Charybdis of the immolation of the discursive structure of monotheistic religions.

KANT'S LEGACY AND THE RELIGION OF REASON

A significant difference between contemporary proponents of tolerance and pluralism, such as Hick and Habermas, and the thinkers of the religion of reason trajectory, centers around the issue of symmetry in the relationship between self and Other. Given the centrality of this issue Kant, or more particularly, the interpretation and legacy of Kant's thought, plays an important role in separating contemporary Kantians from Cohen's specific form of Neo-Kantianism, which is the culmination of the religion of reason trajectory. Kant maintains both the notion of a determinate human *telos* and tolerance-as-inclusion. However, two points must be borne in mind which distinguish Kant's notion of tolerance from 'Kantians' such as Habermas and Hick, who stress tolerance often in the form of tolerance-as-inclusion and pluralism. First, since the trajectory of the history of reason (which is very much a form of *Heilsgeschichte*) has not yet fulfilled itself according to Kant, he is not averse to invoking an agonism with the Other (construed as one who is not yet, but could still become a moral agent) which is of central significance to the discursive structure shared by elective monotheisms. This agonism is absent in 'Kantians' of the likes of Habermas and Hick. Second, the presuppositions that enabled Kant to maintain both a determinate human *telos* and a notion of tolerance-as-inclusion—namely, an a-historic and *a priori* notion of human reason which is sufficiently universal that human beings will inevitably and eventually reach shared norms and values—are no longer philosophically tenable.

In fact, it is precisely the differences in their respective appropriations of Kant that not only enable Cohen to remain within the religion of reason trajectory, while Hick and Habermas are clearly outside of it, but also account for Cohen's relevance today. It is beyond question that claims regarding shared *a priori* moral truths are problematic in today's pluralistic, multicultural world. Whereas Cohen retains Kant's emphasis on a determinate universal *telos* (although with a more sophisticated understanding of the role of history in shaping reason), Habermas and Hick retain Kant's inclusivist proclivities regarding tolerance. Since Hick and Habermas prioritize mutual recognition and symmetry, the central monotheistic notion of a determinate, universal human *telos* becomes either hopelessly abstract (Hick) or is shifted beyond the realm of meaningful discussion, bound as it is to a view of the lifeworld as a whole (Habermas). Without the willingness to assert the truth of one determinate account of the universal human *telos* over against all others, neither Hick nor Habermas can maintain the moments constitutive of the discursive structure of elective monotheism (revelation, election, historical drama, *eschaton*) which are all predicated upon this tension. Thus, they only carry on one side of the legacy of Kant's philosophy; they lose his 'religion of reason.'

The Thinkers of the Religion of Reason Trajectory and Tradition

Mendelssohn, both in his personal life and in his authorial stance (at least in the works written toward the end of his life, which will be the focus of the present work),[18] operates as an explicitly Jewish thinker. In works such as "Gegenbetrachtungen über Bonnets Palingensie"[19] and "Sache Gottes: oder die gerettete Vorsehung,"[20] as well as in his most famous piece, *Jerusalem: Or on Religious Power and Judaism,* Mendelssohn develops an account of Judaism that is at home with both scriptural universalism and crucial aspects of rational universalism such as the respect for the inherent dignity of all human beings in contrast to (his account of) Christianity, which he accuses of operating with a naked scriptural universalism. In these works, Mendelssohn articulates an account of Judaism that is torn between the logics of scriptural and rational universalism. Regardless of the failures which beset this account, he nevertheless succeeds in upholding relatively traditional notions of God, revelation, election, historical mission, and *eschaton* while dramatically reducing agonism toward the Other.

Kant, in sharp contrast to Mendelssohn and Cohen, is at best at the margins of the religious tradition out of which he operates, Christianity. While Christian concepts and prejudices appear throughout Kant's corpus, being particularly apparent in the *Critique of Practical Reason*[21] and even more so in *Religion within the Limits of Reason Alone,*[22] Christianity for Kant is only an instantiation of the 'religion of reason'—it enjoys no qualitative distinctness. Christianity's only distinction is quantitative, as Kant claims that it most perfectly embodies the ideal of the 'religion of reason' and thus, when properly understood, exists in least conflict with the ideal of the 'religion of reason.' Kant's stress on rational universalism prevents any particular monotheistic community from being elected to a special divine mission; Kant seeks to illuminate the dangers of scriptural universalism with his account of Judaism. Rather, like all other particular,[23] historical religions, Christianity is charged with the task of rationalizing its doctrines. For Kant, the process of rationalizing itself necessarily entails embracing the task of the formation of the ethical commonwealth which brings together all rational beings in a community run by autonomous virtue and rationality, rather than political or theological means (although Kant is forced to take recourse to the language of politics and theology to articulate his vision of the ethical commonwealth).

Finally, Cohen elucidates his normative account of monotheism from within the Jewish tradition. In *Ethik des reinen Willens*,[24] and his explicitly Jewish writings, such as *Ethics of Maimonides*,[25] "Religion und Sittlichkeit,"[26] and his posthumous work, *Religion of Reason Out of the Sources of Judaism*, Cohen argues that the Jewish notion of God and the account of ethics that is inextricably bound up with it are universally valid and rationally discernible to all human beings despite their emergence from the literary history of a particular community. God for Cohen is a 'foundational' concept of universal significance that originates in the particular literature of ancient Israel;[27] the Christian notion of God serves as the counter-example of how certain concepts emerge from a particular context and claim to be universal but in fact remain contingent and arbitrary. To use the terminology of the Marburg Neo-Kantianism, the Jewish notion of God is the core concept of Cohen's *Ursprüngslogik* which perpetually unfolds and refines itself in each new manifestation. Thus, Cohen's reading of the Jewish Scriptures elucidates the process whereby this concept struggles to realize the full implications of its rationality (which involves a dialectical interplay, or *correlation*, between particularity and universality) and break free from its mythic roots.[28] Cohen never claims that other religious groups lack rationality, but to the degree that other religions have realized their potential for rationality they will resemble Judaism in terms of its notion of God and the ethics that derives from it. Cohen's account of the election of the Jews is tied to his belief that all human beings possess the capacity for reason, and that reason involves accepting a notion of God and ethics quite similar to those operative in his conception of Judaism. In short, for Cohen the election of the Jews means not merely disclosing the idea of the Unique God—an idea of universal significance nevertheless born in their particular national/religious literature—but testifying to its rationality. Cohen argues that the idea of the Unique God, the founding idea of the national literature of the Jews, is, in fact, the ultimate foundation of morality and generates the ideal of humanity. By proceeding in this manner, Cohen, unlike Mendelssohn and Kant, wholeheartedly embraces the agonism toward the Other inherent in the discursive structure of elective monotheisms. Instead of trying to dilute or eradicate this agonism, he concentrates on rendering it ethical.

At a time when so many monotheistic communities, whether Jewish, Christian, or Muslim, eagerly seek to distance themselves from the epistemological and social constraints of modern liberalism, and when so many philosophers and theologians seek to distance themselves from the Enlightenment, it is worth exploring the religion of reason trajectory. In the wake of the post-modern critique of the Enlightenment, the flourishing of communitarian and non-rationalist philosophies of religion, and the general desire among philosophers and theologians to abandon the legacy of modern liberalism, we must remember that the Enlightenment was not a univocal phenomenon with homogeneous priorities and commitments. While it is no longer feasible or even desirable to privilege the universal over the particular or to confine religion to the private sphere, it is imperative not to overreact and abandon the pursuit of reason and the desire to harmonize it as much as possible with revelation. And while thinkers like Hick and Habermas go too far in stressing the obligations of universality, fundamentalism in all the monotheistic traditions reveals the danger of unfettered particularity convinced of its universal relevance. What is so promising about the religion of reason trajectory, especially as it takes shape in the work of Mendelssohn and Cohen, is that the dialectic of particularity and universality is preserved, but ethics and reason are not abandoned in the process. This is one strand of the Enlightenment which has not yet received a fair hearing in contemporary thought, and which has much to teach us.

Part Two

Mendelssohn: Idolatry and Indiscernibility

3 | Mendelssohn and the Repudiation of Divine Tyranny

History has not been particularly kind to Moses Mendelssohn, the 'father' of modern Jewish thought. While a famous metaphysician, religious reformer, literary critic, and polemicist in his own day, Mendelssohn's legacy has largely been relegated to intellectual history. Not only were his prize-winning metaphysical arguments rendered marginal by Kant's 'destruction' of 'pre-critical' philosophy, but Mendelssohn's account of Judaism, viewed as incoherent and/or too eager to cede central tenets of Judaism to Christianity and the state, failed to establish lasting roots among his descendants.[1] Indeed, he is remembered more for being the first Jew to take up modern philosophy in defense of Judaism, than for what he accomplished in this regard. I offer an alternative reading of Mendelssohn's work which finds fresh urgency in his project, which has too often been read with an unsympathetic eye. As the founder of the religion of reason trajectory, his writings on religion, particularly the 'religion of reason' (or 'natural religion')[2] and its relationship to Judaism and Christianity, have much to contribute to our contemporary concerns about monotheistic intolerance. However, despite his important inaugural contributions to the religion of reason trajectory, there are certain indelible difficulties in his position which require further developments in this school of thought, namely the subsequent innovations of Kant and Cohen.

Mendelssohn's particular strategy for dissolving, or at least relieving, the tension between monotheism on the one hand and tolerance and pluralism (construed here as cultural egalitarianism and not a deep plural-ism)[3] on the other, consists in reconfiguring the moments of the discursive structure of elective monotheism upon a new, more inclusive metaphysi-cal foundation. Mendelssohn reconfigures the monotheistic religion of Judaism such that its primary conception of the Other ceases to be of one ensconced in sin and error, and instead becomes one shrouded in ambigu-ity and uncertainty. Yet in Mendelssohn scholarship, this ambiguity re-garding the Other has not been an area of much concern.[4] The question of the Other surfaces in Mendelssohn's thought in regard to his discussions about the status of the election of the Jews and cultural egalitarianism, themes which innately bear upon relations with the Other. It is precisely with regard to the question of the relationship of election and cultural egalitarianism that Mendelssohn's conception of the Other becomes a sig-nificant object of inquiry and contention among contemporary scholars, as there is an important disagreement about the relationship of these two facets of his thought.

One important school of thought suggests that the election of the Jews and cultural egalitarianism are conflicting agendas in Mendelssohn's thought. Scholars who hold this position argue that these two tendencies are basically irreconcilable, as the election of the Jews entails a qualitative distinction, indeed elevation, of the Jews over the Other, which is incom-mensurable with Mendelssohn's cultural-egalitarian agenda. The disjunc-tion between these directions appears especially entrenched, these schol-ars claim, when one considers that for Mendelssohn the election of the Jews emerges relative to the 'historical phenomenon' of idolatry, which under-mines the hold of other religious and cultural communities on the eternal truths of the 'religion of reason.' As a result, so this school of thought con-cludes, Mendelssohn's position collapses from self-contradiction.[5] In this construction Mendelssohn appears torn between a pre-modern, or perhaps better, scripturally universal conception of election and a distinctly mod-ern Enlightenment notion of universal (moral) reason and egalitarianism.

A significant strand of contemporary scholarship has been relatively unconcerned with this apparent incommensurability between the elec-tion of the Jews and cultural egalitarianism in Mendelssohn's thought. For example, a recent, fairly exhaustive examination of Mendelssohn's work considers this apparent tension to be a relatively insignificant matter, and one not particularly problematic for Mendelssohn's rationalist posi-tion.[6] Other scholarly works, in contrast to the more traditional position sketched above, minimize Mendelssohn's arguments concerning Jewish election and claim, or more often imply through omission, that the center of gravity of his thought concerning the Other is its thrust toward cul-tural egalitarianism or, to use more contemporary parlance, pluralism.

For these scholars, Mendelssohn's Jewish apologetics is secondary to such consummately modern, liberal concerns as constructing a space for multiple religions to peacefully and productively flourish within a shared civil society,[7] or elucidating a general philosophy of religious ritual through an examination of Jewish Halakhic practices,[8] a position which not only supports freedom of religion but tacitly supports religious pluralism.[9] Implicit in such arguments is the claim that the aspects of Mendelssohn's writings concerning the election of the Jews, rather than being seen as his central concern, should be understood primarily as a response to the historical circumstances under which Mendelssohn was compelled to write, i.e., defending himself and other Jews from Christian demands to convert.[10] In these interpretations, Mendelssohn offers a consummately modern form of religious and political thought, without any scripturally universal residue.

While these two schools of interpretation offer much that is compelling in their readings of Mendelssohn's texts, both are insufficient. Neither of them can coherently link both tendencies of Mendelssohn's thought—election and cultural egalitarianism. What these readings miss is precisely what makes his conception of Judaism of major importance for our investigation, not to mention for contemporary Jewish thought and philosophy of religion in general. They miss that Mendelssohn, in fact, manages to retain both the notion of Jewish election *and* openness to the Other by mitigating the effects of monotheistic intolerance through sophisticated metaphysical reflection. Mendelssohn represents the beginning of an alternative strand of modernity which retains the discursive structure of the monotheistic worldview.

In this chapter we will investigate this complex and seemingly paradoxical position which secures Mendelssohn's importance for our discussion. Of particular value in discerning this different, more productive view of Mendelssohn's thought, is supplementing his most widely discussed text, *Jerusalem: or on Religious Power and Judaism*,[11] with two lesser known and un-translated works, "Gegenbetrachtungen über Bonnets Palingenesie,"[12] and especially, "Sache Gottes: oder die gerettete Vorsehung,"[13] in addition to some of his letters and his early work on natural theology, *Phaedon: or the Death of Socrates*.[14] We will begin by discussing Mendelssohn's natural theology, which constitutes the basis of his rational universalism underlying his account of the 'religion of reason.' First we will discuss how Mendelssohn uses the 'religion of reason' as an alternative to the scriptural universalism operative in most forms of the Abrahamic monotheisms. We will then discuss the polemical fashion in which Mendelssohn uses the 'religion of reason' to highlight the problem of the exclusive reign of the logic of scriptural universalism within Christianity. Next, we will discuss Mendelssohn's account of Judaism, which is constructed along the lines of this new scheme of rationally universal natural theology. In chapter 4, we will discuss how this reconfiguring of Judaism allows a less intolerant conceptualization of the Other, and will consider certain indelible problems with Mendelssohn's endeavor as a whole which render it untenable despite its considerable virtues.

THE 'RELIGION OF REASON' AND THE NEW METAPHYSICAL FOUNDATION OF MONOTHEISM

Mendelssohn is troubled, more than the other thinkers of the religion of reason trajectory, by the tendency of the Abrahamic monotheisms to ascribe exclusive access to the means for fulfilling the universal human *telos* to a particular religious community. Given the reliance of these religions upon scriptural universalism, which allows for the promulgation of their revealed truths only through non-rational (and often coercive) processes taking place in history, numerous people are deprived of access to the universal human *telos*. This is simply unacceptable for Mendelssohn, who finds such circumstances incommensurable with a perfect God and the best possible world, beliefs central in the natural theology that comprises the rational universalism fundamental to Mendelssohn's reconfiguration of monotheism. Mendelssohn seeks to counteract the exclusivist proclivity of Abrahamic monotheisms by providing a new metaphysical paradigm, one supplied in his works on natural theology, to underpin the moments of their discursive structures. For Mendelssohn the universe is rooted in, and reflects, God's perfection, and the 'religion of reason' is grounded in the rationally universal truths of this metaphysical theological-cosmic order. That is, these 'eternal truths' which are fundamentally metaphysical in nature, but which undergird morality as well, are readily discernible to all human beings everywhere. As a result, all human beings can discern their place in the cosmos and thus can presumably fulfill their determinate human *telos*.

Two insights about the context in which Mendelssohn writes which are vital for understanding his thought can be found in J. B. Schneewind's magisterial study *The Invention of Autonomy*.[15] First, Schneewind examines the debate between 'voluntarists' and 'intellectualists' that rages throughout the seventeenth and eighteenth centuries, in which both sides posit different relationships between God and morality. While neither voluntarism nor intellectualism offers a one-to-one correlation with our categories of scriptural and rational universalism, there is a clear resonance between the respective positions. Those thinkers rooted in the theologies of Luther and Calvin and the philosophies of figures such as Duns Scotus, and who argue that the rules of morality rest upon an arbitrary fiat of God's will, exemplify the voluntarist position.[16] Voluntarism resonates with scriptural universalism in that it seeks to preserve God's omnipotence and unfathomable nature, which inevitably results in the ultimate arbitrariness of the laws of morality (i.e., actions and behaviors regarding human beings with each other).[17]

In opposition to the voluntarists is the position of the intellectualists, who fall in line with the agenda of rational universalism to the degree that they stress the fundamental comprehensibility of God on moral grounds. For the intellectualist, God's perfection requires God to endorse morality, and thus the idea that morality consists merely of arbitrary rules imposed by a fiat of God's will is rejected. As a result of their insistence upon the rational necessity of the laws and norms of morality, the intellectualist position requires that God be ultimately fathomable to human reason. That is, the intellectualist holds that the laws of morality qua products of God's perfection are rationally necessary, not the result of an arbitrary fiat of an unfathomable will. In fact, God's very will is determined by God's perfection, a perfection that is largely discernible to human reason, and thus by and large comprehensible to human reason. While the intellectualists decouple morality and God in one sense, since morality is no longer simply founded upon God's free will, they nevertheless re-couple God and morality in another way. For the intellectualist, God provides the necessary conditions for morality, as God's power and goodness ensures that human beings live in a morally ordered world.[18] Mendelssohn, at least in his declared allegiances, belongs to the intellectualist camp. In fact, intellectualism is a key component of Mendelssohn's rational universalism. Mendelssohn not only makes knowledge of God's perfection the foundation of his natural theology but he also makes this a truth that is readily available to human reason.

Second, Schneewind provides an alternate theory of the history of moral philosophy which, while now largely forgotten, was once accepted by many reputable thinkers. Today, without question, the dominant theory of the history of moral philosophy is what Schneewind refers to as the "Socrates story,"[19] which argues that moral philosophy consists of truths that must be discovered through rational inquiry. For this account of morality, Schneewind writes, "Although we have not reached agreement about the basis of morality, we know the tasks that we moral philosophers should undertake. We are trying to answer the question Socrates raised: how to live."[20] Disagreements arise, because when it comes to Socrates' fateful question, "it is very hard to get an indubitable answer based on an undeniable foundation."[21] However, in the seventeenth and eighteenth centuries there was a competing paradigm for moral philosophy, what Schneewind terms the "Pythagoras story."[22] In contrast to the Socrates story, for the

Pythagoras story, "Whatever moral philosophy is, therefore, it is not a search for a hitherto unknown . . . knowledge."[23] In the Pythagoras story, the truths of morality have been with us from time immemorial, or at least since some key religious turning point. If the Socrates story is concerned with finding the correct foundation for morality such that it is a fully human pursuit of knowledge, the Pythagoras story understands morality to stem from a disclosure from God, often in a revelatory event of some sort, such that moral theory is *not* a solely human pursuit. While the Socrates story understands error as a result of the difficulty of the endeavor, according to the Pythagoras story, erroneous views about morality are a mark of sin or being disconnected from God.[24]

Where the Socrates story makes morality a human endeavor to find the correct foundations for proper behavior, the Pythagoras story binds morality to God. It operates with the assumption that "reason is one of God's gifts to humanity,"[25] and as a result it enabled philosophers of the Enlightenment to elaborate "a role for reason while not making revelation superfluous."[26] Indeed, a great deal of energy was expended trying to figure out a positive relationship between Pythagoras and Judaism. Since Aristotle credits Pythagoras with being the first Greek philosopher to deal with morality, and since morality and reason were understood to be rooted in revelation and God, it was assumed that Pythagoras somehow had acquired knowledge of Jewish teachings before becoming a philosopher. For many early modern philosophers, it was presumably inconceivable that one could be moral without knowledge of revelation.[27] Other thinkers such as Locke, Clarke, and as we will see, even Kant to some degree, look to Christ rather than Pythagoras for the origin of genuine morality, but they maintain the connection between revelation and morality.

While the Pythagoras story is for all intents and purposes more compatible with the voluntarist position, Mendelssohn's integrates Pythagoras-story commitments with intellectualist, or perhaps more appropriately, rational-universalist ones. Mendelssohn, in order to facilitate the conditions for cultural egalitarianism (and to critique Christian triumphalism), does not link morality to a specific event of revelation, but does credit God and providence with providing all human beings with the innate rational capacities for comprehending genuine morality. Following Leibniz and Wolff, Mendelssohn's notion of morality is inextricably bound up with reason, i.e., a proper understanding of certain basic metaphysical or 'eternal' truths concerning God, providence, and immortality. Mendelssohn's commitment to rational universalism is evident in his argument that these truths which undergird morality are not rooted in any event specific to one religious tradition, but are in fact (or should be) constitutive of different religions, albeit clothed in disparate cultural, linguistic, and symbolic idioms. While, as we will see, Mendelssohn ultimately does think that a notion of revelation rooted in a supernatural event has a key role to play in sustaining moral knowledge, it is not a precondition for discerning the eternal metaphysical truths constitutive of morality.[28] And as we will see, in keeping with the Pythagoras story, Mendelssohn links erroneous notions of morality to sin, or more specifically, to the insidious influence of idolatry.[29]

The importance of Mendelssohn's 'religion of reason' is its ability to serve as a corrective to the shortcomings of scriptural universalism, whose exclusivistic tendencies conflict with his Pythagorean-intellectualist brand of rational universalism. The shortcoming of scriptural universalism and its eighteenth-century European variant, voluntarism, according to Mendelssohn, is that it operates with an inadequate or imperfect notion of God. While Mendelssohn's critique of scriptural universalism has to do with voluntarism—the arbitrariness of a morality imposed by a fiat of God's will—his concerns are more specific. To be sure, Mendelssohn's natural theology argues that morality is rational and, following the intellectualist position, holds that God undergirds morality because it is good and not that it is good merely because God dictates it. However, of greater significance for Mendelssohn than the abstract nature of such questions regarding the constitution of the good and morality, are the implications of these questions for non-monotheists. That is, Mendelssohn's Pythagorean thought takes a step beyond the dispute between the voluntarists and intellectualists, in that his concern is with how these philosophical and theological stances relate to the logics of salvation which are operative in scriptural and rational universalism.

What makes Mendelssohn of such interest for the present investigation is that his subsequent steps do not lead him to a one-sided acceptance of either scriptural or rational universalism, but rather to an attempt to integrate them. A central, although as we will see, insufficiently realized principle in Mendelssohn's enterprise of integrating a rational universalism with scriptural universalism is the task of transforming the unfathomable God of scriptural universalism into a God that is comprehensible, or at least commensurate with reason, while simultaneously maintaining a non-rationalist notion of revelation.

Mendelssohn attempts to render God transparent to reason by means of the principle of God's perfection, which is in keeping with the intellectualist tendencies of the Leibnizian-Wolffian school of natural theology. This principle is supposed to pervade every aspect of Mendelssohn's notion of God, from necessitating God's existence to securing a moral foundation for God's creation. In *Phaedon,* his early work on the immortality of the soul which earned him international acclaim, Mendelssohn reveals an important methodological procedure for acquiring knowledge about God that he more or less retains throughout his writings. Socrates, Mendelssohn's mouthpiece in this dialogue, states, "We must look to [God's] supreme perfection . . . and endeavor to investigate what contradicts or accords with it. When we are convinced that any thing is incompatible with it, we may reject and deem it impossible, as if it were contrary to the nature and being of the things in consideration."[30] This procedure allows Mendelssohn to render God essentially transparent to (human) reason, a feat which is essential to rational universalism. Since perfection belongs to God's essence, a principle which Mendelssohn believes natural theology demonstrates to be true, then any action or characteristic ascribed to God by a religious tradition, theologian, or anyone else that would indicate anything less than perfection must be erroneous.

In "Sache Gottes," his work devoted to the issue of divine providence, Mendelssohn takes up an intellectualist strategy highly influenced by Leibniz. Mendelssohn stresses that to properly understand divine providence it is essential that one correctly understand certain attributes of the divine. Mendelssohn criticizes various schools of philosophy which err by privileging either the goodness (*Güte*) or the greatness (*Größe*) of God at the expense of the other. To privilege one attribute over the other leads either to divine tyranny or divine powerlessness, both of which are indicative of an imperfection in God.[31] However, Mendelssohn points out, "The true religion of reason [*Religion der Vernunft*] considers them both in combination [*Verbindung*] with each other."[32] These divine attributes are equiprimordial, and all other attributes of God pertaining to providence, such as wisdom and might, are derived equally from them.[33] From this equiprimordiality of God's goodness and greatness, Mendelssohn argues that God not only wills the best possible world, but necessarily brings it about. To be sure, this does not mean that evils, i.e., unfortunate events and imperfections, do not exist. It means, rather, that these evil instances are byproducts unavoidably bound up with the best possible state of affairs. That is, if God were to eliminate these particular, less-than-perfect instances it would entail bringing about a less-than-optimal state of affairs, which would be morally impossible for God to do, given God's perfection.[34] Mendelssohn's natural theology implies nothing less than a thoroughgoing accordance of God's nature with human reason, such that God is rendered translucent to human inquiry.[35]

Despite his significant debt to Leibniz, Mendelssohn radicalizes the universalistic core of intellectualism well beyond his mentor. Of great significance for Mendelssohn's reconceptualization of monotheism is that his natural theology, as opposed to that of Leibniz, sees an inherent connection of God's goodness and greatness to the unique place that rational beings enjoy in the created universe. In contradistinction to scriptural universalism, the rational universalism which Mendelssohn makes the foundation for his religion of reason imposes certain moral constraints upon God in order to elevate the inherent worth of human beings. In Mendelssohn's natural theology "rational beings" (*vernünftigen Wesen*), a category in which human beings belong, are different from all other beings in creation. Mendelssohn explains that rational beings "are their own genus," because their rational nature gives them "their own independence" (*seine eigene Selbständigkeit*). That is, through their own means, rational beings inevitably strive after and achieve, however minimally, "an increase in inner perfection" (*einen Zuwachs an innerer Vollkommenheit*).[36] What Mendelssohn means here is that humans, as rational beings, have an ideal of human perfection toward which they unceasingly strive.[37] As a result of their rational faculties and the nature of the universe—which is the most perfect possible, given that the universe derives from God's own supreme perfection—human beings inevitably progress toward this goal, even if some progress at a more rapid pace than others.

This independent, unceasing progress toward their own ideal distinguishes human beings, and any other rational beings that may exist, from animals, plants, and all other creatures. Mendelssohn concludes from this that each individual rational being constitutes "his own small world" (*seine eigene kleine Welt*).[38] As a result, each individual is of infinite worth in and of itself, such that it would contradict God's own perfection for God to sacrifice rational beings for the greater good of the whole, as each rational being represents an irreplaceable whole in and of itself. The best possible world means, then, according to Mendelssohn, that God is concerned not only with that state of affairs which offers the greatest preponderance of good/ perfection over evil, but also that which does not sacrifice rational beings, i.e., terminate the progress toward their ideal of perfection, in its unfolding.[39] From this Mendelssohn argues that eternal felicity (*Glückseligkeit*),[40] which consists in the perpetual increase of human perfection even after bodily death, belongs to all human beings qua rational beings.[41] In contrast to Leibniz's intellectualist position, which upholds the Christian dogma of eternal damnation, Mendelssohn boldly asserts a humanistic rational universalism which holds that "No single individual [*Kein einziges Individuum*] that is capable of felicity is [destined for] damnation, no citizen in the state of God [*kein Bürger in dem Staate Gottes*] is chosen for eternal misery."[42]

With staggering implications, Mendelssohn substitutes this idea of the human being as a *selbständig*, rational being who inherently progresses step by step toward her own eternal perfection, for the account of the universal human *telos* operative in common notions of monotheism. By injecting his humanistic, rationally universal natural theology into the dialectical interchange between particularism and universalism which is at the center of scriptural universalism, Mendelssohn radically reconfigures it. In scriptural universalism the universal God reveals itself to a particular community and provides said community with a set of doctrines bearing universal significance. As a result, the *particular* community takes on *universal* significance, as it alone possesses the means for fulfilling the universal human *telos*. In contrast, Mendelssohn argues that all human beings as rational beings are capable of fulfilling the human *telos*, i.e., the infinite striving after perfection, on their own, without revelation.[43] Mendelssohn finds divine revelation, i.e., the logic of scriptural universalism, to be deficiently universal, in that its salvific message is inevitably limited to a particular community, at least for long historical periods. Since the exclusion of large numbers of human beings from fulfilling their *telos* is irreconcilable with the perfect God of his humane natural theology, Mendelssohn argues that revelation is an unsuitable medium for providing human beings with access to the universal human *telos*.[44]

Rather than accepting the particular laws or doctrines of the scriptural universalisms of the Abrahamic monotheisms, according to Mendelssohn, all that is needed to bring oneself into accord with one's *telos* is a rudimentary grasp on the 'eternal truths' constitutive of the 'religion of reason,' which not coincidentally also serve as the foundation for morality. Hence, Mendelssohn opposes his Pythagorean-intellectualism to any sort of voluntarist, scriptural universalism. He claims that the eternal truths "without which man cannot be enlightened and happy," are provided by the "Supreme Being . . . to all rational creatures . . . inscrib[ing] them in the soul."[45] In marked contrast to the common conceptions of Abrahamic monotheisms, Mendelssohn's account of the 'religion of reason' emphasizes that, "Since all men must have been destined by their Creator to attain eternal bliss, no particular religion can have an exclusive claim to truth."[46] Since Mendelssohn identifies eternal felicity with the human *telos*, we see that Mendelssohn's humanistic natural theology requires nothing less than a complete refusal to invest a particular community with exclusive access to the universal human *telos*, an investment which lies at the heart of the discursive structure of Abrahamic monotheisms. That is, according to his natural theology the universal God provides all human beings with access to their universal human *telos* through the *universal* human capacity of reason. Particularity is essentially minimized, in that all human beings qua rational beings must be capable of grasping the eternal truths and thus more or less able to secure the fulfillment of their *telos*. Particularity only emerges on a surface level, in the particular linguistic and symbolic differences in which various cultures clothe these universal eternal truths.

While the philosophical idiom in which Mendelssohn develops his natural theology and his notion of the 'religion of reason' is clearly a European and Christian one—he often relies more heavily on thinkers such as Leibniz and Wolff than on Maimonides,[47] for instance—Mendelssohn nevertheless finds the Christian religion problematic on natural-theological grounds. Despite the nearly universal view among his gentile contemporaries that Christianity was more rational than Judaism, if not the true 'religion of reason' in and of itself, Mendelssohn argues the contrary, and not simply as a defensive gesture. Rather, Mendelssohn presents Christianity as emblematic of the intolerant nature of Abrahamic monotheisms in general, in that it maintains a logic of scriptural universalism which is not tempered by rational universalism. This renders it incompatible with proper natural theology and therefore also the 'religion of reason.'

The inversion of the dialectical interplay of particularity and universality at the heart of scriptural universalism enacted by Mendelssohn's natural theology creates significant problems for him insofar as he wants to retain connections to Judaism. At first blush, Mendelssohn's position resembles that of John Hick. To be sure, Hick as a contemporary thinker has a deeper appreciation of the differences between religions, but structurally there appears to be a great deal in common between the two: Hick no less than Mendelssohn posits an ultimate unified metaphysical foundation for all religions. In fact, the comparison with Hick is particularly apt, given that Mendelssohn also faces the quandary of having a metaphysics skewed toward universality, which places it at odds with the discursive structure of Abrahamic monotheisms, which requires a tense dialectical interplay between universality and particularity. Unlike Hick, however, who gladly parts with the discursive structure of monotheism, Mendelssohn seeks to introduce particularity into his rationally universal natural theology in order to remain within the ambit of the elective-monotheistic worldview. As a result of this (re-)introduction of particularity, Mendelssohn's thought is less consistent than Hick's. That is, Mendelssohn's account of Judaism is insufficiently self-reflexive in the face of the epistemological challenges raised by the "problem of pluralism" (Hick). While many commentators have been quick to criticize Mendelssohn for this shortcoming, it nevertheless enables him to pioneer a new way of approaching the Other within the strictures of the discursive structure of Abrahamic monotheism.

Fittingly, in order to create the conditions necessary for scriptural universalism (i.e., a dynamic interplay between universalism and particularism) in his cosmology, which remains committed to intellectualism and the Pythagoras story, Mendelssohn proceeds less by rigorous argumentation than by means of retrieving the Abrahamic-monotheistic notion of idolatry, which he establishes as a counterpoint to the 'religion of reason.'[48] While this attempt to counterpoise idolatry, which is a notion embedded in the logic of scriptural universalism, with the 'religion of reason,' which is embedded in rational universalism, is philosophically flawed from the beginning (his account of idolatry's origin remains frustratingly arbitrary and problematic) it nevertheless enables Mendelssohn to inject a sufficient degree of particularity into his 'religion of reason' so as to preserve the dynamic interchange of particularity and universality necessary for sustaining the moments of the discursive structure of the monotheistic worldview intact.[49] In short, despite its dubious philosophical status, the significance of idolatry for Mendelssohn's thought can hardly be overestimated; it is at once the locus of his greatest ingenuity and, as we will see, the site of his greatest weakness.[50] Without it, Mendelssohn would have to forfeit any genuine connection with monotheism. However, given its heterogeneous status, idolatry poses significant challenges for the stability of his rationally universal natural theology.

Idolatry, for Mendelssohn, highlights the tenuous nature of the human grasp upon the eternal truths. It characterizes that sad aspect of human existence whereby knowledge of the eternal truths, despite being of the utmost importance for morality and attaining human felicity in this life, are extraordinarily difficult to preserve. Idolatry manifests itself as those tendencies in religious or philosophical movements such as superstition or anthropomorphism which, as degradations of reason, deflect from and interfere with the normative status of the 'religion of reason,' and thus interfere with their adherents' relationships with the universal human *telos*. The issue of idolatry, tied as it is to particularity in the tense interchange of particularity and universality, is a significant challenge for Mendelssohn's natural theology and for his attempt to elucidate a Judaism free from the moral problems endemic to scriptural universalism. It is at this juncture that Mendelssohn considers Christianity. Christianity is not merely a rival elective monotheism to Mendelssohn's Judaism, but rather represents a wholly unsatisfactory resolution to the tension between particularism/ universalism as it is related to salvific truth. Mendelssohn finds a direct connection between the imperialism and religious persecution practiced by Christians of his day and the discursive structure of Christian monotheism.

CHRISTIANITY: THE LIVING ANACHRONISM

While there are certainly urgent political and social reasons underlying his often polemical discussions of Christianity,[51] it is also important to recognize that Mendelssohn uses Christianity as a foil for Judaism, allowing him to problematize naked scriptural universalism, i.e., a scriptural universalism that is not supplemented by rational universalism. I would like to radicalize Jonathan Hess's point, that Mendelssohn "makes modernity inherently anti-colonial, using Judaism as its prime exemplar to articulate a universalist vision grounded in an appreciation of cultural and religious difference that would relegate Christianity to its status as just one religion among others."[52] Mendelssohn certainly uses a distinctly modern natural theology to radically critique colonialism and to relativize Christianity, but I would like to push Hess's point further and suggest that Christianity serves Mendelssohn as the prime example of the incompatibility of the logic of naked scriptural universalism and modern notions of tolerance and egalitarianism.[53] That is, Christianity is not merely one religion among others, but at least in its current incarnation, Mendelssohn charges, it is the obverse of the 'religion of reason.' Unlike his notion of Judaism, which is rooted both in the metaphysical natural theology of his 'religion of reason' and a domesticated form of scriptural universalism, Mendelssohn's account of Christianity is moored solely in the logic of a scriptural universalism more or less in common to Abrahamic monotheisms, which we discussed in chapter 1. That is, over and above his political motivations, i.e., defending the beleaguered and besieged Jews of Christian Europe, there is much that is theoretically productive in Mendelssohn's polemics against Christianity.[54]

Through recourse to his natural theology, Mendelssohn points out what he considers to be the irrational, and therefore immoral, aspects of Christianity such as its exclusivism, its failure to recognize the self-worth of human beings, and its voluntarism, from which follows a tyrannical notion of God.[55] On the historical level, we see that this allows Mendelssohn to defend the dignity of Judaism by retaliating against its would-be theological attackers, those claiming to demonstrate not merely the theological, but also the rational and moral superiority of Christianity, although many of these writings were wisely kept secret during his lifetime given their volatile nature.[56] On a theoretical level, which is of particular significance for our investigation, we see that Mendelssohn's discussion of Christianity allows him to problematize the logic of scriptural universalism which underpins the discursive structure of the common monotheistic worldview. Moreover, it helps him to elucidate what can be gained by substituting a more 'enlightened,' intellectualist metaphysics for the standard metaphysical paradigm underlying the structural moments of the Abrahamic monotheisms.

According to Mendelssohn's account, at the core of Christianity lies an exclusivist notion of salvation predicated upon the privileged role of revealed doctrine. Mendelssohn focuses his argument around a claim he takes to be central to all forms of Christianity, the tenet that belief in Jesus' messianic status is a necessary condition for the salvation, or eternal felicity, of human beings.[57] In our terms, this suggests that Christianity is an exemplar of unadulterated scriptural universalism, in that it attaches ultimate significance, in terms of the universal human *telos*, to the content of a revealed doctrine.[58] That is, while its revealed doctrines claim to possess universality in scope, they lack any rational necessity and universality, which means that without exposure to these teachings, not to mention some form of (non-rational) persuasion in regard to them, one is barred from fulfilling one's *telos* as a human being.

Mendelssohn argues that Christianity's claim that the human being as such cannot live morally or attain eternal salvation without access to and acceptance of confession of proper revelation predisposes it to an innate and hostile intolerance of the Other. As is common to the logic of scriptural universalism, in Mendelssohn's account of Christianity the human being is incapable of bringing herself into accordance with her *telos* (which pertains to all of humanity), without access to revelation (which belongs to the elected—Christian—community alone). Such a position clearly manifests monotheistic intolerance, in that only the members of a particular community possess the means by which to bring themselves into accordance with the universal human *telos* and, as a result, all other human beings are in error and sin.

Mendelssohn's explanation for Christianity's intolerant exclusivism lies in its metaphysical underpinnings. Christianity's exclusivism, Mendelssohn argues, derives from an erroneous notion of both God and human beings. Unlike the 'religion of reason' which conceives of God's goodness and God's greatness as being metaphysically equiprimordial, Mendelssohn claims that Christianity, which he essentially conflates with voluntarism, ascribes more importance to God's greatness than to God's goodness. In "Sache Gottes," Mendelssohn explains that this error creates a radical disparity in the relationship between God and human beings, making "God into a tyrant" whose "theological despotism"[59] consists in the radical diminishment of the human *telos,* such that human beings lack any inherent worth. This stands in stark contrast to Mendelssohn's account of natural religion, where the primary relationship between human beings and God is one of emulation and dependence. In Mendelssohn's natural theology, human beings strive to emulate God, as the ultimate actualization of perfection, through their perpetual quest to increase their own innate perfection step by step *ad infinitum.*[60] And furthermore, God provides coherence and meaning to the lives of rational beings by insuring that this is the best possible world, a hospitable environment suitable for carrying out their own struggles for perfection. In short, in the 'religion of reason,' God's relationship to human beings is an ennobling one. That is, it nurtures the infinite process of human beings perfecting themselves by bringing themselves into accord with their *telos.*[61]

In Christianity, according to Mendelssohn, God's relationship to humanity degrades rather than ennobles. Mendelssohn argues that it is not simply that Christianity adheres to voluntarism, where God, as an infinite and all-powerful being imposes morality upon human beings as finite and thus infinitely less powerful beings. But rather, Mendelssohn claims there is also an antagonism between God and humanity that lies at the root of Christianity. Rather than the 'rational' teleology of imminent approach to the infinite goal of human perfection, Mendelssohn finds the primary metaphysical orientation of Christianity in the theological notion of original sin. With original sin, Mendelssohn argues, God is by and large placed in an antagonistic relationship with human beings. Such a notion, which clearly violates Mendelssohn's notion of the cosmic order and therefore his notion of reason, "places the creator in a sort of duel [*Zweikampf*] with his creature: man has offended, provoked, and insulted" God.[62] Mendelssohn's concern here is not simply with voluntarism, but with the exclusivism of scriptural universalism, of which he sees Christianity as the prime exemplar. According to (Mendelssohn's account of) Christianity, human beings are incapable of any good on their own, they have no access (or, at least, no longer have access) to the metaphysical *telos* that God ordained for them at creation, and as a result they are rendered innately evil and depraved. The only way for human beings to escape this vile condition, to be brought back into accord with their *telos,* is through God's intervention, through an act of divine grace. Whereas the 'religion of reason,' according to Mendelssohn, holds that all human beings are of inherent, even infinite, worth and therefore destined for eternal felicity, Christianity, he thinks, is content to allow the majority of humanity to be damned for eternity. Those who do not receive God's grace are bound for eternal punishment. They are, as Mendelssohn characterizes those destined for damnation in what he sees as Leibniz's characteristically Christian theodicy, "of virtually no worth" (*fast von keinem Werth*).[63]

However, Mendelssohn perceives the same lack of intrinsic worth in those who are to be saved in Christianity. In a letter to a Christian theologian written in 1771, Mendelssohn warns that Christ, as the returning Messiah, "would, in fact, be the end of both man's freedom and all his noble endeavors to develop and cultivate his innate gifts and thus come closer to salvation. Only if man were to divest himself of his very nature would such a Messianic reign serve the best interests of mankind."[64] Mendelssohn is claiming, then, that any account of salvation which predicates salvific agency to God alone, divests even those who are saved of any inherent worth. That is, those being saved remain valueless in and of themselves; only God's grace can bestow worth upon human beings. According to Mendelssohn, this degradation of human beings in Christianity is a direct result of an erroneous notion of God which privileges God's greatness over God's goodness. Mendelssohn thinks that the inevitable corollary of this subordination of God's goodness to God's greatness, for Christians, is that while God is rendered all-powerful and all-important, the human being is rendered inherently valueless. And since the contrary, the inviolable and inherent dignity of all human beings, is a central feature of Mendelssohn's humane natural theology, this corollary is quite problematic for the (rational) tenability of Christianity.

Christianity, Mendelssohn suggests, veers from the path of reason by placing God's greatness, rather than the conjunction of God's goodness and greatness (whose corollary is the inherent worth of human beings), at the center of importance for human beings. A metaphysics that supports greatness over goodness in the character of God is quite compatible with naked scriptural universalism in its harshest forms, wherein those without access to 'correct' doctrines, i.e., the "greater part of the human race without true *revelation*," are condemned to "depravity and misery."[65] According to Mendelssohn, Jesus' sacrifice could only be viewed as a blessing if one considers God's chief priority in regard to human beings to be that they recognize, respect, and revere God's infinite majesty. According to this logic, God is justified in damning all human beings who lack grace because human beings are innately worthless, finite beings who transgress the infinite majesty of God simply by existing in their fallen states. Since God's majesty is infinite in nature, all sins against God are transgressions that have an infinite magnitude, given that they transgress God's majesty. Thus, according to this logic, God has good grounds to punish sinners most harshly.[66] Of course, by this logic all human beings without grace—which is, at the very least, all non-Christians (all Others)—have offended God's majesty and are therefore doomed to perdition, where they will suffer infinitely, which is adequate to the degree to which they have offended God's divine majesty. The only escape from damnation for the Other is conversion, whereby the Other divests herself of otherness and thereby earns the grace of God and is relieved of her infinite guilt.

The problems of the Christian position clearly emerge, Mendelssohn argues, when one sees that the attempts of Christian philosophers to justify providence through theodicy inevitably encounter "indissoluble difficulties."[67] Mendelssohn, who otherwise considers Leibniz the consummate authority in all things philosophical, finds his defense of providence to be indicative of these difficulties. Mendelssohn thinks it is Leibiniz's Christian presuppositions that constrain him in his works on theodicy to the position that only Christians can attain eternal felicity. As a result, Mendelssohn concludes that Leibniz can defend providence, which pertains to all of creation and not just Christians, only by making it essentially irrelevant to human beings in general. That is, Mendelssohn charges Leibniz with abandoning any real attempt to validate providence for human beings, since he justifies God's goodness through recourse to infinite varieties of angels and to inhabitants of other planets who he claims both greatly outnumber the inhabitants of the earth, and are necessarily bound for felicity.[68] Such a position, Mendelssohn wryly notes, offers "[m]iserable comfort for us poor earth creatures [*Erdgeschöpfe*] who are to be simply [pre]determined for suffering."[69] Even worse, in Mendelssohn's eyes, is the fact that such an attempt to reconcile this exclusivism with God's perfection "makes God into an awful and misanthropic tyrant" (*macht . . . Gott zum ärgsten und menschenfeindlichsten Tyrrannen*).[70] By calling Leibniz's God a 'misanthropic tyrant'—terms Leibniz and other intellectualists commonly used to describe the God of the voluntarists—Mendelssohn indicates that contrary to their claims, the Christian 'intellectualists' are either unwilling or unable (given the constraints of Christianity itself) to incorporate rational universalism into the scripturally universal foundations of Christianity and, as a result, voluntarism rather than intellectualism lies at the core of their positions.

In addition, Mendelssohn claims that the notion of God which is operative in the Christianity of his contemporaries lends itself to a Eurocentric view of the world.[71] Mendelssohn asks the following vitriolic questions in order to draw attention to what he sees as the irrationality of the Christian position in regard to the Other.

> If, therefore, mankind must be corrupt and miserable without revelation, why has the far greater part of mankind lived without *true revelation* from time immemorial? Why must the two Indies wait until it pleases the Europeans to send them a few comforters to bring them a message without which they can, according to this opinion, live neither virtuously nor happily? To bring them a message which, in their circumstances and state of knowledge, they can neither rightly comprehend nor properly utilize?[72]

The vision of the Other engendered by Christianity (qua elective monotheism) is inimical to the idea of inherent human dignity. A central tenet in Mendelssohn's argument against Christian exclusivism and intolerance is that a perfect God would not, indeed could not (according to the logic of this God's own perfection), be willing to permit "the greater part of the human race" to live without the necessary means for a moral existence, and without access to attaining eternal felicity.[73] And yet, Mendelssohn claims, these are precisely the terms in which Christianity views the Other as a result of its subscribing to a scriptural universalism without supplementation by a rationally universal natural theology. According to Mendelssohn, without the proper access to revelation—i.e., the New Testament and the teachings of the Church—Christianity sees humans as being "necessarily depraved and miserable," without access to either "virtue or felicity."[74] Instead, there is only the looming prospect of eternal damnation. Offering some credence to Mendelssohn's depictions of Christianity at least in his time and place, one need only look to the disputes in which he became embroiled, to see how pervasive the belief was among Mendelssohn's contemporaries that non-Christians were incapable of meeting even the minimal requirements for being decent persons in terms of outward behavior.[75]

Ultimately, for Mendelssohn, the problem with Christianity is that its notions of God and humanity are thoroughly determined by a scriptural universalism whose discursive structure, founded upon the utterly irrational and misanthropic notion of original sin, is impenetrable by and irreconcilable with any rationally universal natural theology. Christianity, therefore, even when defended by philosophers of the class of Leibniz, remains, at least in its core, a creature of revelation, giving precedence to scripturally universal brands of theology rather than philosophical, i.e., rationally universal natural theologies. As a result, Mendelssohn concludes that Christianity is not only intolerant, but is ultimately irrational as well and is therefore incompatible with modernity.

JUDAISM: THE EMISSARY OF REASON

In contrast to his account of Christianity, Mendelssohn offers an account of Judaism which attempts to synthesize the scriptural universalism of Judaism with the rational universalism of his natural theology. Mendelssohn's account of Judaism begins with the problem of the tensely interwoven dynamic of universality and particularity as it relates to salvific truth. In this case, the problems of idolatry and the lack of knowledge of the eternal truths necessary for fulfillment of the universal human *telos* among many in 'the nations' are the point of departure.[76]

Unlike his account of Christianity, Judaism for Mendelssohn rejects the notion of exclusivism in regard to the universal human *telos*, eternal felicity. Mendelssohn hopes to evade the exclusivism of strict scriptural universalism by reconfiguring the moments of Judaism's discursive structure upon the rationally universal natural theology of the 'religion of reason.' In sharp contrast to Hick, whose pluralist hypothesis compels him to forego the logic of scriptural universalism *tout court,* Mendelssohn posits that the Jews are God's elected community with a special revelation and a world-historical mission entrusted to them until the *eschaton.* Were Mendelssohn to hold that Judaism is simply one more religion that has the 'religion of reason' as its archetype then it would be, in principle, interchangeable with all other religions, insofar as all religions possess the capacity for a modicum of knowledge of the eternal truths. Since such formal interchangeability is incompatible with the logic of scriptural universalism, and Mendelssohn is not willing to abandon the discursive structure of Abrahamic monotheisms, his thought profoundly differs from Hick's at this juncture.

The complexity, and indeed significant tensions, internal to Mendelssohn's philosophy of religion arise as a result of his attempt to retain the discursive structure of the elective monotheisms while incorporating a rationally universal logic into the heart of scriptural universalism. Although lacking the rigorous consistency of Hick's egalitarian pluralistic theology, Mendelssohn elucidates an account of Judaism that is not entirely amenable to the foundations of rational universalism, yet incorporates many of its key elements while preserving the logic of scriptural universalism intact. Mendelssohn maintains the metaphysical scheme of his natural theology but integrates the discursive structure of elective Judaism with it. According to Mendelssohn, the Jews are the recipients of a special revelation, and as such they have become God's elected community, entrusted to bear witness to reason—to serve as emissaries of reason, to the eternal truths of the 'religion of reason'—in a world ruled by idolatry, superstition, and prejudice. The lived time of history is the time in which idolatry reigns, the 'religion of reason' is at best only partially recognized among humanity, and the Jews live a diasporic existence among the nations.[77] Only in the eschatological conclusion of history will the 'religion of reason' be embraced by all and the rigid distinction between Jew and gentile—enacted on the one hand by the observance of Halakhah and self-segregation on the part of the Jews, and the oppression and exclusion of Jews by the gentiles on the other—disintegrate. For Mendelssohn, the Jews are God's instrument for ensuring that those religions that are degraded by idolatry can (eventually) be led to the 'religion of reason,' although this transformation will not fully take place until an eschatological or messianic conclusion of history.

Mendelssohn's account of revelation discloses the difficulties of his task. On the one hand, he attempts to uphold his commitment to rational universalism by insisting that revelation, i.e., specific doctrines provided by the divine to a particular community, is in no way a prerequisite for human beings in general to bring themselves into accord with their *telos*. "Is revelation therefore unnecessary?" Mendelssohn asks. It is, he answers, at least for "all people who do not have it."[78] Yet revelation nevertheless introduces a profound asymmetry in the relations between the Jews and all other peoples, insofar as God has entered into a revelatory relationship with the Jews alone. Mendelssohn tries to mitigate this asymmetry and prevent any hint of voluntarism in his position, by insisting that this revelation only requires special acts and duties on the part of the Jews over and above what is required by all other peoples to bring themselves into accord with morality and the universal *telos*, and that the non-Jew need not perform these acts and duties to be moral or fulfill their *telos*. Thus Mendelssohn's concessions to scriptural universalism seem insufficient, in that while God reveals himself to the Jews,[79] providing laws and statutes, they are only binding for the Jews. In other words, Mendelssohn seems here to suggest that his scriptural universalism is not a genuine universalism, in that it does not have implications that would bear upon the Other since for all non-Jews (i.e., Others) knowledge of the eternal truths which are accessible to reason is sufficient for bringing oneself into accord with one's *telos*.[80] However, as we will see shortly, the scripturally universal aspects of revelation cannot remain contained, and they challenge and eventually undermine the built-in rationally universal constraints established by Mendelssohn's natural theology.

Mendelssohn attempts to ground his radical theological innovations in the context of traditional Jewish theology, making it appear that he is not actually reforming his religion but merely returning to its original purity. The Noahide laws, which are the seven laws developed in the Talmud concerning the status of non-Jews, focus around the issues of worshipping idols, violence, theft, eating the flesh of a still living animal, and injunctions to courts of law.[81] According to the then-dominant reading of a section of Maimonides' commentary in the *Mishneh Torah* (a reading since rendered controversial), gentiles who observe these basic, minimal laws, and observe them *because they are revealed by God,* are considered to belong to the category of 'the pious of the nations,' and therefore have a share in the world to come.[82] However, Mendelssohn innovates from this interpretation of Maimonides' authoritative position by conflating the Noahide laws with universal human morality, which he claims follows inherently from knowledge of the eternal truths. In addition, Mendelssohn rejects those stipulations of the Noahide laws which require that the laws be observed on the basis of their being commanded by God (conceived along the lines of Halakhic reasoning) in order to provide the observer with the status of 'the pious of the nations.'[83] With this bold maneuver, as David Novak explains, Mendelssohn makes the theologically unprecedented move of privileging universal reason in the form of the Noahide laws over the particular teachings of the revelation at Sinai.[84] That is, Mendelssohn roots the Noahide laws in rational universalism, not scriptural universalism.

It is important for Mendelssohn to undermine the traditional reliance on revelation in the Noahide laws for two reasons. First, Mendelssohn believes that there is universal access to the eternal truths of the 'religion of reason' among human beings. However, these truths are mediated in different linguistic and cultural mediums, such that they take very different conceptual and symbolic forms, which often vary greatly in sophistication and appearance.[85] Thus, that which appears to be idolatry to an outsider might merely be the symbols through which a religious group represents the eternal truths.[86] Second, revelation for Mendelssohn is inherently limited in its reach, and therefore cannot possibly be a prerequisite for the fulfillment of the universal human *telos*. Thus the rabbinic-'Maimonidean' insistence that the Noahide laws must be performed along the lines of Halakhic commandments, which require that they are performed because commanded by God, is in principle no different from the Christian claim that only through specific doctrinal beliefs about Jesus can one be saved. Implicit in both is the restriction that the intentional content of revelation is a necessary condition for salvation. Such claims adhere to a thorough-going logic of scriptural universalism, one which refuses to recognize the very possibility of rational universalism. This stance, which rejects modern rationalism and the egalitarianism that accompanies it, is unacceptable for Mendelssohn.

Mendelssohn attempts to uphold a balance between his rational universalism and revelation by claiming that while God is quite content to allow all other peoples to reach felicity through their reason, the Jews nevertheless require revelation. Mendelssohn insists that the notion of revelation in Judaism is quite distinct from the one which is operative in Christianity. Mendelssohn writes, that for the Jews, "the Creator, for very special purposes [*ganz besondern Absichten*] has found it good to reveal this special law according to which they live, are governed, and attain felicity."[87] With this passage we see two key elements of scriptural universalism emerge in Mendelssohn's thought which coexist uneasily with his rational universalism, namely, the dynamic interchange between particularity and universality and the notion of a God who is unfathomable to human reason. We will address this second element first. The God who reveals himself to the Jews is no longer the God of Mendelssohn's intellectualist natural theology, but rather has recourse to 'very special purposes,' i.e., purposes knowable to God but not ascertainable to human reason. Such 'special purposes' do not easily allow themselves to be reconciled with Mendelssohn's rationally universal natural theology.

Furthermore, this revelation to the Jews entails their election as emissaries of reason, which in turn creates the tense dynamic between particularity and universality. To be sure, Mendelssohn attempts to ameliorate the qualitative distinction between Judaism and all other religions, thus mitigating the dynamic interchange between particularism and universalism as much as possible. He argues that the notion of revelation operative in Judaism is not doctrinal, as in Christianity, but rather consists solely in laws and statutes. This allows him to claim that Judaism is founded on the truths of the 'religion of reason'—as are all other religions, insofar as they have not degenerated into idolatry—and that it is only in supplement to this shared body of salvific truths that the Jews posses a "revealed legislation." Thus, in contrast to Christianity, "Judaism boasts of no *exclusive* revelation of eternal truths that are indispensable to salvation, of no revealed religion in the sense in which that term is usually understood."[88] However, it remains unclear whether or not this distinction regarding the nature of revelation saves Mendelssohn from the problems tied to Christianity's exclusivism. The short answer, as scholars have been quick to point out, is that it does not.[89] The longer and more complicated answer is that the question scholars have been asking may perhaps be the wrong one. This question and the criticism that inevitably follows presuppose that Mendelssohn is attempting to escape altogether from the ambit of scriptural universalism, which would necessarily entail the forfeiture of the election of the Jews, a leap that Mendelssohn is unwilling to take.[90] Rather, Mendelssohn seeks more of a compromise between the two competing and largely incommensurable logics. It is imperative to investigate the nature of this compromise.

Mendelssohn claims that the ordinances commanded by God to the Jewish people at Sinai maintain a special relationship with the eternal truths of natural religion.[91] He explains that within the Jewish Scriptures is contained "an inexhaustible treasure of rational truths and religious doctrines" and that these remain "so intimately connected with the laws that they form but one entity. All laws refer to, or are based upon, eternal truths of reason, or remind us of them, and rouse us to ponder them."[92] That is, these laws, which are largely ceremonial in nature, are intimately bound up with the eternal truths, such that their repetition inspires Jews to perpetually contemplate and recall these truths. The laws are to be followed by the Jews in order that these truths never become lost to them.

Mendelssohn's account of the election of the Jews is founded upon his notion of Halakhah and its capacity to stave off the degeneration of the human understanding of the eternal truths of the 'religion of reason.' This notion of election goes hand in hand with the increasing ambiguity of the Jewish conception of the Other, specifically the Other's status in regard to the eternal truths. On the one hand, Mendelssohn argues that diverse religions are (or can be) in accord with the truths of the 'religion of reason,' although they express these truths in different linguistic and symbolic idioms. With this in mind, Mendelssohn is prone to accept the validity of other religions, including their accounts of miracles, provided of course they do not possess teachings which violate the eternal truths of reason.[93] However, the logic underlying this openness to other traditions and their claims is purely pragmatic in nature. Or as Mendelssohn puts it, "what is of utmost importance is not the historical truth of a [religious] mission but the logical truth of a [religious] precept."[94]

Simultaneous with this openness to the truth of Other's traditions, however, are the doubts which Mendelssohn begins to introduce concerning the Other, specifically the Other's capacity to maintain these eternal truths. In short, as soon as Mendelssohn discusses the Other, idolatry comes into play. In "Gegenbetrachtungen," Mendelssohn reveals that the Jews, bolstered by Halakhah, are qualitatively privileged over other religious communities and cultures in maintaining their grasp on the eternal truths. As a result of the inherent difficulties in sustaining philosophical truths, and apparently because they lack any equivalent to Halakhah to aid in this effort, Mendelssohn laments that "most of these [other] peoples" have turned away from the eternal truths, "harboring incorrect opinions about God and his reign" (*von Gott und seiner Regeierung irrige Meynungen hegen*).[95] In *Jerusalem*, Mendelssohn expands this line of thought into a full-blown historical account of idolatry, finding its origins in abuses of the art of writing. Idolatry, he argues, afflicts the entire world, such that the "history of mankind actually went through a period of many centuries during which real idolatry became the dominant religion in nearly every part of the globe."[96] And while Mendelssohn has been heavily criticized for the dubious nature of his 'historical' argument about the origins of idolatry,[97] this notion of idolatry provides the conditions that enable the election of the Jews to take place.

The election of the Jews, Mendelssohn indicates, is a response of divine providence to this outbreak of idolatry. The election of the Jews, for Mendelssohn, is inextricably bound up with Halakhah, or the revealed legislation, as the latter's precise purpose (or one of its main purposes) is to maintain these eternal truths among the Jews. As opposed to the idolatries that result from the written word, the Halakhah, composed mostly of ceremonies and rituals, is "a kind of living script, rousing the mind and heart, full of meaning, never ceasing to inspire contemplation."[98] The Jews, then, as the observers of Halakhah, are to serve as the preservers of these truths for all of humanity. Mendelssohn argues that the descendants of Abraham, Isaac, and Jacob

> were chosen by Providence to be a *priestly* nation; that is, a nation which, through its establishment and constitution, through its laws, actions, vicissitudes, and changes was continually to call attention to sound and unadulterated ideas of God and his attributes. It was incessantly to teach, to proclaim, and to endeavor to preserve these ideas among the nations, by means of its mere existence, as it were.[99]

This quote would suggest that the Jews are to serve as God's or, perhaps better, reason's emissaries to a world in the mire of idolatry—to serve as a veritable 'light to the nations'. The Halakhah preserves the Jews and their grasp on the truth through the historical epochs of idolatry, in order for the

Jews to testify to these eternal truths for the benefit of the Other, although, as we will see, the Others will not recognize these truths *en masse* until the *eschaton*.[100] Thus, Mendelssohn attempts to cast the historical mission of the Jews, as well as their adherence to the Halakhah—elements of Judaism which are rooted in scriptural universalism—in rationally universalistic terms. The Halakhah, which preserves the knowledge of the eternal truths for the Jews, allows them in turn to preserve and give occasion to ponder the eternal truths among those non-Jews who have lost touch with these truths. The Jews, then, do not and will not provide new knowledge to the Other, but rather restore old, forgotten, and degraded knowledge.

However, the Jews also suffer the corruption of idolatry soon after the experience of revelation.[101] This fall is concomitant with the dissolution of the Mosaic state and the new diasporic existence of the Jews. Nevertheless, Mendelssohn is adamant that the Halakhah is strong enough to preserve the Jews in exile, to maintain their distinction from the Other, and to continue to offer a privileged access to truth even in the face of the degradations of history. In a famous letter that Mendelssohn writes to his friend Herz Homberg shortly after the publication of *Jerusalem,* he explains that Jews must not abandon the Halakhah, must not convert and assimilate, as the age of idolatry is by no means over—and neither, we can infer, is the divine mission entrusted exclusively to the Jews. Mendelssohn explains that Jews are obligated to observe the Halakhah at least "as long as polytheism, anthropomorphism and usurpation of [political] power by religions reign upon the earth." For it is the Halakhah, Mendelssohn claims, which unites "the true theists," i.e., the Jews. To be sure, Mendelssohn believes that Judaism has also suffered historical degradation and idolatrous corruptions, but unlike other nations, the Halakhah prevents the Jews from being decimated by "these plagues of reason."[102] While this letter is somewhat vague, I think it is reasonable to presume that Mendelssohn is here elucidating Halakhah's preventative function, in safeguarding the Jews from a dramatic loss and distortion of the truths constitutive of the 'religion of reason.' That this can and does happen in other religions, according to Mendelssohn, is exemplified in many iterations of Christianity. Given what else we know of Mendelssohn's thought, we can also piece together that because the Halakhah is explicitly recognized by the Jews as revealed legislation which prevents the eternal truths from ever being entirely lost from their memory, so too the Halakhah preserves in their minds their mission to lead the other nations to the 'religion of reason.'

At the structural moment of the *eschaton,* Mendelssohn seems to be committed to a model of conversion. However, this model of conversion is not one which demands that the Other become Jewish. This follows from the fact that the revelation of the Jews is not a fundamentally new form of truth as in naked scriptural universalisms. Rather, Mendelssohn's account of revelation, in accordance with his Pythagorean rational universalism, provides laws and statutes which preserve the eternal truths that all humans once recognized (and some might still), and which all human beings should come to recognize again (albeit according to diverse religious customs, symbols, and languages). Thus, Mendelssohn claims that in (his notion of) Judaism there is the "hope that the differences of religions will not be of an eternal duration [*nicht von ewiger Dauer seyn wird*]," yet without demanding the conversion of the Other to Judaism. Rather, the hope is that the Jews will shepherd the nations mired in idolatry to the true knowledge of God, and at such a time "the divine wisdom" will end the separation of the Jews by publicly declaring the termination of the "the special ceremonial law."[103] Then, Jews and the nations (i.e., the Others) will no longer be separate communities,[104] and "the knowledge of the true God will fill the earth, like *water fills the sea.*"[105] In short, both the religions of the Other and the Jew will become something new, presumably something involving the 'religion of reason' broadly conceived. Due to its deferred nature, Mendelssohn does not devote much attention to the *eschaton,* and rarely mentions it explicitly. However, it is safe to say that in the *eschaton* we see that Mendelssohn tempers the intolerance that inheres in scriptural universalism by utilizing the 'religion of reason' as a mediator between the Jew and the Other.

Nevertheless, Mendelssohn's reconstruction of Judaism does not fully resolve the tensions between the rational universalism and scriptural universalism which coexist uneasily in the foundations of his thought. The most obvious indicator of this tension is in the lack of any equivalent to the Halakhah for the Other, in order to help preserve the Other's access to the eternal truths. Unless we follow the strategy of some recent scholars and marginalize Mendelssohn's discussions of the election of Judaism in general, dismissing them as merely a result of his social and political situation, we seem compelled to recognize a deep, perhaps irresolvable tension in his thought between scriptural and rational universalism, cultural egalitarianism and election.

In light of this tension, Mendelssohn's notion of the Other appears to be deeply problematic. It is far from clear how we are to reconcile his notion of Halakhah with his egalitarian insistence that "no particular religion can have an exclusive claim to truth."[106] His accounts of natural theology and Judaism appear to be incommensurable. Even if Mendelssohn grants non-Jews the same cognitive abilities to discern the eternal truths constitutive of the 'religion of reason,' because these adherents of other religions lack any equivalent to Halakhah, they cannot preserve these truths once they have reached them.[107] If this is the case, then Mendelssohn is presented with a formidable problem. As Alexander Altmann points out, "The same moral considerations that caused Mendelssohn to deny the revealed character of eternal verities should have suggested the need for a universal revealed legislation."[108] To rephrase Altmann's criticism in terms of this chapter, Mendelssohn's account of Judaism does not differ sufficiently from his account of Christianity, as it too is plagued with an exclusivism that is simply inconsistent with rational universalism. Mendelssohn's account of Judaism, no less than his account of Christianity, conceives of only one particular community having the capacity to live in such a way as to fulfill the universal human *telos,* whereas all others exist in error. The only difference would be the means of exclusion, Halakhah instead of faith in Christ. The core of Judaism, it would seem, and not just Christianity, is impenetrable to the rational universalism of natural theology. There is no ultimate reason discernible to human understanding why Judaism is privileged and elected to serve as the guardian of reason. However, Mendelssohn is not unaware of this problem, and provides a subtle attempt to extricate himself from it and in fact achieves a limited success in this venture.

4 | Monotheism and the Indiscernible Other

Judaism and the Other, a Second Look

We concluded the last chapter by recognizing the seemingly intractable nature of the difficulties of reconciling Mendelssohn's notion of Halakhah and election with cultural egalitarianism. At this point, the two poles of Mendelssohn scholarship become all too appealing—claim that the two positions are irreconcilable and Mendelssohn's project failed, or play down his talk of election as determined more by the necessity of his historical milieu than as characteristic of his thought. However, as I suggested, Mendelssohn is not unaware of the difficulties which beset his precarious position. And while these difficulties may be intractable, if we are to stop at this point, we miss what is perhaps most subtle and fascinating in Mendelssohn's thought. Mendelssohn makes fruitful innovations in the monotheistic conception of the Other in order to ameliorate, if not solve, the predicament in which his competing interests land him. It is therefore imperative that we explore these innovations in more depth.

In Mendelssohn's attempt to extricate himself from his philosophical predicament, there is more to be found regarding his conception of the Other—in particular the relationship of the Other to the election of the Jews—than has been acknowledged in the existing scholarship. Mendelssohn makes two claims which, if borne in mind in this context, suggest that his thought regarding the relationship between the Jew and the Other in fact succeeds, at least in a limited degree, in reconciling election and cultural egalitarianism. These claims also help ameliorate the effects of the ultimate predominance of scriptural universalism over rational universalism in his thought. The two claims at issue here are (1) that diversity is the plan of providence, and (2) that there is an uncertain relationship between the individual and the collective. Rather than viewing these characteristic claims of Mendelssohn's natural theology as simply in conflict with the election of the Jews, as Alexander Altmann and many other commentators do, it is more suitable to view them as ways to make his conception of the Other more nuanced. These two claims ease the tensions between the tendencies of cultural egalitarianism and election of the Jews which emerge in Mendelssohn's integration of a rationally universalistic natural theology into the moments of the discursive structure of Judaism, even if they do not fully extricate him from the bind between scriptural and rational universalism.

Mendelssohn's claim that "diversity is evidently the plan and purpose of Providence,"[1] is a corollary of his beliefs that human beings are all destined for eternal felicity and that this is the best possible world. Recognition of this divinely ordained diversity, Mendelssohn thinks, should bring about a sense of humility when examining foreign cultures and religions. He sharply rebukes Christian Europeans who claim that other cultures and religions are idolatrous when, in fact, they are not sufficiently familiar with them to make such a judgment. Mendelssohn states, "In judging the religious ideas of a nation that is otherwise still unknown, one must . . . take care not to regard everything from one's own *parochial* point of view, lest one should call idolatry what, in reality, is perhaps only *script*."[2] In exploring an unfamiliar religion, it is not readily apparent to the outsider if its culturally specific signs/symbols point beyond themselves to the eternal truths, or if they are, in fact, mistaken for the divine. That is, it is not clear to the outsider whether the specific signs/symbols of a particular religion aid in or detract from the knowledge of God's relation to the universe, i.e., whether they are benign and holy or malignant and idolatrous.

The Other's religion is ambiguous, since its mysterious and foreign symbols may point to the eternal truths but may also be debased, no longer pointing beyond themselves, and therefore idolatrous. The status of the Other's religion is often unclear. Mendelssohn's own discussion of the religions of India, which he poses as a counterpoint to the dominant Christian accounts of his day, beautifully demonstrates this ambiguity. While Mendelssohn reprimands the arrogance of the Christian missionaries for their dismissal of the religions of India as idolatrous monstrosities, he then goes on to claim that Hindu symbols exemplify "how easily such symbols and hieroglyphs can lead one into error."[3] He never says that they do lead one into error, but only highlights how symbols such as these can serve as great temptations to idolatry.

Although Mendelssohn does not offer clear criteria by which to ascertain who is or who is not idolatrous, and in fact his thought renders this distinction difficult to determine, he nevertheless believes it is one that with great care can be legitimately discerned. In *Jerusalem*, Mendelssohn explains that travelers "must acquaint themselves very intimately with the thoughts and opinions of a nation before they can say with certainty whether its images still have the character of script," i.e., still point to the eternal truths, "or whether they have already degenerated into idolatry."[4] How intimately must a traveler be acquainted with the culture of the Other in order to make such a judgment? That appears to be a question left open by Mendelssohn. However, it seems clear that Mendelssohn felt sufficiently versed in the doctrines of Christianity and the speculative theologies of Christian philosophers such as Leibniz and Wolff, to make judgments about that religion. Unfortunately, however, Mendelssohn never explains how he is able to do this with any precision.

The second claim of Mendelssohn's which nuances the relationship between election and cultural egalitarianism, is the uncertain relationship between the individual Other and the society or religion to which she belongs. Since Mendelssohn's natural theology requires that access to the human *telos* be available to all human beings qua rational creatures, rather than allotted on a communal basis, Mendelssohn opens a gap for individuals to be distinguished from the communities to which they belong. That is, according to the logic of Mendelssohn's position, we can only really speak of access to and fulfillment of the human *telos* on an individual, not a collective level.[5] In fact, Mendelssohn's philosophical worldview requires that the level of teleological development of humanity as a whole in this life always remains about the same; it is only the individual that can progress toward fulfilling her *telos*.[6]

We are now in a position to examine Mendelssohn's response to the contradiction that haunts his thought, i.e., the incommensurable notions of the Other at play in his respective accounts of cultural egalitarianism and the election of the Jews. Mendelssohn's arguments regarding providence's plan for diversity and the uncertain relationship between the individual and the collective enable him to bring about a limited reconciliation between election and cultural egalitarianism. However, this reconciliation is limited in that Mendelssohn's notion of election requires at least a significant number of Others to remain idolatrous, otherwise there would not be sufficient grounds for providence to warrant the election of Jews in the first place. That is, Mendelssohn cannot allow a full-blown cultural egalitarianism to emerge until the *eschaton*, until the messianic age, because idolatry, an element of agonistic particularism he appropriated from the monotheistic worldview, is the only foundation Mendelssohn has for the election of the Jews.

Mendelssohn achieves a limited reconciliation between the election of the Jews and cultural egalitarianism by means of softening the intolerance inherent in the notion of idolatry, or better, by rendering it more difficult to distinguish the idolater from the non-idolater. Given the arguments about diversity and the possible disparity between the status of the individual and the collective of which she is a member, Mendelssohn makes it necessary to draw a distinction within the category of the Other. One can no longer consider all Others to be idolaters, or even to possess less truth than the Jews.[7] To be sure, humanity-in-general, which characterizes the majority of human beings, is for all intents and purposes idolatrous. However, at any particular time it is unclear who specifically comprises this humanity-in-general. Rather humanity-in-general, as a division within the broader rubric of the Other, represents the background of Others with whom one is not presently concerned. As for the particular Other(s) who are before one—which can be an individual or a specific cultural or social group—her or their status is always, at least at first, uncertain. While the Jews may consider themselves to have a better grasp on the truth than humanity-in-general, it is much harder to accurately determine such a privileged status in regard to the particular Other(s) before them. Rational universalism is still in play to the degree that the Other may possess the eternal truths, albeit in a cultural-linguistic form which is yet indecipherable to the Jews.[8]

The notion of the Other, however—thus split between humanity-in-general and the particular Other who is before one—remains a site of anxiety with regard to the status of her (or their) possession of the eternal truths. That is, the Other's relationship to the eternal truths cannot be a matter of indifference to the Jew, or any adherent of the 'religion of reason' for that matter, since these truths have important practical implications. In *Phaedon*, Mendelssohn explains that moral existence is predicated upon a proper conception of these eternal truths. Without a belief in the afterlife, the perfection of God, and providence, Mendelssohn argues, morality is simply not rationally coherent.[9] And in *Jerusalem*, Mendelssohn explains how incorrect conceptions of God lead to religious "violence and persecution" as well as all the other "evils which from time immemorial have been perpetrated under the cloak of religion."[10] Given these concerns, it is helpful to ask three questions. First, how should a non-Jewish adherent of the 'religion of reason' interact with a particular Other who is before her, whom she has good reason to suspect has a deficient understanding of the eternal truths? Second, how should a Jew interact with this same Other? Third, are these two interactions different, and if so, why?

With regard to the first question, the non-Jewish adherent of the 'religion of reason' should proceed with great caution in approaching a particular Other, even though she is fairly secure in her estimation that this particular Other has idolatrous religious beliefs as a result of a deficient understanding of the eternal truths. In a remarkable letter written to the Swiss Christian theologian Johann Caspar Lavater, Mendelssohn offers important insights into why this caution is required.[11] The context of this letter is a dispute which erupted in August 1769 when Lavater, conscious of Mendelssohn's fame as a philosopher, challenged him to publicly refute a recent philosophical justification of Christianity by the well-known scientist and philosopher, Charles Bonnet, or convert.[12] Instead of accepting Lavater's challenge openly, over the next few years a flurry of letters were exchanged between the men and unfortunately Mendelssohn, who had always striven to avoid religious controversy, thenceforth found himself at the center of it.[13] To be sure, Mendelssohn explains, certain religious and philosophical positions are wholly detrimental to humanity and should not be tolerated if held by the Other. Such idolatrous beliefs, Mendelssohn thinks, produce a "harmful effect on all ethical conduct [which] is so obvious [that] they cannot be expected to yield even some incidental good." Examples of such idolatrous beliefs, for Mendelssohn, include "fanaticism, hatred of one's neighbor and the hatred-spawned desire to persecute him"—an obvious jab at Lavater and his brand of Christianity—as well as "sybaritic opulence, and amoral atheism which bespeak man's waywardness."[14] These two extremes, Mendelssohn thinks, can lead to positions dangerous to humanity as a whole.

Nonetheless, Mendelssohn is quite adamant that in general the religious beliefs of the Other, even if they are erroneous, are not harmful to society as a whole and therefore must not only be tolerated, but should not even be subject to criticism—they must be accepted like differences in taste. According to Mendelssohn, even idolatrous, superstitious systems often serve as pillars of the social order, the destruction of which would do more harm than good. There is, as Mendelssohn had already explained in *Phaedon,* "no system of religion so corrupt as not to give certain sanction to some duties of humanity, which every friend to mankind holds sacred."[15] In addition, Mendelssohn explains to Lavater, there are many sorts of erroneous beliefs which ought to be tolerated by all without criticism, so long as they are not directly detrimental to morality. In answer to Lavater's challenge, Mendelssohn explains that "some of my fellow men's convictions, though erroneous in my eyes, belong to a category of higher theoretical principles so far removed from life's practical concerns that their harmful errors are not immediately felt."[16] He goes on to explain that because the beliefs of Christianity serve as the bedrock of the social order, their theoretically erroneous doctrines should not be undermined, lest one inadvertently undermine the social order as well. Mendelssohn explains:

> Anyone interested more in mankind's welfare than in his own public image will refrain from making his personal thoughts about such matters public.

> *In fact, he will avoid an outright attack on another's religious beliefs and pro-*
> *ceed with the greatest caution, so as not to cause the overthrowing of an ethi-*
> *cal principle*—suspect though it may seem to him—before his fellow men
> are ready to replace it with one he himself regards as true.[17]

Mendelssohn acknowledges that his position in this regard is largely
a result of pragmatic realism. He concedes to Lavater that such erroneous "notions or beliefs" can be conducive to the welfare of humanity "only
incidentally," and that because "wrongly motivated," actions stemming
from such beliefs "hardly deserve to be called moral" in the proper or full
sense. That is, such beliefs motivate proper actions for the wrong reasons,
such as fear of punishment, rather than 'correct' ones such as the love of
oneself and the Other, and the desire to better both. Mendelssohn even
acknowledges further, that "it would be far better and safer to base the
promotion of the good on truth—wherever it is recognized—than on error and prejudice." People with adequate knowledge of the eternal truths,
Mendelssohn believes, act more consistently with moral norms than those
who are motivated by superstition and prejudice. However, Mendelssohn
is profoundly pessimistic about the knowledge of these eternal truths ever
being disseminated sufficiently during history "to have as great an impact
upon the masses as their long-standing prejudices." Popular culture, with
all its superstitions and errors, is nevertheless a more stable and secure
foundation for society, Mendelssohn believes, than the innovations of reformers, however well-intentioned and even rational they may be. As a result, Mendelssohn concludes that not only must "these prejudices" not be
interfered with, but they "must be almost sacred to anyone who cherishes
virtue."[18] Thus, a position of cautious conservatism is to be preferred to
that of radical reform. Mendelssohn may ultimately affirm much concerning the doctrine of rational universalism, but he is rather pessimistic regarding the capacity of human beings and culture to render themselves
commensurable with it.

Mendelssohn's discussion of the power of the state and religious freedom reflects both his ambiguity toward the Other and his pessimism toward a secular answer to idolatry. He explains that the state can legitimately "trouble itself" with religions or organizations that call into question the
proper understanding of the eternal truths of reason, "those fundamental
principles on which all religions agree, and without which felicity is but
a dream, and virtue itself ceases to be virtue."[19] How precisely, we might
ask, will the state 'trouble itself' in this matter? Mendelssohn is, unfortunately, extremely vague in his answer to this question. He explains that
the state "is to see to it from afar that no doctrines are propagated which
are inconsistent with public welfare; doctrines which, like atheism and

Epicureanism, undermine the foundation on which the felicity of social life is based."[20] However, it is not clear what this 'from afar' actually means, especially given the strictures Mendelssohn puts on the power of the state in terms of influencing the beliefs of its citizens. Nevertheless, Mendelssohn's vagueness in this regard clearly highlights the difficulties involved in intervening with the Other even when the Other shows signs of idolatry.

We will now turn to the second question, how is the Jew to approach the particular Other before her, whom she has good reason to believe possesses an insufficient understanding of the eternal truths? The Jewish approach is to remain distinct, to preserve itself as a community apart, through observance of the Halakhah. Judaism, according to its discursive structure, understands its election as the bringing of a 'light unto the nations.' Mendelssohn transfigures this doctrine to accord with his natural theology by casting the Jews as the emissaries of reason in a world that is ruled by prejudice and superstition. The Jews, despite this esteemed function, are, practically speaking, a relatively powerless lot, lacking political position, influence, and military might in the societies in which they live.[21] As a result of Mendelssohn's rather pessimistic understanding of history—with no hope for significant progress in human beings bringing themselves into accord with the universal human *telos* on anything but an individual level—it is simply not feasible to expect any major conversion of humanity as a whole to the 'religion of reason' in any particular era or generation. Thus, the mission of the Jews cannot be conceived in terms of bringing the truth to the Other in any immediate sense. How precisely the Jew serves as a light to the nations remains unclear since Mendelssohn seems to conceive of the mission of the Jews as consisting, practically speaking, in nothing more than their remaining distinct from the Other throughout history by means of the observance of Halakhah.

Although Mendelssohn attempts to frame the mission of the Jews in terms of his rational universalism, it nevertheless becomes apparent that scriptural universalism is the dominant operating logic here. It is no coincidence that Mendelssohn never adequately accounts for precisely how the Halakhah can preserve the eternal truths for the Jews, much less how the Jews' observance of Halakhah can beneficially affect the Other. Commentator Fritz Bamberger highlights the incomprehensibility of Mendelssohn's position, asserting that the "concept of mission—that the Israelites have been called to proclaim divine truths—is completely obviated by the exclusively legislative character of the revelation. The purpose of the Law is limited to one nation alone, even and indeed especially as far as universal truths are concerned."[22] Mendelssohn uses the well-known ability of Halakhah to keep the Jews separate and distinct in the societies in which they live as the basis of a vague and thoroughly inadequate argument about the nature of bearing witness. Mendelssohn claims that somehow this separation draws more attention to the Jews, so that nations lost in the mire of idolatry will somehow be more disposed to watch as the Jews bear witness to the truths of the 'religion of reason' through their rituals and ceremonies.[23]

Ultimately, Mendelssohn's failure in argumentation here stems not so much from any weakness inherent in the bearing-witness modality of promulgation, to which he takes recourse, as from the fact that his thought is, at this point, more thoroughly rooted in scriptural universalism with its unfathomable God, than in rational universalism. That is, having tacitly shifted into the logic of scriptural universalism, Mendelssohn finds himself unable to make viable arguments—he is now dealing with an essentially unfathomable God. All Mendelssohn can do is reiterate traditional arguments of trust in and loyalty to God. There must be some rationale for the Halakhah, and a benevolent God cannot allow the majority of humanity to endure idolatry forever. However, given that he is no longer dealing with natural theology, Mendelssohn is no longer able to utilize his subtle metaphysical arguments about God's perfection and the relationship of God to humanity. In fact Mendelssohn, the thinker who bested Kant in a prize-essay competition on metaphysics organized by the Prussian Royal Academy, can only state:

> God liberated them [i.e., the Jews] from this state of slavery by extraordinary miracles; He became the Redeemer, Leader, King, Lawgiver, and Judge of this nation that He himself had fashioned and He designed its entire constitution in a manner that accorded with the wise purposes of his providence. Weak and shortsighted is the eye of man! Who can say: I have entered into God's sanctuary, looked over the whole of his plan, and am able to determine the measure, goal, and limits of his purposes?[24]

He can only urge trust in God and the mission of the Jews as attested to in revelation. In this sense, while Mendelssohn has blurred the lines between scriptural and rational universalism, there is no question that the status of the pristine metaphysical argumentation for which he was famous has been significantly diminished, and its authority replaced by the logic of scriptural universalism.[25]

At this point, as well, the relationship between the Jew and the Other becomes mediated by God. There is a curious disinterest in regard to the Other that emerges in Mendelssohn's discussion of bearing witness. The witness performed by the Jews becomes something primarily between the Jews and God, and only indirectly between the Jews and the Other. To be sure, in this way Mendelssohn can evade requiring any actions which might appear to be overtly hostile against the Other or her way of life, as there is no need or even expectation that the Other will pay any special heed to the Jews. The Other's attitude toward the Jews, and, even toward the eternal truths, is a matter of concern for the Other alone, not for the Jews. The Jews' sole task is to remain steadfast to the commandments entrusted to them by God, regardless of the consequences.[26] Only at the *eschaton* will there be any dramatic interaction between the Jews and the Others, and this will not concern all Others, but only idolatrous ones—and this is deferred for the foreseeable future. The benefit of Mendelssohn's position is that it not only preserves the Jews as distinct while they bear witness to the Other, but also avoids the inevitable agonism that arises from direct confrontations or critiques of the Other. It both permits the Other to be other for the duration of history and allows for the possibility that the Other may possess the truth, in part or in whole, and therefore to be in no special need of the Jews. However, the cost of this solution is a relative disregard for the Other and her knowledge (or lack of knowledge) of the eternal truths.

To answer the third question, which concerns differences between the adherent of the 'religion of reason' broadly conceived and the Jew's approach to a particular Other who appears to have erroneous conceptions of the eternal truths, it is necessary to discuss the specific religious mission of the Jews. Mendelssohn seems to have little confidence that human beings can achieve a genuine solution to idolatry on a large scale and solely with the aid of reason. While the 'religion of reason' remains the archetype of all existing religions for Mendelssohn, he is skeptical of it ever concretely extending beyond a small elite within any given culture. The best humanity can do is to preserve the dominant social order which, although largely founded upon prejudices and superstitions, nevertheless offers a sense of moral and social order and stability, however skewed and problematic. Mendelssohn considers reform-efforts based on reason alone to be dangerous, as they inevitably uproot the established order and accrue more damage than any possible benefits. As for the Jews, they—or properly speaking God, acting through them in bringing forth truth—and not reformers among the adherents of the 'religion of reason' broadly speaking, are to be the ultimate instrument bringing humanity in general to embrace the 'religion of reason' and to abandon idolatry. It is the Jews, as the keepers of Halakhah, who bear witness to the eternal truths through their very lives, and who will serve as the emissaries of reason in their isolated status from other communities. The election of the Jews, despite Mendelssohn's claims to the contrary, is ultimately rooted in the unfathomable will of God and not in any sort of rationally universal natural theology. Thus, for Mendelssohn, it is the unfathomable will of the God of scriptural universalism which determines the direction of religious history, not the God of rational universalism, whose will is discernible to human reason.[27] At the *eschaton,* Mendelssohn avers—but not before—the 'religion of reason' will emerge as universal among human beings.

Has Mendelssohn succeeded then in reconciling election with cultural egalitarianism, scriptural with rational universalism? Has his account of Judaism, unlike Christianity, allowed itself to be thoroughly permeated with natural theology, with rational universalism? While Mendelssohn's innovations are impressive, we must conclude that ultimately he cannot escape the problem for which he finds fault in Christianity. Let us approach the difficult issue of the relationship of natural theology and election in Mendelssohn's thought one final time. Judaism as an elective monotheism, particularly its sense of election, is predicated upon separation from the Other, and is thus more or less satisfied by Mendelssohn's position. However, while Mendelssohn fulfills this requirement of the Abrahamic monotheisms, in that it provides a robust conception of election, it fails to satisfy the demands of the rational universalism of his natural theology, namely that all human beings should possess equal access to the eternal truths given that they all possess infinite worth. Unlike John Hick, Mendelssohn refuses to dissolve the bind of maintaining both an egalitarian natural theology and the discursive structure of elective monotheisms. Mendelssohn is unable to balance the incommensurable logics of scriptural and rational universalism, and the former becomes the dominant logic. The best Mendelssohn can do is to soften the intolerance endemic in the Abrahamic monotheisms by breaking the identification of the Other with the idolater, making the Other's relationship to idolatry more difficult to discern, and thereby reducing any structural hostility toward the Other to a sort of indifference. While this is clearly a tremendous advance in regard to our project of ameliorating the violent intolerance of monotheisms, one cannot avoid the incoherence that arises with regard to the unfulfilled egalitarian needs of his own version of a rationally universal natural theology. The election of the Jews will always remain a heterogenous element in Mendelssohn's natural theology, which undermines his very endeavor to establish Judaism as compatible with natural theology, and thus with rationality.

WHY WE CAN'T STOP WITH MENDELSSOHN

Mendelssohn attempts to overcome the intolerance inherent in the Abrahamic monotheisms by replacing their traditional metaphysical foundation with that of his Leibnizian natural theology, and thus supplementing the logic of scriptural universalism with rational universalism. While Mendelssohn's endeavors in this direction enable a softening of intolerance, in the end his position is unable to reconcile election with cultural egalitarianism.

The inability of Mendelssohn's thought to bring about a seamless integration of rational universalism into scriptural universalism, I submit, is not a result of the nature of the task itself. Rather, the problems that beset Mendelssohn arise as a result of his basic assumptions and the specific means by which he sets about to achieve this reconciliation. Mendelssohn's natural theology is rooted in his commitments to the Pythagorean story of the history of moral philosophy, which, in conjunction with his rationally universal Leibnizian metaphysics, commits him from the beginning to a premise of radical equality and deep homogeneity across apparent diversity. This assumption is simply incompatible with the discursive structure of Judaism, and indeed all Abrahamic monotheisms. Thus, the specificities of Mendelssohn's Enlightenment commitments present him with an 'Athens' that is incommensurable with any viable 'Jerusalem.' However, Mendelssohn's failure in no way entails that we must accept the position of so much twentieth-century philosophy of religion and theology, namely that (rationalist) philosophy and theology are in principle, at least in their deepest foundations, incommensurable.[28]

The metaphysics of Mendelssohn's natural theology is problematic from multiple perspectives. Most obviously, his natural theology is tied to a conception of metaphysics which has become highly suspect in philosophy. In both Continental and Analytic discourses, as well as their precursors in eighteenth and nineteenth-century philosophy, including the epoch-making thought of Mendelssohn's contemporary, Kant, there has been a rigorous and steady assault on the metaphysical enterprise as a whole. To be sure, natural theology, Mendelssohn's chosen medium of rational universalism, is still by no means a dead enterprise. However, its form has changed significantly, having become far more cautious in the wake of Kant, Heidegger, and many other thinkers, not to mention under the dramatic impact of modern science. Mendelssohn's robust Leibnizian framework takes as self-evident many assumptions about the capacities of human reason which subsequent philosophy has significantly problematized. All of Mendelssohn's eternal truths—the existence of God, providence, and the immortality of the soul—though some more than others—have been rendered questionable if not indefensible in light of subsequent philosophical developments. Mendelssohn's notion of the 'religion of reason,' premised entirely around these metaphysical, eternal truths, is too anachronistic to maintain any useful function today.

Furthermore, and even more importantly for our purposes, the specific metaphysical assumptions implicit in Mendelssohn's Pythagorean natural theology insist upon a radical homogeneity of truth across cultures and religions, and this has two implications that are ultimately disastrous for Mendelssohn's enterprise. The first implication is that his metaphysics forces him to inevitably underestimate the otherness of the

Other. Mendelssohn's metaphysics relies upon the existence of the eternal truths, which are absolute and universal—truths concerning the existence of God, providence, and the immortality of the soul. While these truths have, ironically, a particularly Christian character to them, arising as they do from the Neo-Scholastic philosophies of thinkers like Leibniz and Wolff, Mendelssohn insists that these truths belong to all religions (insofar as they are not debased by idolatry) although they are clothed in diverse symbolic and linguistic frameworks. While Mendelssohn's claim in this regard is, in fact, aimed at counteracting the more chauvinistic views of his contemporaries who tended to regard adherents of non-Christian religions as irrational, Mendelssohn nevertheless configures the Other and the Other's religion in terms which are foreign to them. That is, because Mendelssohn believes that rationality necessarily involves belief in these metaphysical truths, he is compelled to render the Other, at least insofar as she is believed to be rational, as one who believes these same truths. As a result the only legitimate differences between cultures, insofar as they are rational, are the differing linguistic and cultural configurations in which the same eternal truths are clothed. And while Mendelssohn zealously defends maintaining these cultural differences,[29] the differences themselves are rather insignificant. The great exception to this minor differentiation between religions is Judaism, which Mendelssohn clearly distinguishes by means of its elected status, Halakhah, and divine mission as the emissary of reason.

The third problem related to the metaphysics constitutive of Mendelssohn's natural religion is that it is incompatible with Judaism. His natural theology's requirement of sameness and equality essentially precludes the doctrine of election which stands at the very core of Jewish self-understanding. To be sure, Mendelssohn is able to sustain a notion of Jewish election, but it is only by introducing a heterogeneous element, idolatry, into the rational universalism of his natural theology, which ultimately undermines it. Judaism, and elective monotheism more generally, cannot coexist with a metaphysics that is predicated upon equality and deep homogeneity between cultures. Rather it requires asymmetry in some form or other, and Mendelssohn is only able to provide this by introducing heterogeneous elements which contradict his natural-theological foundation.

Mendelssohn is a far subtler thinker than is often recognized, and his innovations regarding the Other and idolatry are of tremendous importance for the philosophy of religion. As the first thinker in the religion of reason trajectory, Mendelssohn discloses new ways of thinking about monotheism—of combining rational and scriptural universalisms—even if his synthesis of these logics is imperfect. The difficulties and failures of his thought also reveal the direction that subsequent thinkers of this trajectory, Kant and Cohen, are forced to take. In order to escape the intractable problems that reliance upon metaphysics poses for tolerance, it is imperative that we look elsewhere for solutions to this problem. Kant diverges from Mendelssohn's position in two ways which prove essential to the success that Cohen will ultimately achieve: Kant begins a shift from a Pythagorean conception of rationally universal morality to a Socratic one, although this shift is only partial, and he shifts religion's focus from metaphysical truths to ethical ones. It is these two innovations which, when perfected by Cohen, can lead to the elimination of violence in the intolerance of monotheistic religions—or at least in Judaism.

Part Three | Kant: Religious Tolerance

5 | Radical Evil and the Mire of Unsocial Sociability

If Mendelssohn's efforts within the religion of reason trajectory are concentrated upon rendering the Other indiscernible and thereby problematizing the automatic characterization of the Other as an idolater, Kant's energies are marshaled in a very different direction. Kant incorporates an awareness of the finitude of human knowledge as well as a radical reflexivity and decentration into the very core of the dynamics of the discursive structure of the elective monotheisms. In short, Kant utilizes the discursive structure of the elective monotheisms to engender the possibility of a genuinely symmetrical relationship with the Other, and as such Kant establishes a notion of tolerance which significantly deviates from the respective accounts of Locke, Rousseau, and even Mendelssohn in its respect for the otherness of the Other, prioritizing mutuality with the Other in processes of reasoning and community-formation.

This new notion of monotheistic tolerance is made possible by Kant's epoch-making philosophical critique of metaphysics and shift toward reason employed in its practical (ethical) varieties. However, while Kant's epoch-making thought offers essential resources to this project, it is not its culmination. Indeed, as we will see there is a profound ambivalence in the heart of Kant's project. As a result, Kant's thought can be developed either in the direction of Cohen's Neo-Kantian 'religion of reason,' or in that of such contemporary 'Kantians' as Hick and Habermas. In this chapter and the next we will explore Kant's profound contributions to the religion of reason trajectory, but also why it is ultimately necessary to learn from his attempt to reform the monotheistic worldview—incorporating essential elements from his project of reconfiguring the monotheistic worldview—while nevertheless taking a different path. In short, we will see both the important contributions as well as the indelible problems of Kantian religious thought, which Hermann Cohen's Neo-Kantian ethical monotheism is able to solve successfully (though he also forsakes certain elements in the process) in a manner that should still hold our attention today.

Radical Evil and Indeterminate Selves

Perhaps the insight in *Religion within the Limits of Reason Alone,* against which the rest of that book—and perhaps even the rest of Kant's philosophy—is ultimately illuminated, is that human beings are mired in an inexplicable evil which keeps them from living as they should. As Philip J. Rossi points out, it is only with the notion of radical evil that the "social dimension of critique" which is present throughout Kant's critical oeuvre "receive[s] its complete articulation."[1] That is, through his discussions of radical evil, Kant elucidates not only that reason is thoroughly social but so also is the act of critique, the act of bringing reason into accord with itself (which Kant takes to be central to his philosophy).[2] As a result of the sociality of reason and critique that it reveals (or reveals most fully), Kant's notion of radical evil provides the self with the capacity for profound reflexivity and decentration. And this radical reflexivity and decentration foster Kant's own account of a rational universalism that is rooted in mutual respect and inclusivity, such that the teleological fruition of history, where ethics remakes nature (which for Kant includes human institutions), is effected through public processes—i.e., processes comprising the self and others/Others[3] in symmetrical relationships of mutuality. These public processes are constitutive of critique, whereby individuals freely recognize and transcend their own selfish inclinations and thereby bring their ends into harmonization with Others' ends. Thus, where Mendelssohn is able to break the troublesome equation of the Other with the idolater, but in other respects remains more or less bound to a scripturally universal worldview, Kant initiates a turn toward a more immanent conception of God (though his notion of God is not solely immanent, but remains immanent *and* transcendent).[4] This enables him to develop a notion of tolerance which is rooted in mutual recognition between rational agents and which fosters a universally inclusive pursuit of the eschatological moment of elective monotheisms, albeit translated into rational universalism and rendered immanent to history.

Kant's explorations of the theme of radical evil maintain a rather ambiguous relationship with the doctrine of original sin. Emil Fackenheim highlights this ambiguity, pointing out that on the one hand the "doctrine of radical evil . . . has so close a resemblance to the Christian conception of original sin as to be practically indistinguishable from it," while on the other hand "the state of original sin is a moral and metaphysical impossibility" for Kant.[5] This ambiguity manifests itself in Kant's vacillating attitude toward original sin throughout *Religion within the Limits of Reason Alone.* For instance, Kant can state, "However the origin of evil in man is constituted, surely of all the explanations of the spread and propagation of this evil through all members and generations of our race, the most inept is that which describes it as descending to us as an *inheritance* from our first parents."[6] In keeping with his ambivalence, however, immediately after this dismissal Kant proceeds to explain that the scriptures from which this doctrine derives are in fact quite helpful narrative explanations of the nature of radical evil, which is a fundamental facet of the human condition.[7] Perhaps Kant's peculiar treatment of original sin stems from a discomfort with its resemblance to his notion of radical evil. It is known that many of the *Aufklärer*'s contemporaries understood his notion of radical evil as nothing less than an affirmation of this most theological of doctrines.[8] And yet, Kant's notion of radical evil is anything but a straightforward acceptance of this doctrine.

Mendelssohn, as we have discussed, was highly critical of Christianity, which he saw as ultimately irrational in its metaphysical foundations given its roots in the theological doctrine of original sin.[9] Mendelssohn's complaint against the doctrine of original sin is twofold: first, it renders human beings incapable of being moral or good in any capacity of their own; second, it implies a tyrannical notion of God willing to offer grace to some and inflict damnation upon a vast many others on a basis which, as far as human reason is concerned, is completely arbitrary. While I do not wish to claim that Kant is influenced by Mendelssohn in this respect,[10] it is quite interesting to note that Kant's account of radical evil takes issue with precisely these two elements of original sin as well.

Kant agrees with Mendelssohn's first objection to original sin, that it is morally unacceptable to consider humans as being incapable of being autonomous moral agents. However, while the two philosophers agree on this point, this same objection leads them in very different directions. Whereas Mendelssohn uses this objection as a basis on which to argue on behalf of the potential moral integrity of the religious Other, Kant remarkably uses it as a means by which to investigate the self's own moral corruption. To be sure, the moral law, which for Kant is an *a priori* 'fact of reason,' tells us that all human beings ought to be moral, i.e., it tells us to make the moral law our supreme maxim. And if we are commanded thus by practical reason, then the fulfillment of such a command must be possible. And yet, when looking at the world of humanity around him—from explorers' reports of distant peoples to personal observations of the moral flaws in his own society, and especially from "the international situation, where civilized nations stand toward each other in the relation obtaining in the barbarous state of nature (a state of continuous readiness for war)"—Kant concludes that the moral law is not the supreme maxim in the hearts of human beings.[11] So what is the root of this 'barbarism,' this *unsocial sociability*,"[12] if not that human beings with the capacity to be moral—to make the moral law their supreme maxims—have instead chosen to subordinate the moral law to self-love?

In contrast to the doctrine original sin, which places the ability and thus ultimately all responsibility (at least for Kant) of remedying humanity's innate tendency to 'evil' in God's hands, Kant develops a nuanced notion of human guilt and responsibility.[13] To be sure, Kant concedes that human beings have an 'original propensity' to evil. That is, bound up in the very nature of being human, and as such beyond any choice of an individual's will (i.e., freedom), are the propensities to self-love of the animal and human varieties. This means that human beings qua sensible creatures are naturally predisposed to be affected by the senses and sensual pleasures and thus susceptible to such vices as gluttony and lasciviousness.[14] Additionally, insofar as they are admixtures of sensibility and rationality, human beings are caught up in a dialectic of unsocial sociability wherein "we judge ourselves happy or unhappy only by making a comparison with others," which nature uses in order to foster "rivalry . . . as a spur to culture."[15] Human beings, then, are inevitably tempted by self-love (either in its animal or human varieties), but this temptation is not itself evil. The propensities to self-love, as Fackenheim puts it, "exist prior to my act of will, and independently of it. I am under their control, not they under mine."[16] Since good and evil have to do with freedom and the will, the propensities themselves, which are not under the jurisdiction of our freedom, cannot be the root of evil. Rather, good and evil are the result of what a human being does with the inclinations inherent in their propensities, and thus there remains a free choice of the will even though this will is already delimited. Kant asserts, "Man *himself* must make or have made himself into whatever, in a moral sense, whether good or evil, he is to become. Either condition must be an effect of his free choice; for otherwise he could not be held responsible for it and could therefore be *morally* neither good nor evil."[17]

And yet Kant argues that all human beings are evil. They are evil, however, only contingently and not necessarily. That is, every actually existing human being is in fact evil, and thus Kant can say "evil can be predicated of man as a species."[18] Nevertheless, evil is not something inherent in the human species, such that every human being would possess it of necessity. If that were the case then the will and its free choice to incorporate something *other* than the moral law into the foundations of its supreme maxim—i.e., the disposition which underlies all particular maxims—would be removed from the process, and no one would bear moral responsibility because they could not have done otherwise.

However, the *radicality* of this evil is not so much in the fact that it is universal (though not necessary) in humanity, but rather that this evil "corrupts" precisely this "ground of all maxims"[19]—it corrupts this basic disposition underlying all specific maxims. As commentator Leslie A. Mulholland explains, "Every specific maxim concerning a specific action must cohere with the agent's supreme maxim. Thus Kant insists that all unlawful conduct is a consequence of the evil maxim."[20] Mulholland is highlighting that human beings as moral beings are fundamentally free and thus can and should (in the sense of *ought*) make the moral law in all its purity their supreme maxim, and yet they inevitably fall short. Since nowhere is the moral law the supreme maxim of anyone in actuality, Kant concludes that in human beings the "ultimate subjective ground of all maxims" is corrupt.[21] Not only are human beings corrupt in the ground of their maxims, i.e., human beings possess evil dispositions, but they are responsible for their own evil dispositions. That is, it must be regarded as a choice of each individual's own will to make something other than the moral law as its supreme maxim or else morality itself is impossible. But we know morality is not impossible since the moral law is an apodictic 'fact of reason.'

However, if one's supreme maxim is corrupt, then all subsequent willing and acting will be corrupt. It remains unclear, then, how one can extricate oneself from this situation when one's basic disposition underlying all particular acts of willing is corrupted. That is, if one's supreme maxim/basic disposition is corrupt, then all specific maxims will be corrupt. Therefore, it seems impossible that one can pull oneself free from the quagmire of corruption once one has fallen into it—and we have all fallen into it. And yet, Kant remains adamant, even though we cannot help but recognize that the supreme ground of all of our maxims is corrupt, because we are free and obligated to the moral law, it must be possible to overcome this corruption.[22]

Tellingly, in order to clarify his position, Kant alludes to the doctrine of original sin. Kant argues that it would be wrong to ascribe the term "*wickedness*" to account for the radical evil that afflicts human beings, but "we should rather term it the *perversity* of the heart." Whereas a wicked person has a "diabolical" disposition that eagerly adopts evil into her maxim, a person with 'perversity of the heart' is such that her 'evil' disposition can "coexist with a will which is in general good." The essential difference for Kant, is that the genuinely wicked person, which for Kant is an impossibility in actuality, seems to delight in evil,[23] and is thus monstrous, whereas the person with 'perversity of the heart,' along Pauline lines, delights in the good (i.e., recognizes the inherent value of the moral law) but lacks "sufficient strength to follow out the principles it has chosen for itself" and fails to preserve the moral law in all its purity due to other incentives.[24] Kant stresses that the scriptural account of the fall correctly represents

> man . . . as having fallen into evil only *through seduction,* and hence as being *not basically* corrupt (even as regards his original predisposition to good) but rather as still capable of an improvement. . . . For man, therefore, who despite a corrupted heart yet possesses a good will, there remains hope of a return to the good from which he has strayed.[25]

Kant finds additional merit in the mythical nature of the scriptural account of the 'fall' from which the doctrine of original sin arises in Christian theology. The account in Genesis gives a narrative form to something that remains rationally unintelligible to us. Kant explains that "the rational origin of this perversion of our will [*Wille*] whereby it makes lower incentives supreme among its maxims, that is, of the propensity to evil, remains inscrutable to us." The problem, as Kant sees it, is that evil "could have sprung only from the morally evil," and yet if we freely chose to let this reign in our supreme maxim, which again is the only case in which human beings can be held morally accountable, then this would imply that prior to this 'fall' into evil, human beings had a natural "predisposition to good." But if this is the case, then how did the 'morally evil' ever enter the picture in the first place?[26]

Kant, however, breaks with the traditional doctrine of original sin in his response to the problem of this innate corruption. Unlike the Christian doctrine which emphasizes God's role in the redemption of human beings from this corruption, Kant defers questions about God's role, stating that knowledge about what God does to help us in terms of our moral self-renewal, if anything, is not essential, at least from the perspective of practical reason. What is absolutely imperative is "to know *what man himself* must do in order to become worthy of this [divine] assistance."[27] However, it is precisely at this juncture, where the human being and not Jesus' vicarious atonement is to overcome this corruption, that ironically God and a notion of grace come to play a positive role in Kant's account. However, both the notions of God and grace are radically reconfigured in such a way that human beings and reason remain the primary focus of *Heilsgeschichte* even if, in keeping with the tone of his earlier works, they are brought to humility in a process of radical reflexivity and decentration.

In agreement with Mendelssohn's second objection to original sin, Kant finds the notion of God bound up with that doctrine to be problematic. If we recall, Mendelssohn finds the notion of God which is compatible with the doctrine of original sin to be not only metaphysically erroneous, but also tyrannical and monstrous: This notion of God is incompatible with the modern ideal of egalitarianism since it justifies oppression and imperialism. Kant is equally troubled by this notion of God and any (scripturally universal) foundations to Christianity rooted in the nexus of original sin and grace, at least as traditionally conceived. But Kant goes further than Mendelssohn in problematizing the "mystery of *election*." Kant rejects as irrational those teachings of Christianity in which "a heavenly *grace* should work in man and should accord this assistance to one and not to another, and this not according to the merit of works but by an unconditioned *decree*; and that one portion of our race should be destined for salvation, the other for eternal reprobation."[28] Such teachings could only refer to a God who is incompatible with rationality, i.e., to the unfathomable God of scriptural universalism, which is wholly unacceptable to Kant.

Kant repudiates scriptural universalism, which he more or less equates with the operating logic of historical religions in *Religion within the Limits of Reason Alone,* recognizing legitimacy solely in a rational universalism. By making morality a 'fact' of practical reason, Kant not only imbues morality with necessity and universality; he also makes it the basis of rational universalism and thus the 'religion of reason.' In *Religion within the Limits of Reason Alone,* Kant explains that it is not God who invests morality with legitimacy, but conversely, it is morality which invests the idea of God with rational legitimacy.[29] In short, Kant dramatically reverses the traditional theistic conception of the divine command by claiming that it is morality that gives us access to God, it is morality which "leads ineluctably to religion,"[30] rather than it being God's revelation which founds or provides access to morality.[31] With this move, Kant disqualifies revelation axiomatically by means of the rather radical claim that reason is the sole legitimate access to God.[32] And since metaphysical speculation about God transcends the limits of reason strictly laid out in the *Critique of Pure Reason,* Kant claims that one is only rationally justified in speaking about matters of God insofar as they pertain to the moral law, which is a fact of reason. Thus, the idea of God is only rational and thus only legitimate to the degree that it is a necessary presupposition for the moral law. In doing so, Kant undermines the unfathomable God of scriptural universalism, transfiguring it into a God fully in accord with his ethical rational universalism.

It is useful at this juncture to contrast Kant's conception of God to Mendelssohn's, in that there is a major divergence between them whose significance cannot be overstated for the purposes of this investigation. Mendelssohn initially attempts to maintain the coexistence of the logics of rational universalism and scriptural universalism. However, due in no small part to their incommensurable notions of God, the perfect God of his rationally universal natural theology gives way to the mysterious and unfathomable God of scriptural universalism. Kant, on the other hand, decisively rejects the unfathomable God of scriptural universalism in favor of a God who is rooted in his account of rational universalism with no vacillation whatsoever.

Kant critiques the historical religions, and thus scriptural universalism, by asserting that the conceptions of God and concomitant forms of worship inherent in these religions of 'mere worship' systematically prevent the human being from fulfilling the demands of the moral law and the entire realm of morality. These religions do not grant reason autonomy in that they still adhere to a theocentric notion of the universe, such that both the right and the good are predicated upon an anthropomorphic conception of God. With striking clarity, Kant's philosophy of religion highlights that there is no room for both an autonomous (human) reason and an autonomous God (i.e., the unfathomable God of scriptural universalism). Since the entire foundation of Kant's thought is predicated upon the priority of autonomous reason, historical religions err in that they privilege God's will over (autonomous) reason. By elevating God above the moral law, such that God cannot be a fellow rational being bound to the rational law as human beings are, adherents of historical religions fall into idolatry and superstition in that they compromise the absoluteness of the moral law, which is degraded and rendered relative. Kant argues that unlike a pure rational religion, in which God and human beings are both members of the same moral community working to establish the ethical commonwealth,[33] historical religions play to their own inclinations, and privilege God in order to either quell fear or to enlist the aid of the divine in satisfying desires.[34]

Kant binds all legitimate discussion of God to the moral law, which both respects the infinite worth of *all* human beings qua rational agents and categorically rejects any sort of special aid that would circumvent the arduous journey of moral self-improvement, which is the sole condition of salvation. As a result, any scripturally universal account of the Christian God is rendered not only speculative but idolatrous. Thus, while Mendelssohn does his best to rein in those elements of scripturally universal Judaism which conflict most sharply with a rationally universal egalitarianism, he nevertheless ends up with a notion of election in regard to the Jews which privileges them in terms of access (or ability to retain) the eternal truths of reason, if not earthly power or even salvation. Kant, however, rigorously effaces all such traces of scripturally universal election, and even if he argues for Christian superiority, it is on solely rational grounds and not on theological ones.[35]

Rather than rejecting Christianity's metaphysics specifically, Kant rejects metaphysics and speculation altogether and rigorously conceptualizes sin and grace in terms of practical reason. Given the demands of both his strict subordination of scriptural universalism to his account of rational universalism, and his project of critical reason, Kant renders more traditional solutions to the problems raised by original sin—such as the idea of vicarious atonement,[36] concomitant claims on behalf of the priority of faith,[37] and rituals such as church worship[38]—problematic. Such 'solutions' are untenable given the privileged position Kant accords to the moral law. That is, unlike the moral law, which is apodictic and indubitable, Kant claims that "we cannot know anything at all about supernatural aid."[39] Thus, if the claims of supernatural aid contradict the indubitable moral law, one should trust the moral law.[40]

Nevertheless, Kant is unwilling (and perhaps also unable) to part with the notion of grace entirely. The problem that remains for Kant is that the corruption described in his discussions of radical evil lies in the innermost core of each person's supreme maxim, and thus one cannot gradually reform oneself through behavior in accordance with the moral law. For Kant, this would at best render one legally and not morally good, and the difference between the two, as we will soon see, cannot be overstated. For Kant, in order to attain the morally good status one must effect "a revolution" in one's inmost "disposition" so that one can be rendered a new person.[41] This raises a significant problem for Kant. In the absence of God's active and mysterious grace, how can someone who is "corrupt in the very ground" of her maxims bring about a revolution by herself, in order to become morally good? How can her will, perverse and corrupted in its very core, change what it itself is, without help from something outside of it? And yet, "duty bids us to do this, and duty demands nothing of us which we cannot do."[42]

Kant's solution to this impasse is to utilize the same inscrutability that enshrouds the 'fall' into radical evil, to hold open the hope for the possibility of a restoration of our original good disposition. Kant states:

> How it is possible for a naturally evil man to make himself a good man wholly surpasses our comprehension; for how can a bad tree bring forth good fruit? But since, by our previous acknowledgment, an originally good tree (good in predisposition) did bring forth evil fruit, and since the lapse from good into evil (when one remembers that this originates in freedom) is no more comprehensible than the re-ascent from evil to good, the possibility of this last cannot be impugned.[43]

That is, just as it is inexplicable and inscrutable how an originally good disposition chose to incorporate evil into its supreme maxim and thus fall from innocence, so too must it be utterly inscrutable (but no less possible) for a disposition which is corrupted even in the core of its most basic maxim, to reform itself in a radical moment of decision.[44]

Whatever the merit of this argument philosophically, Kant fruitfully exploits the relationship between the ground of the supreme maxim and particular actions. First of all, the radical revolution in one's inner disposition, the change of heart or (self-enacted?) inner revolution into a new person, which Kant argues must be possible for all human beings, is nevertheless something that no particular individual can ever be certain that she has attained for herself. As Kant puts it, "Man cannot attain naturally to assurance concerning such a revolution, however, either by immediate consciousness or through the evidence furnished by the life which he has hitherto led; for the deeps of the heart (the subjective first ground of his maxims) are inscrutable to him." What is key for Kant is that one "must be able to *hope* through his *own* efforts to reach the road that leads thither, and which is pointed out to him by a fundamentally improved disposition, because he ought to become a good man and is to be adjudged *morally* good only by virtue of that which can be imputed to him as performed by himself."[45] In other words, what is important for Kant is not the knowledge that you yourself *are indeed reformed* but only that *it is possible for you to be reformed,* for otherwise morality itself would become irrational, since it would be impossible.

Kant's account of the possibility of inner revolution or moral regeneration is both parasitic upon and transformative of his postulates of practical reason—i.e., God, freedom, and the immortality of the soul[46]—as they are discussed in the *Critique of Practical Reason.*[47] For the Kant of the second *Critique,* God ensures the deep coherence between the right and the good and thus the rationality of moral endeavor. Since moral actions have never necessarily entailed positive results in Kant's ethical theory, God ensures that ultimately the proper (i.e., moral) ordering of one's maxims will have some positive effect on the world lest a radical cleft form between one's prudential interests and the moral order, which would threaten the very coherence of the moral project. However, Kant insists that the 'highest good'—the object of morality itself, which in the second *Critique* consists in a more individualistic correlation of happiness and virtue—is impossible without the additional postulate of immortality.[48]

Immortality is a necessary postulate of practical reason in the second *Critique,* Kant argues, as a result of the moral obligation incumbent upon all human beings to enact in themselves a "*complete adequacy* of attitudes to the moral law." However, "Complete adequacy of the will to the moral law . . . is *holiness,* a perfection of which no rational being in the world of sense is capable at any point of time in his existence."[49] Human beings as admixtures of the sensible and the rational will always fall short of holiness, of complete adequacy to the moral law, and therefore the best they can do is approach such adequacy as a regulative ideal.[50] That is, the individual can perpetually approximate it, getting ever closer but never attaining this goal of holiness. However, Kant's notion of the 'highest good'—the point at which the sensible self's desire for happiness is reconciled with the rational self's demand for virtue—has this complete adequacy as its supreme condition. On these grounds, Kant justifies postulating the immortality of the soul as ethically necessary, since moral coherence requires that the human being is "proceeding *ad infinitum* toward that complete adequacy,"[51] which will in turn bring about the reconciliation of happiness and virtue.

Now it is important to bear in mind that Yirmiahu Yovel is certainly correct in his groundbreaking argument that in Kant's later works, such as *Critique of Judgment* and *Religion within the Limits of Reason Alone,* the emphasis of the highest good shifts from the otherworldly to a this-worldly future. That is, with the *Critique of Judgment* Kant's position in regard to the highest good fundamentally shifts from a personal and otherwordly emphasis to a collective and this-worldly one.[52] However, Yovel overstates the case when he argues that one's personal highest good (which requires the immortality of the soul) transitions entirely into a universal and immanent highest good, namely, "the *complete realization* of this moral world."[53] While Yovel is correct in that the immanent future of the collective, earthly realm of human existence becomes the central focus of Kant's discussions of the highest good, the role of the individual, particularly the individual's concern with her own extraworldly salvation, remains significant. In fact, it is precisely the reflexivity and decentering capacities that accompany the individual's concern with her own salvation in *Religion within the Limits of Reason Alone* (in light of radical evil) which create the conditions for the immanent, collective highest good.

In *Religion within the Limits of Reason Alone,* emphasis is taken away from God as the being that secures the correct apportionment of virtue and happiness on an individual basis,[54] such that God now becomes necessary as that being which can provide the conditions of the possibility for an inner-revolution away from radical evil and into the long road toward virtue and holiness. Of course, Kant never abandons the epistemic and moral strictures established by his earlier critical works.[55]

The question of God's help in terms of grace inevitably raises the question of immortality. God may be willing to help one become worthy of entering the infinitely long path of righteousness toward holiness, but one must first make oneself worthy of this help. But how can we know if we ever achieve this worthiness? In the second *Critique,* Kant already elaborates an infinite gap between all human striving and the ideal of holiness. *Religion within the Limits of Reason Alone,* however, radicalizes this gap by throwing into doubt whether the individual ever truly embraces holiness as her ideal, and thus escapes corruption of the will. In other words, the change of heart from perversity and corruption to the good, if it does indeed ever take place, only gets the individual to where she was at the beginning of the *Critique of Practical Reason.*

It would be a mistake, however, to think that Kant has simply added a supplement of little consequence to his argument for the necessity of the postulate of immortality, or that his notion of God now simply offers a different version of the same transcendental-ethical function served by the God of the second *Critique.* Rather, the character of these postulates has changed significantly, such that a profound degree of reflexivity and decentration is injected into the self that finds itself compelled to postulate them.[56] According to the *Critique of Practical Reason,* as an individual one not only knows what one's duty is, but there is a relative security in one's good faith in that one knows what one is doing is right (or at least is on the right track for approximating the unattainable ideal). However, in *Religion within the Limits of Reason Alone,* the individual cannot know if she has in fact made the 'inner revolution' and changed herself into a new person, created for herself a new disposition. Mulholland claims that it is in this context of humanity being situated "in a condition of radical ignorance regarding its own salvation" that grace comes to play such an important role for practical reason. According to Mulholland, far from releasing people from moral responsibility, Kant's account of grace serves "the function of reminding everyone 'to continually test himself as though summoned to account before a judge.'"[57] Since grace is only a postulate, and one that is conditioned upon one doing all that one can to be morally worthy of it—a status that again is uncertain—grace serves as a constant lever supporting moral behavior.

Sharon Anderson-Gold highlights the social nature of radical evil and the concomitant reflexivity—indeed indictment of oneself—that this doctrine brings with it. She argues that "if evil exists, if we are moved to protest its existence, we must suspect its power is pervasive."[58] That is, we must question "our own conduct," and given that "we have no privileged access to our own disposition,"[59] we are forced to recognize the following disconcerting insight: "The disposition as such can only be good or evil,[60] and as the conditions of the exercise of our freedom are the shared conditions of social existence, we have no reason to apply different standards to others and to self. The world must be a mirror to our souls."[61] That is, just as the world is a morass of evil rather than of good, so too we must conclude that we ourselves are sunk in the morass of radical evil, rather than deluding ourselves into thinking that we have somehow pulled ourselves loose from the mire. Anderson-Gold's statement raises an intriguing point that has far-reaching consequences: Radical evil is not solitary but, as she and Philip Rossi have elaborated in their respective works, is inextricably connected to our social relationships with other human beings.

RADICAL EVIL AND POLITICS

Kant's historical political writings explain the origins and progress of reason and culture by means of 'nature,' where the dialectic of 'unsocial sociability' is regnant rather than morality, which is more a-temporal in character and which, in fact, arises from the unfolding of the dialectic of unsocial sociability.[62] The recent scholarship of Anderson-Gold and Rossi have fruitfully brought Kant's account of radical evil in *Religion within the Limits of Reason Alone* into discussion with his account of unsocial sociability. As Anderson-Gold puts it, "Kant's theory of evil provides an important interpretive bridge for the historical, cultural and social dimensions of his moral philosophy."[63]

As finite rational beings, humans are driven by the desire to have their inclinations sated. This desired compensation and satisfaction of needs and wants, Kant argues, derives from a more foundational desire for happiness. While many philosophers base their moral philosophies on the universality of this desire for happiness, Kant argues that happiness is only problematically universal. To be sure, Kant concedes that "although the concept of happiness *everywhere* underlies the practical reference of *objects* to the power of desire, it is still only the general heading for subjective determining bases and determines nothing specifically."[64] That is, although happiness is desired by all human beings, its particular contents vary significantly from case to case. Happiness is universal in name only; since its specific contents differ from person to person, it is incapable of founding a universal principle. The content of each individual's happiness is particular to herself, and thus it is unsuitable to be the foundation for any sort of consensus, given that it is bound up in the fundamental differences between individuals.

Not only is happiness not a genuinely universal principle, it is also a futile one. First, nature, which Kant states is clearly "very far from having adopted [humanity] as its special darling," often thwarts our desire for happiness; but second and even more significant, is that humanity's own natural proclivities hinder its realization. Kant explains that "man's own absurd *natural predispositions*" lead human beings to "put others of his own species in great misery through oppressive domination, barbaric wars, etc."[65] Human nature is, according to Kant, peculiar because it craves happiness more than anything else, and yet is constituted in such a way as to be incapable of it, even if all the material conditions for it are met. Kant asserts that the primary element of this discord in humanity, this innate inability to be happy, lies in humanity's social nature. This element of social discord is quite productive in that this overwhelming desire for a happiness which cannot be achieved has, according to Kant, an essential function in the development of the human species toward its destiny, which is to make itself into the very purpose of creation. Kant envisions this teleological process in which reason develops as a struggle of wills between human beings, resolving itself in the engendering of an ethical commonwealth and a cosmopolitan federation of nations which live in perpetual peace with one another.

Human beings thus unknowingly serve nature's end, the development of reason and society, through their individual pursuits of happiness via the attempts to satisfy their inclinations, which of necessity bring them into conflict with other human beings. It is not simply that sociability and the pursuit of happiness conflict with each other, but that sociality in general is at once inextricable from human nature and yet a source of immorality and thus unhappiness. Moreover, not only are individual human beings rooted in the dynamic of unsocial sociability, but nation-states are as well. Thus nation-states, just as individuals, are unable to exist peacefully with one another, but rather exist in a state of perpetual envy and hostility with one another.

The example of unsocial sociability that Kant uses in *Religion within the Limits of Reason Alone* is the interminable wars of historical religions.[66] The disputants in wars of religion are the 'historical religions' or religions of 'mere worship.' These historical religions are utterly corrupted by radical evil in that they are predicated upon the logic of self-love, which privileges the desire for happiness over moral duty in one's maxim. However, self-love—rooted as it is in the merely sensuous, where happiness in and of itself is the end—is unable to generate the universal consensus which, Kant argues, only morality can.

The implications for our investigation of this identification of radical evil (which is driven by self-love) with the operating logic of historical religions are substantial. Since Kant essentially treats all historical religions as operating according to the logic of scriptural universalism, the dialectic of unsocial sociability permeates the logic of scriptural universalism through and through such that it is by no means free from the mire of radical evil. According to Kant, self-love and scriptural universalism share the same fatal deficiency: They lack the fundamental conditions of rational universalism, in that they do not grant autonomy to reason, and as a result of their reliance upon external authorities they are unable to generate a genuine universality.[67] Kant recognizes that historical religions (and thus the logic of scriptural universalism) have universal pretensions to peace and harmony, but he insists that given their problematic foundations and logics, they can only engender endless conflict and strife.[68]

To understand how Kant envisions overcoming this endless strife between historical religions, it is imperative to discuss his notion of morality in a bit more depth than we have up to now. While human beings are sensible creatures and thus given to self-love (governed by fear of punishment and desire for reward), they also possess practical reason (the foundation of his notion of rational universalism), and thus are capable of possessing a good will, i.e., a will that is capable of willing what is good in and of itself. Human beings possess practical reason, which demands that the human being qua moral agent recognize the moral law and act accordingly even if it conflicts with their inclinations and desire for happiness. Kant insists that human beings possess this capacity to recognize the moral law, to bring their own will into accord with it for no other reason than that it is rational and moral, such that one wills the moral law for oneself. In other words, Kant claims that human beings posses the capacity for 'autonomy.'[69]

However, we must understand that the moral law is not simply a feature of the intelligible world of practical reason, but is rather the very foundation of it. Recognition of the moral imperative discloses that human beings possess autonomy, or at least the capacity for autonomy, and thus that human beings qua moral selves are independent on a foundational level from the order of nature. It is precisely this capacity to adhere to the moral law despite their sensible natures, which makes each individual human being an end in itself, because each human being possesses this capacity to be a moral agent.[70]

Just as theoretical reason, once subjected to critique, is to become a source of harmony in the intersubjective realm—disclosing a shared framework for verifying truth-claims—so also rational morality possesses a harmonizing capacity. Autonomy, as the self-willed subjection to the lawful rulings of rational morality itself, is the foundation of an intersubjective unity since the moral imperative is shared by all rational beings. Kant is adamant, however, that when one proceeds in self-willed subjection to the rulings of morality one is not heteronomously subjecting oneself to the will of another, or even to the will of the whole, but rather to the dictates of one's own practical reason, which happens to be shared by all other rational beings: Morality is quintessentially rationally universal. The dictates of the moral law, the ends that the autonomous individual recognizes and toward which she acts, are nevertheless "in systematic connection" with "a whole of rational beings as ends in themselves as well as a whole of particular purposes which each may set for himself. . . . Thus there arises a systematic union of rational beings through common objective laws."[71] As Rossi helpfully points out, "the morally legislative self" qua autonomous being should not be thought of "as an individual isolated from social relations, but as one whose morally legislative capacity bears fundamental reference to the [universally] legislative community of which she is a part by virtue of her rationality."[72]

Kant makes a rigid distinction between religions of 'mere worship' and the 'religion of reason,' claiming that the former are bound up with self-love—the inclinations and other concerns of sensibility—while the latter privileges morality and the autonomy of reason. The 'religion of reason' is not one concrete religion, but rather an ideal that should be held by all religions. It is an ideal whose content consists in the rationalizing of all particular rituals and dogmas of a religion with the aim of giving a decisive predominance to moral concerns.[73] The religions of 'mere worship,' on the other hand, which according to Kant constitute all historical religions, prioritize the sensible over the moral (often drastically, stifling the realization of the latter). Kant acknowledges that these religions have some rational and thus moral content, but this content remains latent, buried beneath rituals and dogmas which are designed to accommodate the sensible preoccupations with self-love. Kant claims that it is precisely this prioritization of the sensible aspects of the self that is the root of inter-religious discord and violence, i.e., unsocial sociability.

Religions of 'mere worship' enjoy enormous power over the human mind because of the innate constitution of the human subject, especially its sensible components. Kant recognizes that the vast majority of human beings seem to be simply incapable of accepting the abstract nature of the 'religion of reason,' which demands only that one be moral in order to be pleasing to God. He believes that the root of this error lies, at least in part it seems, in the tendency of human beings to conceive of God anthropomorphically, such that God is understood to be an essentially infinitely powerful human overlord. As a result of this mistake, people feel that just like "each great worldly lord stands in special need of being *honored* by his subjects and *glorified* through protestations of submissiveness," so likewise does God, only on a grander scale.[74] Thus human beings enjoy a particular sort of satisfaction in devoting actions and rituals to God, believing that thereby they show obeisance and win divine favor.[75]

In *Religion within the Limits of Reason Alone,* Kant radically problematizes the operating logic of historical religions, i.e., scriptural universalism, based on its rationally deficient form of universalism. For Kant the only legitimate form of universalism is rational universalism, because only this possesses the capacity for genuine universality in that it is rooted in the autonomy of human reason. Kant claims that every religion craves universal domination, or in his words, "cherishes the proud pretensions of becoming a church universal."[76] However, unless such a religion is fully in accord with the 'religion of reason,' such a desire will go unrealized, because its content (i.e., theology and modes of worship) merely possesses a universal scope while lacking the resources to ever generate any sort of consensus among human beings. Given this inability to generate a consensus, these religions too often take recourse to coercive violence.

Kant thinks that historical religions must utilize violence to try to fulfill their universalistic pretensions because they are unable to rationally communicate with Others. This inability to communicate rationally stems from their remaining beholden to revelation as their source of authority. Revelation as a source of authority is contingent and historical in nature and therefore is inherently external to reason. Historical religions neglect autonomous reason, which extends to all human beings everywhere, and instead rely on sources of authority that are "grounded solely on facts," such that they "can extend [their] influence no further than tidings of it can reach," given that they are "subject to circumstances of time and place."[77]

Unlike the reflexive practices of reason, where an ever-expanding community of reasoners who share the same basic moral foundations construct a basis of life and order,[78] revelation claims to be absolute but relies on an authority that is inherently contingent and particular to a specific time and place. In addition, not only are sources of authority grounded in revelation external to reason as well as historically and geographically contingent, but they are also "dependent upon the capacity [of human beings] to judge the credibility of such tidings."[79] However, Kant argues, human beings are incapable of legitimately ascertaining the validity of one set of claims proffered by a specific religious tradition's account of revelation as opposed to those of another. According to Onora O'Neill—in the terms of Kant's famous essay "What Is Enlightenment?"—systems of revelation are inherently private, in that in all of their communications with the Other there is "a tacit, uncriticized and unjustified premise of submission to the 'authority'" about which they speak. Only that which is open to scrutiny, to the free use of one's reason, is public.[80]

For example, while historical religions all indulge in anthropomorphic notions of God according to Kant, because these notions are rooted in authorities external to autonomous human reason, there is no possibility of communal practices of discussion and debate, or at least none that can reach rational consensus regarding the nature of God or how He wants to be worshipped.[81] As Kant puts it, if one goes beyond the strict morality implied by the 'religion of reason,' and thinks that statutory practices advocated by some historical religion or other are required to serve God, then "everything . . . is arbitrary."[82] That is, by relying on dogmatic authorities external to the regulations of reason, one forfeits the capacity to deliberate with the Other in a reflexive and decentered manner about mutual concerns regarding the divine, morality, or anything else. When external authorities are privileged over the autonomy of human reason then there is no longer any common ground shared with the Other on the basis of which disputes can be resolved. Thus, it is not surprising that a diversity of mutually exclusive religions emerge, religions which not only conceive of God differently, but which employ contradictory methods for honoring, glorifying, and generally worshipping the divine.

Reason and revelation essentially serve as contraries in Kant's philosophy of religion. Reason appeals to faculties possessed by all human beings everywhere, and is public through and through insofar as it is thoroughly reflexive, decentering, and inclusive of all (given, of course, that they respect the autonomy of reason). Revelation, however, is thoroughly contingent in nature, given that it is rooted in (putative) events which took place at particular times and places, and thus affected particular communities. Therefore in contradistinction to the moral law and the 'religion of reason' which is parasitic upon it, and despite their universal scope insofar as they assert their relevance to all human beings, the historical religions and their revelations are not genuinely universal to all human beings in all times and places because their specific claims are not recognized or shared by the Others to whom they speak. Rather, a teaching of revelation "like all empirical knowledge . . . carries with it the consciousness not that the object believed in *must* be so and not otherwise, but merely that it *is* so; hence it involves the consciousness of its contingency."[83] In short, because historical religions, despite their universal scope, lack any genuine necessity (and thus lack true universality), they are deficient when juxtaposed to the moral law which is available to all rational human beings at all times and all places.

As with the metaphysical thinking Kant so famously critiqued, the claims of any particular scriptural universalism, given their transgression of the bounds of human reason—in this case reliance on an external authority—preclude the very possibility of ever reaching a rationally legitimate consensus. Kant writes that a "church dispenses with the most important mark of truth, namely, a rightful claim to universality, when it bases itself upon a revealed faith. For such a faith, being historical (even though it be far more widely disseminated and more completely secured for remotest posterity through the agency of Scripture) can never be universally communicated."[84]

Thus, when rival religious traditions put forward contradictory claims based on incommensurable accounts of revelation, there is no possibility of resolving the dispute through rational discourse and argumentation, because their claims exceed human methods for ascertaining verifiable knowledge. As a result, the only possibility for solving such disputes is war. In fact, according to Kant, the long history of religious persecution and conflict is the result of this failure to satisfactorily bring religion into the realm of rational discourse, i.e., to establish the limits of reason and thus the legitimate conditions for discourse and argumentation between religions. Despite the universal pretensions of the scriptural universalisms, which are all historical religions, they are unable to secure any genuine universality. These religions are unable to lead to a comprehensive and therefore inclusive order, but rather inevitably lead to a multitude of fractured religious groups in competition and combat with one another. And this is precisely what history has seen—a series of seemingly interminable wars between mutually exclusive historical religions.

In the dialectic of radical evil and the dialectic of unsocial sociability, as Kant's example of the recurrent wars between historical religions illustrates so well, violence and coercion are as important to social developments as are processes of reasoning—if not more so. If there is a serious deficiency *between* different religions in terms of mutual recognition, the problem *within* (both religious and secular) societies is no less significant.[85] According to Rossi, so long as there is a lack of mutual recognition—of a symmetrical relationship between rational agents which is engendered by respect for practical reason—coercion will be the modus operandi and the state of unsocial sociability will reign. Corruption of reason entails a lack of recognition of the human dignity (and thus rationality) of our fellow human beings, and thus an unwillingness to engage them as free and equal partners in what Rossi terms "inclusive" attempts to take perspectives which, "over against our own particular interest and beyond alliances," attain "the universal interest of humanity."[86] Instead there is mutual antagonism, on both personal and international levels, which as Kant points out "does not just consist in open hostilities, but also in the constant and enduring threat of them."[87] Thus coercion remains necessary for order, but this is an order which is not rational and thus not ultimately legitimate in its most foundational grounds, and as a result cannot escape the dialectic of unsocial sociability. While Kant clearly attributes a great deal of progress[88] to the dialectic of unsocial sociability in terms of driving human beings toward a "*universal* **civil society** *administered in accord with the right,*"[89] he is nevertheless adamant that unsocial sociability is a state that humanity must transcend.[90]

At best, the dialectic of unsocial sociability can lead to historical progress on a societal (i.e., governmental) level.[91] However, there remains a significant gap between politics and morality. According to Kant, this dialectic tends to nurture civil societies that are regulated by laws which, at least externally, are in accord with reason (that is, the laws of these societies do not blatantly conflict with morality, even if they do not conform to the strict requirements of purity of motives that morality demands). Politics—particularly republican politics, which is the only valid form of government according to Kant—can rein in the "self-seeking inclinations" of human beings, ameliorating their destructive tendencies and thus enabling an organized and functional society to arise. A republican government can bring internal peace to a particular society by compelling all individuals "to submit to coercive laws and thus to enter into a state of peace, where laws have power." However, such a society "does not require the moral improvement of man," and in fact, Kant makes the remarkable claim that "the problem of organizing a nation is solvable even for a people comprised of devils (if only they possess understanding)."[92]

A society of devils would recognize the practical benefits of maintaining peace within its borders, but would not see the rational necessity of laws conforming (outwardly at least) to morality, nor to peaceful coexistence with other nations, if either ceased to be conducive to the happiness of its citizenry in some form or other. That is, if it became possible for a nation of devils to circumvent its treaties or go to war with another nation without succumbing to defeat, there would be no real reason for them to forego such an opportunity. Such a society is only externally reflected in its laws and treaties; it only abides by them because of fear of punishment or desire for reward—such a society does not itself *will* them. Only when states are genuinely moral, when rulers and constitutions genuinely recognize and reflect the necessity and universality of the laws of morality, can the clashes between individuals, nations, and religions cease and perpetual peace emerge, because then the irrational and divisive arbitrariness at the root of mutual antagonism between these individuals, nations, and religions will give way to the necessary universalism of morality. Or, as Kant eloquently puts it, "true politics cannot progress without paying homage to morality . . . all politics must bend its knee before morality, and by so doing it can hope to reach, though but gradually, the stage where it will shine in light perpetual."[93]

Since radical evil, the dialectic of unsocial sociability, is incapable of engendering its own overcoming, in *Religion within the Limits of Reason Alone* Kant posits the idea of the ethical commonwealth as the way to transcend this impasse. In the ethical commonwealth morality and tolerance-as-inclusion (of the Other) are simultaneously achieved since, in the words of Anderson-Gold, human beings freely adopt "an orientation towards others whereby our ends are systematically integrated with the ends of others."[94] However, this is by no means easy to accomplish, especially in light of Rossi's observation that in a world mired in perpetual antagonism and violence, reason "may not authorize the use of coercion to combat radical evil."[95] That is, in a world which operates according to mechanisms of antagonism and coercion, reason (as Kant understands it) must necessarily eschew all forms of coercion, violent and otherwise. Further insight into Kant's discussion of the transition from the radically evil order of unsocial sociability to the ethical commonwealth can be gleaned by exploring his discussion of Christianity's supersession of Judaism. It is to this topic that we turn in the following chapter.

6 | Kant and the Religion of Tolerance

Kant's account of the ethical commonwealth is particularly tantalizing in the context of our investigation. This is so because it concerns the climactic realization of the teleological trajectory of history in which a radically new, non-violent ethical order emerges upon the earth, but also because this new order and its manifestation are inextricably bound up with, and yet transformative of, the structures of elective monotheism. In this new order of human affairs wherein human beings transform nature to reflect the interests of practical reason,[1] humanity ceases to be mired in radical evil and rather, as Philip Rossi puts it, embarks upon "a form of social dynamics quite different from unsociable sociability."[2] This new social dynamic, which is the epitome of tolerance-as-inclusion, is constituted by a "mutual moral recognition of one another from which we, each and all, can thereby envision the possibility of constructing, on the basis of our freedom, a shared world."[3] Such a radical transformation, however, requires that the political world as we know it, a world constituted of the stuff of unsocial sociability, be transcended. To explain this movement of profound, world-historical change, Kant takes recourse to a discussion of the relationship of Judaism and Christianity.

A New Supersessionism

Kant sees his own philosophy as coming at a crucial point both in history and the history of philosophy.[4] Kant understands himself to be living in an "age of *enlightenment*" although, to be sure, this is not the same as an *"enlightened* age."[5] What this means is that human beings do not yet use their reason autonomously, but rather remain in "self-imposed immaturity,"[6] i.e., they look to external authorities to make their decisions rather than thinking for themselves, particularly in regard to issues relating to religion. However, Kant believes his own age, as an 'age of enlightenment,' is distinct, in that many of the impediments to the free thinking of individuals, especially the domination of ecclesiastical religious authorities over the hearts and minds of the masses, are beginning to weaken. The diminishing power of clerical authorities opens up the possibility for free thought and the possibility for a new world order to emerge, one that is based on autonomous reason.

The Enlightenment, while primarily a European phenomenon, is understood by Kant to have world-historical implications.[7] To be sure, Kant claims that all human beings, as possessors of practical reason, are aware, at least on some level, of the obligation to bring their religion more and more into accord with the 'religion of reason.' And yet, while it is incumbent upon all religions to make this transition, Kant makes no secret about the fact that he considers Christianity to be the most accomplished of all extant religions in achieving this concordance with the 'religion of reason.' The conditions necessary for fulfilling this transition, Kant believes, are emerging in this 'age of enlightenment,' when people (needless to say, primarily in Christian Europe) are beginning to think for themselves rather than submitting to the 'self-incurred immaturity' which allows ecclesiastical religious authorities to think and decide for them.[8] In *Religion within the Limits of Reason Alone,* Kant explains,

> If now one asks, What period in the entire known history of the church up to now is the best? I have no scruple in answering, *the present.* And this, because . . . the seed of the true religious faith [i.e., the religion of reason], as it is now being publicly sown in Christendom, though only by a few, is allowed more and more to grow unhindered.[9]

Thus, in this 'age of enlightenment,' Christianity is increasingly purging itself of the dogmatic dregs that have prevented it from realizing the rational ideal. This will allow Christianity to serve as a vanguard, with its example galvanizing other religious traditions to bring themselves into accordance with the 'religion of reason.'[10]

Like Mendelssohn's conception of Judaism, Kant understands Christianity as an amalgamation of a historical, revealed religion and a universal, rational religion. However, whereas Mendelssohn sees these two elements—revelation and reason—as ultimately symbiotic, Kant sees them as being in profound tension with one another. Thus, in sharp contrast to Mendelssohn, Kant sees his task as one of purifying Christianity of all that is tied to revelation and by doing this, of giving supremacy to its rational side. To be sure, Kant tries to make it appear as if he believes that the actual 'revealed elements' do not, in fact, contradict morality. However, the form of the historical/revealed elements is such that it is still arbitrary and mythical rather than universal and necessary.[11] Thus Kant rationalizes the various stories and dogmas of Christianity in order to render them "divested of [their] mystical veil," which in turn reveals that their "spirit and rational meaning have been valid and binding for the whole world and for all time."[12]

However, to understand Kant's rationalization of Christianity it is essential to return to the 'Pythagoras story' of morality. Whereas Mendelssohn's philosophy of religion is thoroughly bound up with the Pythagoras story of morality insofar as everyone possesses access to the eternal truths, Kant's relationship with this paradigm is somewhat more ambivalent. Kant recognizes Jesus to be the greatest moral philosopher, "whose wisdom was purer even than that of the [Greek] philosophers, as pure as though it had descended from heaven."[13] As J. B. Schneewind points out, Kant is a good Pythagorean insofar as he views his own moral philosophy as simply restating Christ's teachings—which disclose the moral nature, and the implications that follow therefrom, for all human beings—without ever going beyond these teachings in terms of content.[14] That is, Kant thinks that Jesus' teachings conform to practical reason, and as such express, albeit in sometimes mystical terms (due to the constraints of his environment), nothing else than "the moral relation of God to the human race." This teaching has universality and necessity in that the idea of this moral relation "spontaneously presents itself to human reason everywhere,"[15] even if it took a 'philosopher' of Jesus' stature to elaborate it in a way that is sufficiently convincing to challenge humanity's predisposition to self-love. Kant, as a Pythagorean, sees his own moral philosophy as in keeping with the legacy of Jesus qua philosopher, adding nothing new in terms of content.[16]

However, as Schneewind points out, Kant is not entirely committed to the scheme of the Pythagoras story, in that "Kant has contributed to the progress of morality by showing that it rests on a purely rational principle, which itself dictates the essentials of religious faith."[17] That is, as Kant sees it, he is not simply translating the content of Jesus' teachings into a new philosophical idiom; he is also showing how it is thoroughly grounded in pure practical reason. Thus Kant remains with the Pythagoras story of morality insofar as he thinks he does not offer anything that transcends the teachings of Jesus in terms of content, but he goes beyond Jesus and thus the paradigm of the Pythagoras story insofar as he uncovers the rationally universal nature of the foundations of these teachings. Kant's achievement is to translate the content of Jesus' teaching into a form that is adequate for it, i.e., into a form that accords with the universality and necessity of its content.

In addition to treating Jesus as a historical human being who happened to be a great philosopher and moral teacher, Kant redirects concern from the supernatural and refocuses it squarely upon practical reason. Kant's primary strategy in this vein is to emphasize that the Jesus-figure qua the God-man is an archetype of reason, and thereby he hopes to evade any discussion of divinity. Kant resists the tendency to discuss the concrete individual Jesus of Nazareth as the God-man (although he goes to great lengths to never explicitly deny his divinity), since such a move would be reliant upon revelation and therefore contingent and arbitrary.[18] Kant appeals to the "idea" or "archetype . . . already present in our reason" of a being who is morally pleasing to God, which idea maintains objective validity and necessity even if no empirical individual corresponding to it ever existed.[19] Rather than being the agent of vicarious atonement, for Kant the 'son of God' is an instantiation of the regulative ideal in a practical context, serving as a guide for which we as human beings are ever to emulate.

Judaism, as is well known, does not fair as well as Christianity in Kant's writings. At first blush, Judaism plays a remarkably similar role for Kant's thought as Christianity does for Mendelssohn's. Judaism functions as the cipher for the common monotheistic worldview which Kant hopes to overcome with his 'religion of reason,' and as such it serves as a foil against which the features of the 'religion of reason' are highlighted. However, there are important differences to bear in mind. Mendelssohn engages in polemics against Christianity from a precarious position—he represents and defends a persecuted minority which is ridiculed and despised not only on social and political levels, but also in the theological discourse of the larger population. Kant's juxtaposition of his rationally universal 'religion of reason' to Judaism, on the other hand, is not primarily concerned with empirically existing Jews or Jewish establishments—much less is it any sort of defensive response to them.[20] Rather, Kant's tendentious account of Judaism should be understood in terms of the larger discourse about Judaism that was prevalent during the Enlightenment.[21] As Jonathan Hess points out, "For so many intellectuals concerned with imagining new forms of political community in Germany [during the Enlightenment], Judaism . . . appeared to offer up the perfect antithesis to the norms of the modern world." Hess continues that for the *Aufklärers,* "Judaism seemed to provide the perfect point of contrast" for political orders "grounded in the principles of rationalism and universalism."[22]

Perhaps as a result of this Enlightenment discourse on Judaism, of which *Religion within the Limits of Reason Alone* is a part,[23] Kant's notion of Judaism maintains a rather ambivalent relationship to other religions. This ambiguity derives from the association of Judaism with legalism. On the one hand, Kant associates legalism with the logic of scriptural universalism as such,[24] in which case Judaism is a cipher for all more traditionalist elective-monotheistic worldviews and indeed, for Kant, for all historical religions. On the other hand, Kant understands 'authentic' Judaism as the theocracy depicted in Old Testament.[25] In this light, Kant sees Judaism and its legalism as indicative more of a form of government than of a religion.[26] While Kant's conception of Judaism is imprecise in that it often fluctuates between these two associations, both of its iterations are negative and undesirable in his view.

This ambivalence serves Kant's rhetorical purposes well, since Judaism is used as a grotesque foil for the 'religion of reason' and the ethical commonwealth, which is—or ought to be—ushered in by it. Judaism is not simply an ancient, anachronistic elective monotheism, with a scripturally universal conception of a mysterious and utterly *transcendent* God who rules human beings by irrational and even tyrannical commands; it is also emblematic of the merely juridical or political system of organization which is destined to give way to an order that is pristinely ethical, if nevertheless also in some sense political. Christianity, or at least the rationalized version which Kant hopes will serve as the gateway to the 'religion of reason,' is eminently modern (i.e., rationally universal), and emphasizes divine *immanence* in terms of God's partnership with humanity (though not eliminating God's transcendence) in the task of realizing the ethical commonwealth here on earth.[27]

Judaism serves as a foil which highlights two essential aspects of Kant's enlightened, rationalized Christianity. Kant fruitfully highlights the differences between (his versions) of Judaism and Christianity regarding the relationship between God, ethics, and politics. According to Kant, the Jewish God "desires merely obedience to commands,"[28] attaches "prime importance to mechanical worship,"[29] and has no genuine concerns with the moral disposition or conscience.[30] The God of Judaism, at least in Kant's rendering, seems virtually indistinguishable to the account of God in superstitious and statutory forms of faith.

However, what distinguishes Judaism from other historical religions in Kant's understanding is the relationship between God and the Jews, in that the Jews take God as their "earthly regent."[31] Since the Jews and God are bound to one another through the form of a (theocratic) governmental bond, the connection is legalistic, i.e., political and not moral. And since according to Kant's account of the 'religion of reason,' the sole legitimate service to God is moral, Judaism lacks any genuine religious core. That is, since the Jews take themselves "as a special people chosen by God for Himself"[32] and set themselves in a political relationship with God rooted in the Mosaic Law, they cannot, as far as Kant is concerned, maintain a genuinely religious relationship with God. As a result of this, while Kant posits that all religions bear traces of rationality and are as a result capable of rationalization, Judaism is not.

The Jewish theocracy serves as a negative counterpart for Kant's account of the 'religion of reason' in terms of its conception of the relationship between God and morality, and morality and politics. It is helpful to briefly juxtapose Mendelssohn and Kant in terms of the relationship between God and morality. A key distinguishing feature between the two thinkers pertains to the status of God in terms of transcendence and immanence in their respective philosophies. God is transcendent for Mendelssohn not only in his writings on natural theology but also and especially when he speaks of Judaism and the Mosaic Law in *Jerusalem,* where he passes into a full-blown scriptural universalism. God is utterly transcendent and imposes laws upon the Jews—laws which do not contradict reason, but which are nevertheless heteronomous. While Kant, even as late as the *Religion within the Limits of Reason Alone,* retains some degree of transcendence in his account of God, insofar as this God is the foundation for grace and immortality, he nevertheless places primary emphasis on the *immanence* of God—as the ground of, and partner in, the realization of the ethical commonwealth. While God is the transcendental condition for the improvement of the self and the world, for Kant, this role is nevertheless carefully conscribed by practical reason, which places the primary responsibility and agency for these tasks in the hands of human beings. Schneewind remarks that for "Leibnizians God sees to it that the world is necessarily the best world there can be," whereas "Kant leaves with us the responsibility for perfecting the world as well as ourselves."[33] Mendelssohn, whose natural theology is rooted in a Leibnizian conception of God and whose turn to scriptural universalism never departs from this conception entirely, is unwilling to depart from a vision of the universe in which God is the primary agent. That is, for Mendelssohn a transcendent God is not only the foundation of order and morality but also (when he shifts to scriptural universalism) the primary governor of history (even if this history is itself non-teleological).[34] While Kant retains a notion of God with transcendent and immanent functions, this God is tightly constrained by the rules of rational universalism and rigorous attention to the limits of knowledge. By this means, Kant enacts a fundamental shift away from God's agency in order to emphasize the importance of human agency.

To this end, Kant elaborates how disastrous it would be if actual, theoretical knowledge of God were to be established. In a manner somewhat similar to Mendelssohn's critique of original sin and grace—because individual human beings would have no intrinsic worth, having only so much worth as God arbitrarily bestows upon them (should God choose to do so)—Kant argues that any sort of direct theoretical knowledge of God would undermine morality and thus human worth and dignity *en toto*. Kant writes, "*God* and *eternity* with their *dreadful majesty* would lie unceasingly *before our eyes*."[35] As a result, human beings would lose their autonomy, in that they would be unable to think but in terms of consequences—i.e., of punishments and rewards for their actions—and thus would inevitably be reduced to heteronomous beings. As Kant puts it, "The conduct of human beings . . . would thus be converted into a mere mechanism, where, as in a puppet show, everything would *gesticulate* well but there would be *no life* in the figures."[36] There can be no genuine freedom, given that one would *know* that there will be consequences that inexorably follow every action one takes. In such a situation, human nature being what it is (an amalgamation of the sensible and the rational), it would be impossible to choose to do duty for duty's sake rather than out of self-love (out of fear of punishment or desire for reward). Thus there could be no genuine morality, only legality. If there were to be anything more in terms of knowledge of God than a practical postulate, it would overwhelm human beings, destroy autonomy—which is the source of human dignity—and undermine the anthropocentric mission of improving self and world.

Judaism, however, is rooted precisely in such a knowledge of God, or considers itself to be. Unlike a 'genuine religion,' the basis of Judaism is a theocracy, where "the spiritual natures of the subjects of this government remained responsive to no incentives other than the goods of this world; since consequently they chose to be ruled only by rewards and punishments in this life."[37] Jews, then, have no choice but to follow the dictates of their pseudo-religion and thus forfeit their autonomy and with it their status as moral beings; in short, as a result of having God as their king, they forfeit all that gives human beings their dignity. It is only when theocratic government and the rigid hierarchy of priests begins to diminish and Greek philosophy begins to penetrate the landscape of Jewish legalism that genuine moral and therefore religious thoughts could arise among the Jews.[38]

This raises the second way in which Judaism serves Kant as a foil for the 'religion of reason': It highlights the difficult nature of the relationship of morality and politics. Since autonomy is of foundational importance to Kant's account of morality, and since morality is the sole form of legitimate service to God, legal religions—which he contends are premised on heteronomy[39]—are incommensurable with morality and the rationalization of religion. In his ethical writings, Kant is perpetually troubled by the difference between the 'letter of the law' and the 'spirit of the law.' Since morality is internal for Kant, arising in the ordering of one's priorities and not in the actions one takes, it is virtually impossible to distinguish between a "man of good morals (*bene moratus*) and a morally good man (*moraliter bonus*)," the one who "obeys the law according to the *letter* (that is, his conduct conforms to what the law commands)"[40] and the one who "obeys the law according to the *spirit* (the spirit of the moral law consisting in this, that the law is sufficient as an incentive)."[41] And yet, while they appear indistinguishable, the first man is good while the other, "despite all his good deeds, is nevertheless evil."[42] Thus, the difference between the letter and the spirit of the law, and our epistemological inability to distinguish between people driven by one or the other motivation, bring us back to the problem of radical evil that we discussed in the previous chapter.

Given his distinctly Pauline language, one can already sense that Judaism (at least as he understands it) is acutely problematic for Kant, since it cannot recognize anything other than the letter of the law as legitimate. However, the problem is deeper, insofar as Kant seeks to elucidate how God is to relate to morality and politics. This is an issue which is particularly relevant in *Religion within the Limits of Reason Alone,* where Kant is trying to elucidate the necessary conditions of the ethical commonwealth which will emerge from the 'religion of reason.' It would seem then that the problem for Kant is not the merging of religion and politics as such—since the 'religion of reason' and the ethical commonwealth are also inextricably connected—but rather the manner in which religion and politics relate to one another. Judaism serves as the foil for Kant's depiction of rational Christianity and the proper relationship between the 'religion of reason' and the ethical commonwealth because "in its original form" Judaism is a commonwealth whose relationship with God, and in fact its entire basis for social order, is predicated upon "purely political laws" rather than morality.[43] If Kant is to show that authority derives not from God's infinite power and the teachings of revelation (which lack strict necessity and universality), but rather from a universal notion of reason, then Judaism exemplifies everything about elective monotheisms that his project seeks to de-legitimize.

While the ethical commonwealth is the world-historical turning point at which reason breaks free from the dialectic of unsocial sociability/radical evil, Judaism remains enmeshed in this dialectic. Kant conveys Judaism's rootedness in radical evil in two forms—through his comments on the narrative of Adam, and through his depiction of Judaism as mere politics. First, in Kant's summary of the Old Testament through the lens of critical reason, Adam's fall consists in the elevation of self-love over the moral law as his supreme maxim. According to Kant's reading, Adam knew the moral law in its pristine vitality, but nevertheless called into "question the severity of the commandment which excludes the influence of all other incentives." Adam's sin then is that "by sophistry he reduced obedience to the law to the merely conditional character of a means (subject to the principle of self-love)."[44] In a strikingly similar fashion, the laws of the Jews are not genuinely ethical because "they relate merely to external acts" which lay "no requirements upon the *moral disposition*," which is something only Jesus rediscovers. Instead, Judaism is exclusively preoccupied with the conditional nature of the "consequences of fulfilling or transgressing the laws"[45] which relate merely to this world, i.e., with self-love in the basest sense, reward and punishment in this life.[46]

Second, if Judaism concerns itself solely with the political, Christianity is focused upon the genuinely moral. And as Howard Williams points out, "The aspects of man with which Kant deals with in the philosophy of right are different from the aspects of man with which he deals in the . . . pure moral philosophy."[47] Legality most clearly differs from morality in two respects. First, legality is concerned with external conformity and not internal motives. That is, since it is concerned with sustaining external social bonds, Kant thinks that recourse to coercion is a necessity for legality. While society can and must enforce its external laws, it cannot coercively enforce morality since morality is rooted in autonomy.[48] And second, due to the influence of radical evil and the incomplete nature of history, no system of justice in any commonwealth is ever pure or complete. As a result, Williams argues, "Juridical laws, although necessary . . . are not wholly free from contingency."[49] That is, juridical laws are essential for human existence and in fact, if properly ordered, can support external freedom and serve as a condition for morality, but they never have the necessity and universality of morality. Thus, Judaism qua theocracy lacks universality and necessity, even if its laws literally come from God.

Both Judaism and Christianity touch upon aspects of the ethical commonwealth, which is somehow to be both ethical and political. However, by critiquing the political and thus arbitrary nature of Judaism and privileging the moral and thus rational elements of Christianity, Kant is highlighting the peculiar nature of the ethical commonwealth which will transcend the mire of unsocial sociability and radical evil. In *Religion within the Limits of Reason Alone,* the only potential escape from radical evil is recourse to the ideal of the ethical commonwealth. Through Judaism's example, Kant illustrates the inability of 'traditionalist' elective-monotheistic orderings of religion and politics to engender the ethical commonwealth and thus escape radical evil. And yet, Kant's own solution mirrors Judaism insofar as he insists that to "found a moral people of God," which is another way of expressing the ethical commonwealth, "is . . . a task whose consummation can be looked for not from men but only from God Himself."[50] Thus, Kant must elaborate a commonwealth rooted in God that simultaneously parallels and yet nevertheless radically differs from the theocratic commonwealth of 'authentic' Judaism.

Kant's account of the ethical commonwealth is rather mysterious in that it is a form of politics rooted in morality and not politics as such, a *non-politics* to counter worldly politics,[51] which as we know by now is for Kant tainted by radical evil and unsocial sociability.[52] Kant argues that there is a peculiar moral obligation, a duty *"sui generis,* not of men toward men, but of the human race toward itself,"[53] that grounds this collective ethico-political endeavor in practical reason. It seems that in the wake of the discovery of radical evil, it is no longer sufficient or even ethically tenable for individuals to remain isolated and work on their moral perfection by themselves.[54] However, specifically eschewing any sort of theocratic model, indeed any political model at all, Kant advocates the familial model of the church,[55] albeit one that rejects all sectarian exclusivism and embraces "all right thinking men" as "its *servants.*"[56] Unlike political regimes, the ethical commonwealth grows forth from diverse churches gradually bringing themselves into alignment with the ideal of the 'religion of reason' and in the process casting off their historical, particularistic, and thus arbitrary practices and beliefs. The ethical commonwealth derives its legitimacy from the universal and necessary order of practical reason. As such it is radically superior to the contingent order of coercive juridical law, even if that juridical law is handed down by none other than God.

If Kant rejects the 'Jewish' idea of a transcendent God imposing His will upon human beings as being unsuitable for the proper relationship between religion and ethics/politics, then he must be able to offer a better and more feasible account. The question remains as to how Kant's churches, these vehicles of the 'religion of reason,' can emerge much less prosper in a world mired in radical evil and unsocial sociability. Just as it is unclear how an individual who is corrupt in her basic disposition can bring about an inner revolution into goodness, so too it remains unclear how a humanity rooted in radical evil can free itself from the cycle of unsocial sociability to bring about the ethical commonwealth, or as Rossi puts it, to establish *"a set of ordered social relationships and practices based on a noncoercive authoritative principle."*[57] Kant is aware of the problem, pointing out that the duty of bringing about the ethical commonwealth "involves working toward a whole regarding which we do not know whether, as such, it lies in our power or not." As a result, given that striving for the realization of the ethical commonwealth is a moral obligation, "this duty will require the presupposition of another idea, namely, that of a higher moral Being through whose universal dispensation the forces of separate individuals, insufficient in themselves, are united for a common end."[58] Just as Kant requires a carefully delimited notion of God in terms of the individual and radical evil, so too is recourse to God required for the collective endeavor in regard to the ethical commonwealth. It is simply untenable to even rationally hope, Kant claims, that diverse people, rooted in radical evil, can reform themselves and their world, without the aid of God. And yet, if Judaism's transcendent and law-giving God is the model of unsuitability, what form can this aid take without violating the autonomy of human beings, which is foundational for morality, in the process?

Kant begins his solution by paralleling the ethical commonwealth with Judaism's theocracy. Mirroring Judaism, Kant not only stipulates that the ethical commonwealth requires public legislation, but also that God alone is fit to be the law-giver. However, his reasoning for placing God as the law-giver diverges significantly from what he takes to be the Jewish-theocratic model. Whereas the laws of God in the Jewish theocracy derive their authority from the infinite power of the divine to enforce them (and perhaps also from their prudential value given that the laws and mores resemble ethical principles in their external form),[59] Kant's ethical commonwealth has God as the law-giver because no individual or group of human beings can provide public legislation without that legislation becoming heteronomous in nature and thus undercutting the morality that is to serve as the very basis of the ethical commonwealth.[60] Unlike the transcendent God who proclaims laws in a way that undermines autonomy in Kant's account of Judaism, the God of the ethical commonwealth serves as the public 'law-giver' precisely because this rationally universal God does not violate human autonomy in the slightest, and thus can be obeyed by all human beings qua moral agents. In the ethical commonwealth God can be said to 'issue laws' but these laws are ethical, *not* political/juridical, and as such the laws derive their authority from "the free duty of virtue" not "the coercive duty of law."[61]

Kant preserves the notion of divine commands albeit in a non-heteronomous sense. Unlike the arbitrary quality of the Mosaic Law, which in the final analysis unifies a group of people on the threat of punishment by an infinitely powerful divine will, the God of the ethical commonwealth is the locus of divine commands in a very different sense. The God of the ethical commonwealth can be said to issue divine commands in that this God is the foundation of morality insofar as it can see into the innermost recesses of the individual's heart and thus divine his or her true motivations, which radically decenters the self as well as providing the conditions for the self to hope and desire to continue to strive for individual and collective moral regeneration. Anderson-Gold helpfully points out how all members of the ethical commonwealth not only must share a belief in "a moral governor,"[62] but must also each find herself in an individual and collective relationship with this "holy will."[63] Anderson-Gold argues, correctly I think, that it is only on this basis that individual and collective moral regeneration from radical evil becomes possible. God is the public 'law-giver' insofar as God secures the very coherence and intelligibility of the moral endeavor itself on both the individual and collective level.[64] These traits of God, Kant claims, enable us to regard God as the supreme law-giver which brings a public face to the ethical commonwealth while preserving the autonomy among the individuals that constitute it.[65]

KANT'S *RELIGIOUS* TOLERANCE

Kant elaborates his own vision of an inclusive, tolerant society, somewhat ironically, on the basis of his tendentious critique of Judaism. Rooting his notion of society in tolerance-as-inclusion, Kant finds it necessary to challenge that tendency of elective monotheisms to prioritize divine authority and human access to that authority over the apodictic certainty of the moral law which demands recognition of the inherent dignity of every human being. In light of these concerns, Kant brings fascinating questions to the discourse surrounding monotheism, challenging the importance of the numerical unity of the divine itself. And, perhaps most importantly, his heavily rationalized monotheism renders tolerance (qua tolerance-as-inclusion) into a principle to be valued in and of itself rather than a mere pragmatic, and all too necessary, tool needed to cope with the diverse nature of the modern world.

Just as Mendelssohn radically problematizes the 'Christian' notion of God on metaphysical grounds, Kant finds in the 'Jewish' notion of God a source of moral (and political) error. When speaking of the Jews, Kant writes, "we should not rate too highly the fact that this people set up, as universal Ruler of the world, a one and only God who could be represented through no visible image."[66] That is, for Kant, neither the *one-ness* nor invisibility of God is what is truly important for morality. Kant continues, "For a God who desires merely obedience to commands for which absolutely no improved moral disposition is requisite is, after all, not really the moral Being, the concept of whom we need for a religion," i.e., a 'religion of reason'.[67] The Jewish God, according to Kant, subverts morality, in that this God demands obedience to His laws from fear and desire for reward. Kant then makes the rather striking claim that genuine, rational religion

> would be more likely to arise from a belief in many mighty invisible beings . . . provided a people conceived of these agreeing, amid their 'departmental' differences, to bestow their good pleasure only upon the man who cherishes virtue with all his heart—more likely I say, than when faith is bestowed upon but one Being, who, however, attaches prime importance with mechanical worship.[68]

This claim is rather remarkable for two reasons. First, like Mendelssohn before him, Kant is creating a tremendous gap between his revised Christianity (at least insofar as it embodies the 'religion of reason') and a rival monotheism which serves as a symbol for those aspects shared by the elective-monotheisms that are in need of reform. In fact, Kant claims that the 'religion of reason,' which is best exemplified by his version of Christianity, differs more sharply from Judaism than from virtually any other religion. Here Kant is saying that polytheistic religions, those religions against which all three elective-monotheistic traditions have traditionally (at the very least) polemicized at great lengths, are potentially more in tune with the 'religion of reason' than is Judaism. The similarities between Judaism and Christianity in terms of discursive structure, shared scriptures, and so on, do nothing to alter the tremendous gap that separate them regarding practical reason, which, for Kant, is all-important.

The second reason that Kant's claim in the above passage is remarkable is that while it may appear at first blush that Kant's account of monotheism and polytheism is disingenuous, it is in fact not only sound (according to the tenets of his thought) but also enormously significant to his endeavor. What makes Kant's position appear disingenuous is that it seems as if Kant ignores the process intrinsic to monotheism, described by Lenn Goodman as the "integration of the idea of divinity"[69] which involves a concomitant "integration of all values."[70] That is, monotheism is not simply about belief in one God, but rather involves a belief in the deep coherence of morality itself, such that there is one authoritative notion of the human *telos* as well as an ultimate harmony between values. Polytheism, on the other hand, is precisely the ontological plurality of values and visions of human *teloi*, and this value-pluralism is ontologically embodied in the existence of rival deities.[71] Thus, by saying that morality could "arise from a belief in many mighty invisible beings . . . provided a people conceived of these agreeing, amid their 'departmental' differences, to bestow their good pleasure only upon the man who cherishes virtue with all his heart," Kant is essentially only conceding that morality could easily arise from a polytheism that is monotheistic in everything but the number of gods. That is, Kant is saying that polytheism is acceptable as long as it meets all of what he considers to be the essential background conditions of monotheism, i.e., the integration of all values and the singularization of the human *telos*. In short, Kant only renders the question of number in regard to God unimportant; he is unwilling to sacrifice any other aspects of monotheism.

However, if we probe beneath this apparent disingenuousness we reach an intriguing insight into the heart of Kant's thought. Kant has claimed that all religions, which would include polytheistic ones, possess a rational component, a moral core, and therefore have a capacity to be rationalized.

In addition, we know that Kant repudiates the human capacity for any theoretical knowledge about the divine, and thus only the practical implications of notions of the divine contain significance. Questions about the number of gods are entirely moot so long as the practical dimension, the only legitimate one, is stressed. Also, and more importantly, in regard to traditional monotheisms, to the degree that they are not based on universal reason but rather on claims to revelation—claims which Kant asserts are historical and therefore contingent and particular in nature—these traditions are unable to provide any genuine necessity and universality, rooted as they are in unsocial sociability, and thus their gesture toward the integration of values is deceptive. Therefore in a very real sense, for Kant, to the degree that an elective-monotheistic religion does not cohere to the 'religion of reason' it is *not genuinely monotheistic* because it leads to exclusivism and thus further fragmentation rather than universalism, and enmity and war rather than peace, harmony, and unity. That is, by subscribing to the logic of scriptural universalism rather than the rational universalism of the 'religion of reason,' the elective monotheisms inhibit and obstruct the realization of what Kant sees as the most important aspects of monotheism, the harmonization of values and the singularization of the human *telos* in the moral law, virtue (individual), and the ethical commonwealth (collective). If it is not conducive to autonomy and the rise of the ethical commonwealth, to overcoming the mire of radical evil and unsocial sociability, then it is not a true monotheism—it is idolatry.

Scriptural universalism, lacking necessity and sufficient universality, lacks the necessary resources for such a world-historical task. Such a task, Kant believes, requires nothing less than the rational universalism of the 'religion of reason.' Judaism, for Kant, is only the most egregious example of the ironic paganism of the elective monotheisms, but Christianity can be quite 'Jewish' in this regard as well. As Kant points out, Christian history tells

> how, with a hierarchy forcing itself upon free men, the dreadful voice of *orthodoxy* was raised, out of the mouths of presumptuous, exclusively "called," scriptural expositors, and divided the Christian world into embittered parties over creedal opinions of faith (upon which absolutely no general agreement can be reached without appeal to pure reason as the expositor).[72]

In short, elective monotheisms, at least insofar as they rely upon the logic of scriptural universalism, remain far short of the universality of the ethical commonwealth. If exclusivism and reliance upon revelation render elective monotheisms idolatrous, then *only the 'religion of reason' is genuinely monotheistic.* The 'religion of reason' for Kant, as the religion of universal human morality, alone fulfills the conditions of the monotheistic worldview—the harmony of all values, the singularization of the human *telos,* and a deep universalism. These conditions are far more significant for Kant's understanding of *the one true religion* than theoretical claims about the number of divinities.

Indeed, Kant's writings on religion and the ethical commonwealth show a remarkable disregard for virtually all discussions about God and theological dogmas except insofar as they relate to morality. This lack of concern is quite systematic and forms the basis of a rigorous account of religious tolerance. Rossi points out that Kant's account of the ethical commonwealth emerges as an "ever-enlarging circle of communication, inquiry, and argument to find and construct an enduring and inclusive world for social interaction on the basis of mutual respect for one another's freedom."[73] That is, in contrast to the agonistic tendencies of the traditional elective monotheistic worldview, human beings must forge a "*common world for the mutual exercise of freedom.*"[74] Unlike the structural moment of election in the Abrahamic-monotheistic worldview which is premised upon a structural asymmetry between the self and Other, Kant's ethical commonwealth, which is to transcend the mire of radical evil/unsocial sociability, is rooted in a profoundly symmetrical relationship with the other. This symmetry arises by means of recognition of the finitude of (human) beings—recognition that extends to the limits of our knowledge of the theoretical nature of God—and the moral constraints and obligations this finitude places upon the self regarding the Other. As finite beings we cannot trust any extant scripture as being imbued with supernatural authority and thus being able to tell us how to live and that we ought to judge those who do not accept its authority as living in error, and thus as enemies of God and worthy of violence and/or exclusion. Indeed, Kant condemns such a mentality in the sharpest possible terms.

A major factor in Kant's doctrine of religious tolerance is the fateful link he finds between revelation and hierarchy. It is not surprising for Kant that Judaism, rooted in external and supernatural revelation, is directly linked, or so he thinks, to hierarchal forms of government and order, or as he puts it, "an aristocracy of priests or leaders, who boast of instructions imparted directly by God."[75] Similarly, the "humiliating distinction between *laity* and *clergy*"[76] in various forms of Christianity, which again is rooted in access to revelation, is destined to be overcome by reason, which is equally accessible to all. However, Kant thinks that it is precisely because his notion of reason possesses necessity and universality that it can only sanction gradual reform and not external revolutions, since these are rooted in particular historical circumstances and embrace violent means—both of which are indicative of contingency.[77] More significantly (for our purposes at least) relative to tolerance is Kant's remarkable discussion of conscience.

With his doctrine of conscience, Kant systematically privileges ethics over all theoretical doctrines (especially ones grounded in revelation) by stressing the ethical importance of the radical finitude of human knowledge. Kant defines conscience as "a basic moral principle, which requires no proof that *one ought to hazard nothing that may be wrong.*"[78] In conscience, reason, taking stock of what is certain and what is uncertain, makes reflexive judgments regarding its own intended actions. It is by no means coincidental that the example Kant uses to illustrate conscience is "an inquisitor, who clings fast to the uniqueness of his statutory faith even to the point of [imposing] martyrdom, and who has to pass judgment upon a so-called heretic (otherwise a good citizen) charged with unbelief."[79] Kant argues that a revealed faith, given its historical nature, is contingent and thus without the apodictic certainty of the moral law that categorically forbids murder, but he additionally points out the danger of human error creeping in through interpretation or delusions. In all forms of faith, "the *possibility* ever remains that an error may be discovered in it."[80]

Remarkably, in arguing on behalf of religious tolerance, Kant takes recourse to the certitude that morality provides to the practical notion of God. That is, Kant uses his moral notion of God to infuse a sense of radicality to the reflexivity that conscience imposes upon statutory religions. Kant states:

> Let the author of a creed, or the teacher of a church, yea, let every man, so far as he is inwardly to acknowledge a conviction regarding dogmas as divine revelations, ask himself: Do you really trust yourself to assert the truth of these dogmas in the sight of Him who knows the heart and at the risk of losing all that is valuable and holy to you?[81]

Kant achieves an intense decentering of all religious identity by using conscience as a means of calling people to judgment, at least a postulated one, before the moral God who knows the 'depths of their hearts' which they themselves do not, and cannot, know. That is, since the moral status of all human beings is forever unknown to us—at best a matter of hope—recourse to God does not involve obedience to statutory commands, which can only lead to further division among human beings. Rather, God serves as a source of radical reflexivity and decentration, a radical calling of the self and the self's most cherished beliefs into question, such that the very thought of one who thinks herself fit to judge another's religious beliefs is not only morally impossible but utterly absurd.

Kant's vision of conscience revolutionizes the relationship with the Other, opening up a radical vision of inclusivity on a communal level. Morality, which alone is certain in the sense of conscience, not only demands that we refrain from harming Others on the basis of their conceptions of the divine; it also enjoins us to positively engage them in the shared, ongoing efforts of reasoning and critique and on this basis to unite, and, through discourse and argumentation, form the foundation for a common vision of the world. Kant's account of tolerance, namely tolerance-as-inclusion, differs substantially from standard notions of tolerance and pluralism in which difference between the self and Other is emphasized. That is, in tolerance one suffers the otherness of the Other and values one's own position over the Other (tolerance), or views one's own beliefs and practices as ultimately incommensurable with the Other although one accepts that there is no way to judge between them in regard to merit (pluralism). In contrast, Kant now proposes that what is *religious* is engaging that Other in processes of reflection and mutual critique, such that the difference between the self and the Other is incorporated and overcome in a shared process of discourse from which an ethical commonwealth grounded in symmetrical relationships can emerge.[82] For Kant, the principle of tolerance as a form of inclusivity and mutuality is now itself religious. The otherness of the Other, the site of agonism in the discursive structure of the elective monotheisms, is incorporated, indeed made central to, Kant's notion of tolerance. Indeed, this otherness *of* the Other, and one's own otherness *to* the Other, are to be overcome through mutuality, symmetry, reflexivity, and decentration in processes of reasoning *with* the Other.

The root of the difference between Kant's doctrine of tolerance and Mendelssohn's, which meanders between tolerance-as-restraint and non-violent intolerance, has to do with their respective accounts of reason. Mendelssohn remains beholden to a Lebinizian rationalism, which is predicated upon human reason discovering metaphysical truths about God, the universe, and humanity that are fixed and final. However, as Onora O'Neill explains, Kant's critical rationalism sharply diverges from this conception of reason insofar as reason for him is a "process" involving "connection and integration rather than [a] once and for all laying of foundations."[83] That is, unlike Mendelssohn's rationalism, Kant eschews all metaphysical foundations which take themselves as certain and all metaphysical methodologies which derive knowledge in an "algorithmic" fashion.[84] Whereas Mendelssohn's notion of reason involves a passive process of discovering the eternal truths which are inscribed in the universe, for Kant reason is an active, self-constructing teleological process generated by an ever-expanding community of reasoners thinking reflexively together in such a way that a gradual unity can be achieved, above all on ethical and social grounds. This unity to be achieved is one which will transform the social and natural worlds in which humans dwell. Mendelssohn's rationalism is beholden to a thoroughly theocentric universe, whereas Kant's, despite its retention of the notion of God, is anthropocentric, and prioritizes a socially constituted notion of reason.

There is no doubt that Kant provides a profound consideration of theological and indeed monotheistic motifs even as he interweaves them with more secular concerns. The question that I want to consider in conclusion, however, is the degree to which his thought remains compatible with the monotheistic worldview. It is my contention that inheritors of Kant's thought, in light of contemporary epistemological concerns, are faced with two choices. One of these is to further the process-focused notions of rationality stressed by thinkers such as Habermas and John Rawls—of which I think Hick's religious pluralism maintains a peculiar but nevertheless very real kinship—which are fundamentally antithetical to the discursive structure of the monotheistic worldview (and this does not, of course, count as an objection in terms of their potential tenability in and of themselves). The other is to develop the humane intolerance of Hermann Cohen's ethical monotheism.

Kant's new anthropocentric, anti-foundationalist conception of reason is public in nature, and rooted in discourse rather than the dogmatic algorithms of (non-critical) rationalist metaphysics. However, it maintains a connection with key moments of the discursive structure of the monotheistic worldview such as the world-historical mission and the *eschaton*. In common iterations of elective monotheisms, the relationship between the elected community and the Other is such that the particular community has a universal message which can only be brought to the Other through agonistic relations, i.e., bearing witness (usually in a hostile world), conquest and conversion, or proselytizing. While Mendelssohn sought to soften this agonism, Kant's thought aims at undermining it altogether, albeit gradually, and not by way of the elimination of the Other (by conversion or annihilation) but through a profoundly inclusive version of tolerance in which both self and Other will equally shape the community together. It is this process which will bring about the *eschaton,* the kingdom of ends, whereby the otherness (at least any meaningful otherness) separating the self and the Other is overcome and politics as we know it ceases to exist. When this happens, the world as it is will reflect the world as it ought to be, and morality will be instantiated in nature.[85]

Kant's strategy is to undermine the dialectical relationship between particularism and universalism which is inherent in scriptural universalism, such that it gives way to a harmonious rational universalism. He not only marginalizes revelation but transfigures the notion of election to encompass all human beings regardless of their settings and religious communities, since all religions have the capacity for rationalization, or bringing themselves into accord with the 'religion of reason.' For Kant, either a religion is rational—and thus in accord with the strictures of morality—or it is rooted in a superstition that is in turn grounded in anthropomorphic conceptions of God. A serious weakness of Kant's conception of religion, which is shared by Mendelssohn, is the common Enlightenment belief that all religions are fundamentally alike. Since Kant tends to treat all religions (with the exception of Judaism, which is not recognized as a religion) as rooted in anthropomorphism and as a result prone to the errors of scriptural universalism, 'rationalizing' means reconfiguring their structural moments upon a conception of universal ethical reason. Presumably, as we saw above, polytheistic religions can meet this criterion, but Kant never really acknowledges non-theistic religions, much less what rationalizing them would entail.

Since Kant's notion of religion is profoundly rooted in the monotheisms, it makes sense that his understanding of 'rationalizing' religion is a process of reversing the trajectory of the discursive structure of monotheistic religions, which revolve around the dialectic of particularity and universality. Kant's entire endeavor to interrupt this dialectic is grounded in his notion of tolerance-as-inclusion, which seeks to undermine the asymmetrical relationship with the Other at the heart of the monotheistic worldview. Ironically, in the very process of undoing the agonism between the elected community and the Other, the particular and the universal, Kant has recourse to a very similar agonism between those on the vanguard of the 'religion of reason' and those who are in need of 'conversion.' In short, his attempt to undo the intolerance of the discursive structure of the elective monotheisms leads to the instantiation of a new *Heilsgeschichte*, that of the maturation of reason *in history*.

Thus, Kant must make use of the discursive structure of the elective monotheisms, even if he ultimately hopes to do away with their driving principle (agonism toward the Other). In short, Kant's thought has recourse to the universal human *telos*, the idea of God, and the *eschaton* (the ethical commonwealth) while nevertheless maintaining a notion of religion grounded in a notion of *a priori* ethical reason rooted in universality. Such a position, which is still rooted in the Pythagoras story of morality,[86] may have been convincing in the eighteenth century when fundamental changes were taking place in the understanding of morality and rationality itself,[87] and engagements with other cultures, when they did happen, were deeply parochial. Given these background conditions, Kant posits an extremely robust notion of reason and an optimism concerning the possibility for cross-cultural consensus that seems quite anachronistic in our postmodern, fragmented, and war-torn world. This problem with Kant's thought concerning reason, especially the 'religion of reason,' is quite convincingly illustrated by Philip Quinn and Joseph Runzo. Quinn challenges the rational universalism of the ethical foundations of Kant's 'religion of reason,' describing it as "excessively ambitious" from "an epistemological point of view."[88] In short, Quinn charges Kant with eliding the problem of reasonable pluralism in moral theory.[89] Runzo extends this charge to the realm of theology, arguing that if the conditions of free inquiry are present then it is extremely unlikely that there will be any sort of universal consensus.[90] And yet Kant's notion of the 'religion of reason,' which is to provide a fixed point of certainty by which to eliminate the divisive multiplicity of the historical religions, requires an apodictic notion of morality and consequently a uniform notion of God that accords with morality and reason. In today's epistemological climate, we simply cannot say with any intellectual integrity that the thickness of Kant's rationality, the apodicticity of his moral law and all the conceptual baggage that accompanies it, is genuinely universal and necessary in the sense Kant thinks it is. In short, Quinn and Runzo problematize the very idea of rational universalism, at least as Kant formulates it, and if that is rendered untenable then the overarching thrust of Kant's philosophy of religion is undermined.

Another problem that besets Kant's philosophy of religion, which is particularly troubling in the wake of Quinn's and Runzo's objections, is raised by Rossi regarding the ethical commonwealth. Rossi points out that Kant not only fails to fully elaborate the "final concrete form that the ethical commonwealth will take,"[91] he also fails to "provide a full account of *the means by which* reason extends its social authority" in regard to "the external order of human conduct."[92] To rephrase Rossi's objection, the trouble with Kant's position lies in what I have termed the *non-politics* of the ethical commonwealth: It somehow operates at the juncture of ethics and politics, serving the function of politics but operating according to the rules of morality. Rossi points out that Kant fails to explain how it is possible that one can leave radical evil and unsocial sociability without recourse to coercion. And yet the ethical commonwealth, given that it is eminently rational and ethical, is prohibited from coercion at all costs, as one cannot bring about morality through coercion.[93] Not only is Kant's ecclesiology insufficient to account for the establishment of the ethical commonwealth in a world dominated by radical evil, but "he does not provide an adequate account of the *concrete social means* (or the *concrete forms of social relationship*) by which such a true church makes it possible for agents freely to adopt, as an end for their action, the social intent required for establishing and sustaining an ethical commonwealth."[94] Rossi surmises that the source of the problem with Kant's account is that it tends to use the ethical commonwealth in a negative fashion, to show "what the noncoercive exercise of reason is not," but insufficiently elucidates what it is and how it functions in its own right.[95] However, since it is a moral duty to strive to realize the ethical commonwealth in history, Kant must account for these concerns. I would like to add that the problem Rossi raises is particularly exacerbated, given that the thickness Kant wants to ascribe to human reason is now simply no longer conceivable. Kant, who is so critical of scriptural universalism, must, if he wants to give priority to the necessity and universality of rational universalism and the moral certainty of ethics, "articulate in concrete terms how reason, by nonceoercive means, brings about in each and every agent the intent to social union constitutive of an ethical commonwealth."[96] Yet without an impossibly robust notion of rationality, Kant cannot accomplish this.

As a result, contemporary interpreters of Kant's thought are left with two alternatives. The first option is that one can thin out Kant's notion of reason and move in the direction of procedural rationality. This option is certainly viable, and numerous contemporary interpreters are taking this path.[97] However, given its stress on inclusivity, this strategy must move away from or at least weaken such things as the apodicticity of the moral law, and distance itself from the 'religion of reason' and its moral notion of God which follow upon the moral law. Hence, those who follow this path tend to sever the ties that Kant still maintains with the discursive structure of the monotheistic worldview. Let us explore this path via one of Kant's inheritors, Habermas.

There are profound affinities between Kant's account of reason, which "recognizes no other judge than that universal human reason in which everyone has his say,"[98] and Habermas's discourse ethics. Habermas's thought seeks to point "to a way out of the modern dilemma" where the once-agreed-upon "'transcendent good'" is now lost amid a whirlwind of conflicting discourses. Habermas argues that this lost 'transcendent good' "can be replaced in an 'immanent' fashion only by appeal to the intrinsic constitution of the practice of deliberation."[99] To be sure, Habermas's procedural notion of reason is more modest than Kant's, but both advocate a social notion of rationality, rooted in processes of deliberation and argumentation that are grounded in the symmetrical relationships between reasoners.

Given their structural similarities, it is particularly useful to see where they differ. Like Kant, Habermas takes recourse to discourse (often in the form of argumentation) with the Other. This discourse with the Other takes place in the public sphere, which is an inheritance from Kant's public notion of rationality. However, unlike Kant, Habermas is unwilling to recognize any 'narrative' or 'tradition' (except maybe that of secularism) as definitive, since these can only expound a worldview but cannot actually argue with one another.[100] Philosophical reason, then, is preoccupied with the procedures of deliberation which can render the public sphere neutral of any particular 'narrative' or 'tradition,' rather than the perpetual antagonism of mutually exclusive worldviews.[101] Unlike Kant's grand conception of rationality, which is to provide a new foundation for the entirety of human culture, Habermas advocates a modest procedure of deliberation in order to bring diverse interlocutors together and solve "practical conflicts in need of regulation,"[102] given the contemporary situation which is characterized by an epoch-making disintegration of the metaphysical foundations from which people once derived their ethical orientations. His decisively 'post-metaphysical' philosophy is much more conscious than Kant's is, of "the transition to a pluralism of worldviews in modern society." That is, Habermas recognizes that there is no longer (as if there ever was) any shared ethos, and that "the validity of *universally* binding moral rules can no longer be accounted for in terms of reasons and interpretations that presuppose the existence and the agency of a transcendent Creator and Redeemer." The result of this is the loss of "metaphysical validation of objectively rational moral laws."[103]

Whereas Kant's position remains driven by a profound hope for the realization in the ethical commonwealth in history, a hope grounded in rationality itself, Habermas proffers a far more modest proposal regarding cross-cultural communication and recognition of the rights of human beings in a war-torn, fragmented world. For Kant, the tenability of his position is hope, which as Rossi points out, Kant thinks creates the conditions for the possibility of "*persever[ing] with one another in deliberative exchange* in the hope of reaching agreement about the terms of our living with one another, a hope that includes within its ambit substantive social ends."[104] Hope is rooted in practical reason itself—not only in the rational recognition of the unique destiny of human beings as creatures located at the nexus of nature and freedom and destined to create themselves and their world in light of their own freedom, but also because without hope there is despair, which undermines the moral endeavor. Hope in the possibility, indeed in the necessity, of the ethical commonwealth is therefore eminently rational.[105] Habermas offers a much more modest hope in the wake of the collapse of metaphysics and the undermining of the traditional foundations of societies worldwide in the age of globalization. Habermas hopes to reconstruct "the contents" of moral traditions that are rooted in religious traditions which have foundered in modernity; he does not hope to replace them with a religion of modernity. At best, Habermas can offer "a morality of equal respect and solidaristic responsibility for everybody";[106] he cannot provide the promise of a radically new order of social and individual existence rooted in profound peace and harmony.

To be sure, this proceduralist option advocated by Habermas and other luminaries such as Rawls, not to mention Hick's version of this in the realm of religion, has much to offer. Nevertheless, it is also alienating to many monotheists.[107] Hermann Cohen takes a different route from Habermas and the proceduralists, but it is one which remains rooted in Kant's rationalism and which continues the religion of reason trajectory. In contrast to the proceduralists, Cohen remains committed more to the content of Kant's thought, i.e., the 'religion of reason' and the absolute nature of morality, while he rejects the form, i.e., the emphasis on the inclusivity and mutuality of reason. By breaking with the procedural commitments to inclusivity, Cohen is able to take a stance that is far more firmly entrenched in the discursive structure of the worldview of elective monotheisms while nevertheless maintaining a rigorous morality that is rooted in the universality and necessity of the innate dignity of all human beings.

Part Four

COHEN:

ETHICAL

INTOLERANCE

7 | Cohen and the Monotheism of Correlation

Hermann Cohen is the third and most successful member of the religion of reason trajectory.[1] Cohen's approach to the problematic intolerance inherent in the monotheistic worldview constitutes a significant departure from the respective approaches of Mendelssohn and Kant. What most dramatically distinguishes Cohen's efforts from those of his predecessors, at least in regard to the problem of monotheistic intolerance, is that he completely embraces what J. B. Schneewind has termed the 'Socrates story' of morality, in contrast to Kant and especially Mendelssohn, who remain ensnared in the 'Pythagoras story.' Whereas the Pythagoras story disputes the possibility of progress in moral understanding, given that morality is bound up with an event of revelation or disclosure of some sort in the past, the Socrates story holds that morality is a matter of discovery, of breaking with the past. Since both the Pythagoras and Socrates stories are intimately connected with basic philosophical/theological understandings of the world, it should not be surprising that the story or paradigm one holds has great implications for one's treatment of monotheistic intolerance. The Socrates story as a paradigm for understanding morality, and knowledge in general, is more reconcilable with the discursive structure of the worldview of elective monotheisms than is the Pythagoras story.

The philosophical commitments of Mendelssohn and Kant are driven by their Pythagorean philosophies in the direction of symmetry with regard to the Other, and as a result are ill-equipped to deal with the demands of an asymmetrical relationship with the Other which is inherent in the discursive structure of the elective-monotheistic worldview. Consequently, Mendelssohn struggles to keep his natural theology coherent with his scriptural theology, and Kant virtually sacrifices all Christian commitments to an ideal 'religion of reason' which is rooted in ethics. Cohen, however, in rejecting the 'Pythagoras story' for the 'Socrates story,' and in embracing the notion of discovery concerning the truths of ethics[2] and religion (the two fields are inseparable, if also irreducible for him,[3] as we will see), also rejects the value of tolerance, a key component of the respective positions of both Mendelssohn and Kant. In short, Cohen's solution is to embrace the intolerant orbit of the monotheistic worldview, and to accept the asymmetrical relationship with the Other that results from it. The success of his endeavor derives from his ability to render this intolerance humane and ethical, rather than trying to diminish or banish it entirely.[4]

If we recall, Mendelssohn and Kant each attempt to dissolve the potential for violence plaguing elective monotheisms by introducing heterogeneous elements, elements constitutive of their respective notions of the order of rational universalism, into the scripturally universal structure of the monotheistic worldview. In doing so they hoped to thereby soften or eradicate the conditions in the latter which generate intolerance. In both cases the integration of the rationally universal elements with the scripturally universal ones remains problematic. Cohen, however, utilizes rather than subverts the asymmetry at the heart of the monotheistic worldview that is incompatible with the modern notions of tolerance and pluralism. Rather than attempt to dismantle or reconfigure the moments of the discursive structure of the elective-monotheistic worldview, Cohen argues that these monotheisms can produce, or develop from within, a form of intolerance that is nevertheless ethical. While Cohen's position eschews all forms of religious violence, it cannot be said to be tolerant since it actively works for the conversion of the Other through the bearing-witness modality of promulgation. Unlike Mendelssohn's conception of bearing witness, Cohen's account is not content to wait until the *eschaton* for the conversion of the Other but takes action now. However, since in Cohen's account, the notion of religion is itself a rational and therefore universal concept, what it means to either bear witness or convert is quite complex and rather counter-intuitive and thus requires explication. This modality of intolerance is thus at once both compatible with the monotheistic discursive structure and with the basic conditions for existence within a multicultural society, even if it itself does not approve of pluralism or tolerance.

Since Cohen does not follow his predecessors in attempting to ameliorate and/or eliminate the intolerance inherent in the Abrahamic-monotheisms, but rather engages in the more feasible project of rendering monotheistic intolerance humane, he has no need to import heterogeneous elements which undermine the moments of the discursive structure of elective monotheisms. Rather, using the structural moments of elective Judaism itself, read through a rationalizing hermeneutic, Cohen harnesses the moral resources within Judaism to reconfigure monotheistic intolerance so that it is permeated with ethical and rational significance. In contrast to Kant, Cohen rejects the notion of a dichotomy between scriptural universalism and rational universalism. To be sure, Mendelssohn also rejects such a dichotomy. However, Cohen is more successful than Mendelssohn in bringing these two universalisms into a fruitful and dynamic relationship.

Cohen argues that the order of rational universalism, which begins as only a seed inherent in scriptural universalism, emerges and unfolds through the development of the scriptural literary tradition until it becomes dominant in the relationship. Nevertheless, although Cohen follows Kant in thoroughly rationalizing God—i.e., depriving God of an active, unfathomable will and personality—unlike his predecessor this rationalization does not imply any diminishment of the vigorous relationship between the universal and the particular characteristic of scriptural universalism. It is precisely Cohen's ability to subordinate scriptural universalism to his account of rational universalism while nevertheless preserving a viable relationship between the two that enables him to conceive of elective monotheisms in a totally new light, wherein dyads like 'universality and particularity' and 'reason and revelation' cease to be cast in opposition to one another. This shift proves essential in the ethical transfiguration of monotheistic intolerance.

Despite its ingenuity, Cohen's philosophy of religion has not been met with much appreciation in the twentieth century, for four major reasons. First, Cohen's thought was seen as an attempt to harmonize German and Jewish thought, which is seen as being undesirable as well as impossible.[5] Second, Cohen's thought was associated with the Neo-Kantian project which lost favor in the wake of the phenomenological revolution.[6] Third, the critical idealism of his Marburg Neo-Kantianism was linked with the broader rubric of German Idealism, whose totalizing tendencies have been adamantly resisted by so much twentieth-century thought. However, Cohen's thought is radically distinct from, and in fact, quite critical of these other idealisms, and is not susceptible to the same critiques.[7] Fourth, even before the Holocaust there was a decisive shift in Jewish thought away from rationalism, toward existentialist and more explicitly theological trends. However, the current state of the world political situation, coupled with the urgency of recent critiques of monotheism which decry its tendency to promote violence and intolerance, make manifest the need to reassess Cohen's important legacy. It is my contention that Cohen's conception of monotheism provides a more responsible foundation for contemporary Jewish thought, especially in regard to the concerns of our time, than that of either his forerunners or his successors. As such, it bears considerable significance not only for Judaism but for Christianity, and perhaps Islam as well,[8] in that it offers powerful resources for mitigating the potential violence of monotheistic intolerance while nevertheless preserving the integrity of their discursive structures.

COHEN'S METHODOLOGY

In order to understand Cohen's rationalist recasting of Judaism, it is essential to appreciate his Neo-Kantian methodology. Cohen, the founder of Marburg Neo-Kantianism, was no slavish follower of Kant. Indeed, he was known for his innovate ways of interpreting Kant in order to solve certain philosophical problems in the Kantian legacy.[9] Cohen frequently utilizes elements in Kant's philosophy, often in original and unorthodox ways, to establish his own philosophical position, which profoundly opposes the Romantic turn in German idealism. Methodologically speaking, of particular importance for Cohen is Kant's notion of the regulative ideal, where reason presents ideals that human knowledge strives to approximate but can never reach given that they exhibit a level of completeness which is impossible for the finite nature of human knowledge.[10] The regulative ideal manifests itself in two essential respects in Cohen's methodology: in his active, task-oriented account of knowledge, and in his notion of correlation. These two aspects of Cohen's methodology are not only of significance in his systematic philosophical works, but are also in play in his religious thought.

First, and most obviously, Cohen's theory of knowledge makes heavy use of Kant's notion of the regulative idea, insofar as it is rooted in knowledge as a future-oriented, perpetual task which ever approximates but never reaches its goal. In contrast to Kant, however, Cohen removes any passivity from the process of gathering knowledge, claiming that it constitutes an activity of the mind. Not only does this innovation extricate his position from any sort of metaphysical questions that remain unresolved in Kant, but it also facilitates the rendering of the regulative ideal more explicitly along the lines of scientific thought.[11] Knowledge is an ongoing activity; a process which perpetually tests and corrects itself. Thus, rather than being the simple grasping of a datum, or of reaching a conclusion once and for all about the world as it is, knowledge constitutes an ideal for Cohen. And, in the words of Dieter Adelmann, "the 'ideal' . . . does not constitute some form of the facts of the case in themselves [*Sachverhalt für sich*] against which one would oppose the thinking of 'actuality,' rather it is much more the task to idealize 'actuality' [*sondern vielmehr die Aufgabe, die 'Wirklichkeit' zu idealisieren*]."[12] For Cohen, the present lacks stability and reality, whereas the future alone possesses genuine being. Thus, knowing is an active process initiated by the mind, and knowledge is a perpetual task which is oriented toward the future, not the present.[13]

The specific term Cohen uses for his theory of knowledge is *Ursprüngslogik,* or "logic of origin," which refers to the complex, dialectical nature of his methodology. Cohen's philosophy began as a philosophy of science, rooted in the production of knowledge by means of testing the validity of knowledge-claims, rather than exploring an empirical given.[14] Testing validity, however, requires the laying of foundations—a hypothesis, which is how Cohen defines the Platonic notion of 'idea.' That is, Cohen's account of "foundations" (*Grundlagen*) is non-foundationalist, in that one is perpetually "laying the foundations" or, as Cohen puts it in his characteristic style, "The foundations are the laying of foundations" (*Die Grundlagen sind Grundlegungen*).[15] Given that the 'laying of foundations' is rooted in a regulative ideal rather than any sort of absolute foundation, Cohen's Neo-Kantian methodology rules out metaphysics from the outset.[16] Whereas metaphysics provides a stable foundation from which certain and absolute knowledge is derived, Cohen's 'laying of foundations,' like the body of scientific knowledge, is self-correcting and self-reforming in light of its perpetual task of calling itself to account. Thus, Cohen transforms Kant's notion of a regulative ideal of reason into a foundation of a philosophy of science and a general theory of knowledge.[17]

The second respect in which the Kantian regulative ideal manifests itself in Cohen's own methodology is with his notion of 'correlation.' The relationship between correlation and the Kantian regulative ideal is not as immediately apparent, but is no less central. Correlation as a methodological term first emerges in Cohen's *Logik der reinen Erkenntnis,*[18] and becomes a decisive concept for the rest of his system of philosophy and his religious thought. Cohen explains that the correlation is: "*Not an exchange* [Wechsel], *but rather a preservation* [Erhaltung] *simultaneously of distinction* [Sonderung] *and unity* [Vereinigung]. *In the distinction unity is preserved, and in the unity distinction is preserved* [In der Sonderung erhält sich die Vereinigung, und in der Vereinigung erhält sich die Sonderung]."[19] That is, in a correlation two different terms are related, unified and yet held distinct. They remain isolated and distinct from one another and yet, at the same time, they are not left unaffected by one another. Each term of the correlation is changed and influenced by the other in the process of being held in orbit with it, even though each term remains distinct from the other. Martin Kavka explains that it is precisely the unattainable, infinite quality of the (regulative) ideal that Cohen has made central to his own methodology, that prevents the Cohenian correlation from becoming a Hegelian *Aufhebung*. Kavka writes that with the correlation, "Cohen never uses the Hegelian language of sublating and dissolution (*aufheben*), but stays on its perimeter in his use of the verb *heben*. In this movement of elevation towards the ideal, opposites flow into each other and interpenetrate, without dissolving and producing something new."[20] That is, since each term of the correlation (or at least one, when the correlation involves God), stands in an independent relation to a transcendent ideal, Cohen is able to preserve the significant difference between each term.[21]

The concept of correlation plays a significant role in the entirety of Cohen's system, and beyond, in his writings on religion. In order to understand the three correlations in play in Cohen's account of Jewish monotheism in *Religion of Reason Out of the Sources of Judaism,* which will be of central concern to us in this chapter, we must first understand God as the function of Truth, established in *Ethik des reinen Willens.*[22] In the *Ethik,* Cohen establishes God as truth (*Wahrheit*), as the deepest function of reason, which secures the "combination" (*Verbindung*),[23] or better, the "accord" (*Einklang*),[24] between the spheres of science and ethics, i.e., the respective logics of the way things are and the way things ought to be. This *Einklang* between ethics and logic ensures that a fruitful relationship can be established between ethics and logic, and that the two distinct elements of the system must become connected (by means of a correlation, not sublation) if ethics is both to be secured against pantheism and rendered immune from "all pietism and all quietism."[25] Cohen states, "God signifies that nature has permanency so that it is certain that morality is eternal,"[26] a condition which ensures that "no contradiction between nature and morality [*kein Widerspruch zwischen Sittlichkeit und Natur*] should remain open."[27] Truth as the *Einklang* of logic and ethics, of nature and morality, provides the necessary conditions for the possibility of the moral endeavor, i.e., ensuring that actuality (as nature) is not so constituted as to render the ethical task impossible.

Since there is a harmonization (but not an identity) of logic and ethics, the 'is' and the 'ought,' God, understood here strictly as an idea, exerts influence upon actuality by securing the grounds for the 'ought' in the heart of the 'is.' In other words, actuality is permeated by this possibility for transformation into the 'ought'; the 'ought' has grounds in actuality, i.e., the 'ought' *can* be at least approximated in actuality, if not realized. This ensures that the 'ought' becomes a perpetual, infinite task for the subject striving to become an ethical Self. This means that while the ethical ideal, what ought to be, will always be an infinite task it will nevertheless have an influence on actuality, on nature. Thus for Cohen, the genuine Self of the human being is not the givenness of the empirical human being, nor any sort of biologistic or psychologistic concept of the subject, nor a subjectivity conceived as thrownness nor even any sort of Levinasian passivity.[28] Rather, for Cohen, the Self is constituted by the active striving after the ethical ideal which must be pursued perpetually. This self-generation of the ideal toward which one perpetually strives, bringing oneself (qua actual or given) through one's actions increasingly into accord with it, Cohen calls the 'ethical concept' of the human being. Helmut Holzhey helpfully explains this ethical concept of the human being as a subject who "stands . . . in an indissoluble tension [*Spannung*] between the natural conditions of his drives and needs and the rationally determined, unconditional Ought." Holzhey explains further that this "tension is not simply factical, but rather one that is inscribed in the ethical concept of the human being."[29] The genuine Self is that which is projected, the ideal, for which the given subject strives to attain though it will perpetually fall short.

However, the discussion of the ethical concept of the human being is still more complex since, as Holzhey points out, "Cohen did not conceive of an individualistic ethics,"[30] but rather is concerned with the interface of the individual with the universal. In *Ethik des reinen Willens*, Cohen posits that we cannot discover the human being per se, in its isolated purity, but rather only in discrete forms. We find the human being both in the collective, i.e., plurality (*Mehrheit*) and totality (*Allheit*), and in the singular, i.e., particularity (*Einzelheit*) and the individual (*Individuum*).[31] The given, empirical subject is the particular member (*Einzelheit*) of the plurality (*Mehrheit*), whereas the individual or Self (*Individuum*) is a task that can only be determined in relation to totality (*Allheit*).[32] In conjunction with the two forms of the singular human being, there are two forms of universality—one fully rational, which is rooted in totality, and one incomplete and relative, which is bound to plurality. Totality, which is the legitimate universalism, is not any sort of Hegelian Absolute Spirit; it never exists in the sense of a present actuality.[33] Rather, it is a regulative ideal to be perpetually striven for.

Cohen contrasts totality with plurality, arguing that genuine foundations of the ethical concept of the human being, the Self, must be derived from the totality and not from relative groups or pluralities of human beings. That is, for Cohen, there are many pluralities, or groups with special interests. The particular constituents of these pluralities are not yet individuals in that their foundations do not lie with the ideal rational universality of the totality. The danger with pluralities, then, is not that they have not realized the ideal—given that no one has ever realized the ideal—but rather, that they often claim to have reached the ideal, to be the totality in some form or another, but in fact are not. One of Cohen's favorite examples of this is the medieval Church, in that it excluded and persecuted those who were outside of it and yet insisted it was universal and inclusive for all.[34] Pluralities lack genuine universality, and thus they are unable to generate the proper foundations for a methodologically pure ethics and the genuine individual of ethics that only totality can generate. As a result, ethically erroneous and therefore dangerous ideologies such as religious persecution, racism, and nationalism arise when a plurality is confused for a totality.[35]

Now to be sure, Cohen does not think we can do without pluralities. In fact, he elaborates a system of virtues in *Ethik des reinen Willens* as a way of negotiating the need for universality while simultaneously dwelling in pluralities. Given that the individual human being exists in the tension between the ideal of the ethical Self and the empirically given self, one inevitably exists in and between a variety of pluralities, a variety of distinct, particular communities. These communities are legitimate and even morally useful so long as one does not confuse them with the genuinely universal totality, which is the true foundation of ethics. That is, Cohen is arguing that all communities are not only of relative significance and validity in light of the universal, ideal totality, but they are also morally obligated to strive to help the larger community, the state, to ground itself in totality,[36] a vision of collective humanity ensconced in ethical-socialist states united in a cosmopolitan confederation.

JUDAISM AND THE 'RELIGION OF REASON'

In transitioning from the *Ethik des reinen Willens* to Cohen's explicitly religious works, particularly *Religion of Reason Out of the Sources of Judaism*, we must ask about the relationship of ethics to religion as well as that of Judaism to the concept of the 'religion of reason.' For Cohen, religion is an aspect of human culture which is (or ought to be) ultimately rooted in reason.[37] For Cohen, religion operates with a rationality which opens new insights that are closed to ethics, such as the correlation between God and the human being, the correlation between human beings themselves, the I and Thou encounter, and the recognition of the suffering of the Other. As such, it too has an *Ursprung* that develops according to a principle of lawfulness. As a result of this principle of lawfulness, "the religion of reason" is an ideal which is "represented in the consciousness of different peoples." Cohen continues by claiming that "in no particular people's consciousness is the religion of reason exhausted."[38] In other words, insofar as all human beings have the capacity for rationality, all human beings have the capacity to render their religions rational. Similar to Kant, the 'religion of reason' is an ideal rather than a concrete, empirical religion. And as in Kant, all human beings, insofar as they possess the capacity to be rational, also possess the capacity to approximate the 'religion of reason.' However, unlike Kant, Cohen does not think the 'religion of reason' has already been discovered and fully elaborated by a religious figure in the past (i.e., Jesus qua philosopher), but rather the 'religion of reason' is always to be extracted further from the sources of one's religion—it is always to be further elucidated.

The subject of the relationship of Cohen's works on religion to his system of philosophy, particularly his ethics, has been a source of much scholarly dispute. It is not my intention to rehash this intricate and important debate here.[39] Rather, I will only touch briefly upon the matter insofar as it bears upon the issue of monotheistic intolerance.[40] Cohen claims that the relationship between ethics and the 'religion of reason' is peculiar, inasmuch as both have the human being as their subject matter, yet in very different ways. For Cohen, ethics means 'scientific' or 'critical' ethics, which means that the "scientific method," i.e., his transcendental method of reconstruction, and not the teachings of "holy books," is central. That is, through his 'scientific idealism' Cohen thinks that knowledge can be secured according to which "*any person should be enabled to reason and to account about right and wrong, about good and bad, as much as about true and false.*"[41] In short, Cohen believes there is truth in ethical matters, just as there is truth in scientific matters. However, Cohen claims that just as scientific truth is always a task to be accomplished, always in the future, so too ethical truth is a perpetual process whose conclusion is always infinitely delayed. That is, this ethical truth is a task and not an achievement.

Ethics, given its rigorous, 'scientific' methodology, approaches the human being in a fundamentally different manner than religion, even the 'religion of reason.' Thus, a strict line of demarcation must be drawn between ethics and religion regarding their methodologies and understanding of the human being. Ethics is rooted in the Greek methodology of 'science,' in prioritizing universality and necessity above all else. However, since ethics is rooted in discovery (again, Cohen follows the Socrates and not the Pythagoras story of morality), as a discipline it has garnered much from the sources of Judaism, such as the prophetic notion of the ideal future.[42] However, such 'borrowings' have been and must be methodologically purified in order to thoroughly accord with the universal, 'scientific' foundations of ethics.[43] While ethics may have received historical influences from religious sources, it does not grant authority to holy books but only to critical reason.[44] In addition, ethics is concerned solely with the human, with the relationship between human beings,[45] and this only on the level of universality. Ethics cannot forgive the individual for her particularity (*Einzelheit*), nor can it recognize or respond to or console her particular sufferings.[46] Its exclusive concern is the rigorous nature of its demands for purity and universality in action (*Handlung*), as to their concrete actualization of this (infinite) action it is indifferent, for the task of ethics must remain perpetual and thus always incomplete.[47]

However, Cohen insists that religion and ethics both have human beings as their subject matter. As Cohen stresses, "There cannot be two kinds of reason with regard to the doctrine of man."[48] Kenneth Seeskin offers a helpful gloss on this when he states that there is "only one law and one goal; what differences there are between ethics and religion have to do with the method we use to articulate them."[49] Cohen's ostensible position in *Religion of Reason Out of the Sources of Judaism* regarding the 'religion of reason' is that religion serves as a supplement to ethics, providing support for the particularity or concreteness of the individual which is elided by the formalism of ethics.[50] Religions (insofar as they approximate the ideal of the 'religion of reason') are to be complementary and supplementary to ethics, and therefore have to fully subscribe to the task of ethics, i.e., the construction of the ideal self, the universal human *telos* which is inextricably bound up in the relationship of all human beings to one another.[51] Cohen can then claim that the formality and universality of ethics and the 'religion of reason' rooted in it serve as a point of mediation for the different particular religions, thus enabling them to become more universal, i.e., rational. This will enable a plurality of different religions and cultures to be harmoniously correlated into a larger unity. Like Kant, it would appear that in his discussion of the 'religion of reason,' Cohen hopes to establish universal ethics as a sphere in common between the divergent religions. Ethics, given its unified, 'scientific' character, is not open to plurality; but religion is, it would seem, at least to some degree.

Cohen's 'religion of reason' is therefore eminently practical rather than speculatively or metaphysically inclined. As Cohen puts it, "Religion . . . is concerned more with man than with God."[52] Or, putting religion in explicit proximity to ethics, Cohen asserts that since "religion has been defined as religion of reason, *man* is established as its sphere as well as its content."[53] And the concern with the human being is not with the nature of human beings as an object of speculative inquiry, but rather with the question of how to render them properly in tune with totality, with all human beings. Religions, then, insofar as they are rational, diverge from ethics only in that they have *different* means of reaching the *same* goals.

This position put forward by Cohen is untenable in that it cannot allow for the possibility for plurality in religion—understood here in such a way that the plurality of religions would be mediated by their participation in the universal 'religion of reason'—for two reasons. First, as we will see, the ecumenism of his 'religion of reason' is at best half-hearted, in that it is rooted in an account of Judaism which remains fervently committed to its ultimate messianic justification and the subsequent conversion of the nations.[54] Second, Cohen's attempt to reconcile the plurality of religions with the unity of ethics remains hopelessly mired in his Euro-centrism, given that the sources from which he constructs his ethics are almost exclusively Greek, Christian, and Jewish.

To be sure, a number of distinguished interpreters reject the Jewish specificity of Cohen's 'religion of reason,' pointing to Cohen's reluctance to claim that Judaism alone is *the* 'religion of reason,'[55] as well as his arguments about the contributions religion as a generic category can make to ethics in general and consequently to the entire system of philosophy as an *Eigenart* of ethics.[56] Such a position, however, whatever its merits, is ultimately untenable for two reasons. First, Cohen not only openly confesses a monotheism-centrism in the formation of the 'religion of reason,' but also emphasizes that Judaism has a superiority over Christianity and Islam. Judaism has an "undeniable spiritual and psychological advantage" in that its literary sources are the "primary origin" (*Ursprünglichkeit*) for these other monotheistic religions.[57] Additionally, as Poma points out, "the only faith [that Cohen] did not ignore, apart from Judaism, in his research, i.e., Christianity, not only did not constitute a positive point of reference for the concept of religion, but was criticised and denied legitimacy as a source of the religion of reason."[58] In fact, as will become clear, I take Poma's claim further and argue that Cohen treats Christianity as the very antithesis of the 'religion of reason.'

Second, as we will see, Cohen's account of Judaism, by virtue of its idealistic rather than empirical tendencies, maintains a necessary inclusivistic function, such that all human beings who recognize and act upon religious truth (the two are synonymous when it comes to religious truth)[59] are incorporated into Judaism as the 'righteous of the nations.'[60] Thus, there is no room for a genuine pluralism, given that the more a member of another faith-tradition realizes the 'religion of reason,' the more 'Jewish' she becomes. However, as Poma points out, since Judaism is always an ideal, an infinite task that is by no means limited to ethnic Jews, Cohen resists absolutizing Judaism, i.e., closing the gap between the 'is' and the 'ought' on its behalf or in its regard.[61]

And yet, even if one were to grant that Cohen's 'religion of reason' is not limited to Judaism, it is nevertheless readily apparent that his account of the dialectical interplay between 'scientific' ethics and the different religions which strive for rationalization is bound to fail, if only for his problematic insistence on the universality of his ethics. Cohen's ethics, however post-metaphysical, remain clearly rooted in a monotheistic framework, which renders all claims to neutrality and the capacity to serve as a common ground problematic. That ethics requires a transcendent God to secure the ideality of actuality, in order to render it immune from the dangers of relativism and quietism, is particularly problematic at a time when philosophy is struggling to elucidate a framework that is free of religious and cultural presuppositions and in which members of different cultures can equally participate.[62]

While this may appear to be a weakness for Cohen's thought, it is actually what makes the contemporary appropriation of it possible. Cohen is far more aware of his monotheism-centrism than are Kant and Mendelssohn, who simply take monotheism and its background assumptions to be universal. This is a great strength of Cohen's thought, especially when we consider that he, unlike Mendelssohn and Kant, never attempts to elide the agonism inherent in monotheistic religions. In fact, one feature of Cohen's thought that insures his continued relevance from a contemporary point of view is that he is unwilling to soften the demands of his Jewish monotheism in a vain attempt to secure philosophical neutrality. While this may make his thought hard to appropriate from a pluralist, multicultural notion of philosophy, it makes it easier to appropriate as a specifically Jewish or even specifically monotheistic vision.[63] For monotheistic religions, the unique God is essential for morality.

To be sure, if ethics is to serve as a neutral realm binding upon all human beings, then it is highly problematic that Cohen only takes into account Jewish, Christian, and Greek sources. However, as we have seen above, it is clear that for Cohen, ethics is not a merely secular endeavor, but one that is deeply rooted in monotheism. Thus, Cohen's insistence on systematicity and objectivity in regard to ethics, at least from a contemporary vantage point, is more of a burden to his position than an advantage. Beginning with an elective-monotheistic and indeed, an explicitly Jewish commitment, should not be counted against him. This is, in fact, what provides his thought with vitality regarding the questions of religious tolerance and pluralism over against the secularist approach exemplified in a thinker like Habermas, whose solution to monotheistic intolerance involves the vitiation of the discursive structure of the monotheistic worldview.

THE CORRELATION OF PARTICULARITY AND UNIVERSALITY IN JUDAISM

In Cohen's system of philosophy, and especially in *Ethik des reinen Willens*, where the idea of God serves as the warranty of truth—as that condition which secures the relationship between logic and ethics, between 'is' and 'ought'—God remains radically transcendent and inessential to the constitutive aspects of either logic or ethics in and of themselves;[64] God's role is essential only in the harmonious connection of ethics and logic to one another. Only in Cohen's religious writings does God move to the center, and in fact, rather than merely securing the correlation between logic and ethics, God now enters into correlation with human beings themselves. While God still remains the warranty of truth for Cohen (as that which secures the ideality of actuality), the late writings on religion move away from the radically transcendent and abstract notion of God and from the formality of ethics. In the religious writings, by means of the correlation between God and human beings, it now becomes the task of human beings to close the gap between 'is' and 'ought' and thus fulfill the promise vouchsafed by the God of truth.[65]

Given that religion is rooted in the God of truth, and that truth is the deepest foundation of science, there remains a connection between critical idealism and religion. To be sure, the central role Cohen gives God in his works on religion transcends the limits of his scientific idealism. However, as Cohen repeatedly points out, while the Israelites had no share in science, they nevertheless had a share in reason. Thus, through his works on the philosophy of religion (or better, on Jewish monotheism) Cohen develops an analogous methodology of critical reason that parallels his methodology of scientific reason and which is in accordance with, but is nonetheless irreducible to, his ethics, given that it derives not from science but from that reason derived by the Hebraic tradition's theological literary sources.[66] As Poma puts it, "The alternative character to science, though not in contrast, but rather complementary to it, consists precisely in the theocentrism of religious correlation, i.e. in monotheism itself."[67] God, who remains a liminal concept in the scientific idealism of Cohen's system, becomes the dynamic center from which the 'religion of reason' unfolds.

In *Religion of Reason Out of the Sources of Judaism* the correlation between God and human beings, as uncovered in the sources of Judaism, is in fact the center of three inter-related correlations. As these correlations unfold into each other, the tendency toward violence or hostility toward the Other is extirpated. The most prominent, and in a sense, most basic of the three correlations is that between God and human beings. Parasitic upon the correlation between God and human beings, is the correlation between human beings themselves. And finally, there is the correlation that is tied to the peculiar status of the people of Israel, the Jews. This is a correlation between particularity and universality. It is this *particular* people with their *particular* history that is to bear *universal* (in terms of the totality) significance by bequeathing to the world the previous two correlations, as well as serving as a permanent witness to them. That is, in the particular history of this people, or at least in the ideal of their history as conceived in their literary sources, Cohen argues that the emergence of these other two correlations is to be found. And it is in these correlations, which shape and are shaped by the history of the Jews, that Cohen makes progress over both Mendelssohn and Kant in terms of solving the problem concerning the violence of monotheistic intolerance.

Cohen's idealism emerges immediately in the manner of defining the topic of study in regard to Judaism, i.e., its literary sources.[68] That is, rather than finding race, ethnicity, or even the actual history of the empirical Jewish people to be the essential foundation for his study, Cohen argues that it is the literary sources of Judaism that constitute the historical point of origin which brings forth into the world the correlation between God and human beings, as well as the concomitant correlation between human beings themselves. Cohen does not read these texts as a historian, and thus his method of proceeding diverges sharply from scholars of rabbinic or biblical literature. Similarly, inasmuch as reason is privileged over the doctrines and teachings of the texts themselves, his method of approach is also unlike that of the rabbinic tradition or of theological exegesis in general.[69]

Cohen's hermeneutical method is a procedure of 'idealizing' the sources. What this means, methodologically, is that Cohen aims at reading these sources in a rationalizing manner. That is, he views them in terms of their highest possibilities according to reason rather than conceiving them so as to possess merely historical or dogmatic value.[70] Nevertheless, history still plays a vital role in that "history, literary history, is the factor by virtue of which the actuality of Judaism comes to its realization."[71] That is, Cohen traces the development of concepts within Judaism as they evolve and become more sophisticated and rational through the development of Jewish literary history.

The correlation which Cohen claims animates the form of Jewish literary sources is between the specific and the general (*Allgemeinheit*), i.e., between the particularity of the Jewish people and the universality of reason. That is, while these "literary sources" are the "true sources for the workings of the spirit, of a national spirit,"[72] a reason that is universal in scope is nevertheless "able to wrestle its way into the history of the particular people."[73] It is this correlation, which often takes the difficult form of conceptual 'wrestling,' that plays out and finally resolves itself in the literary history of Judaism. This correlation emerges quite early on in the Jewish literary sources themselves. The correlation consists in the particularity of Judaism, its national literature, being rooted in a universal idea, the unique God (monotheism). In fact, the idea of the unique God is the primary origin (*Ursprung*) of the national literature of the Jewish people. As a result, "Everything that comes forth from the spirit of Israel comes forth just as much from the unique God as it does from the national spirit in its primary origin and peculiarity."[74] Significantly, the two other correlations, that between God and the human being and that between human beings themselves, emerge in the process of this dialectical interplay taking place within the correlation of particularity and universality within Jewish literature. In sharp contrast to Mendelssohn's thought, which is undone by the antagonism between particularism and universalism, Cohen's account of monotheism derives vitality and power from it. With it, Cohen is able to preserve the dynamism of scriptural universalism and the discursive structure of elective monotheisms even as he makes significant alterations to them.

Cohen places the seeds of his account of rational universalism in the dialectical unfolding of scriptural universalism such that it gradually emerges and becomes dominant, but in this unfolding the particularities of scriptural universalism are never effaced. These particularities are not seen as impediments to rational universality, but rather play an essential role in its disclosure and unveiling. For example, in scripture and through its interpretation, including later scriptural texts which interpret earlier scriptural texts, the notion of revelation is harnessed in the direction of morality, albeit a conception of it that is religiously infused. According to Cohen, the primary idea of revelation is the unique God, which in turn entails the election of a *particular* community to promulgate this idea to the world as its historical mission, which when complete will establish universal harmony throughout the diverse plurality of particular human communities. Thus Cohen recognizes and validates all four moments (revelation, election, history/historical mission, *eschaton*) of the discursive structure of traditional elective monotheism. However, these structural moments serve as conditions for, and are put in service to, the emergence of rational universalism as Cohen conceives it.[75]

Religion of Reason Out of the Sources of Judaism, along with Cohen's other Jewish works, reflect Cohen's attempt to work out this harmony. Let us explore this process in more depth. The first moment is revelation. Revelation is the necessary condition for the possibility of the correlation between God and human beings.[76] Although a particular people is required for the promulgation of the teachings of revelation, the actual content of revelation, once purified of its mythic dross, is a notion of the unique God and its correlation with human beings which Cohen argues is inextricably bound to the rational, universal ideal of the totality.[77] Revelation, then, is thoroughly rational and universal, even though it initially appears in the national literature of a particular people and in the mythological form of miraculous encounters with the divine.[78] Cohen offers a reading of *Deuteronomy* which stresses that the miraculous and otherworldly aspects of revelation are to be sloughed off. True revelation "is not in the heavens," rather "the thing is very close to you, in your mouth and in your heart, to observe it" (*Deut.* 30.12, 14). Similarly, Cohen seizes upon the author of

Deuteronomy's claim that it is these laws and statutes "that will be proof of your wisdom and discernment to other peoples, who on hearing of all these laws will say, Surely, that is a wise and discerning people" (*Deut.* 4.6). For Cohen these passages, which he uses as proof-texts, indicate that the laws and statutes of revelation appeal to reason as such, so that all human beings and not just Jews can recognize them. The basis of the laws and statutes commanded by revelation is not a divine knowledge that is beyond the ken of human beings. Rather, despite their particular origin and locus in the people of Israel, the validity of these laws and statutes is or will be universally evident to human beings on the basis of reason.

By making revelation coeval with reason, Cohen is able to create the conditions through which bearing witness becomes comprehensible as a mode of promulgating the divine message *in history*. As a result Cohen avoids the problems associated with Mendelssohn's account of bearing witness, which is rooted in the logic of scriptural universalism—a logic ultimately unfathomable to human reason. If revelation is ultimately and thoroughly rational, then even if its point of origin is with the particular people of Israel, all human beings will be able to recognize its validity through their reason. Thus bearing witness for Cohen, unlike Mendelssohn, is not an enterprise that ultimately defies human understanding because not only is the Other capable of recognizing the validity of the contents of revelation, but also there is no unfathomable mystery regarding the source of the mission to bear witness, or the means by which one engages in this activity.

Judaism has no share in 'science,' but Cohen argues that it nevertheless discovers its own share in rationality through its 'laws and statutes' and its theology, i.e., the correlation of the unique God with human beings. This correlation between God and human beings establishes a version of ethical idealism which is compatible with the 'scientific-idealistic' account of ethics Cohen gives in *Ethik des reinen Willens,* where logic and ethics are correlated. In *Religion of Reason Out of the Sources of Judaism,* God's correlation with human beings establishes the ideality of reality, the gap between the 'is' and the 'ought.' In this later, explicitly 'religious' work, God's role as the condition of the harmony between logic and ethics is not cancelled, but rather the correlation between God and human beings becomes the religious foundation (or non-foundation, given the post-metaphysical nature of Cohen's thought) of ethics. As a result, the moral demands upon human beings become more direct and urgent.

With the correlation of God and human beings, God takes a direct role in rendering human beings themselves into infinite ethical tasks. The correlation, which in the case of human beings and God involves a "reciprocal dependence," is rooted entirely in reason. Thus for Cohen—like

Kant, and like Mendelssohn in his natural theology but *not* in his account of Judaism—reason is a concept in "common to God and man."[79] And like Kant, Cohen rejects the unfathomable God of traditional elective-monotheistic religions for a God that is commensurable with reason. However, unlike Kant, Cohen's process of bringing God into accord with rational universalism derives from sources within the Jewish tradition;[80] Cohen cites biblical, rabbinic, and medieval Jewish philosophical precedents, rather than making arguments from a philosophical position which is external to any specific Abrahamic tradition. While Cohen does ultimately subordinate scriptural universalism to rational universalism in this matter, the logic of scriptural universalism is by no means rendered superfluous.

The correlation between God and human beings thrusts the task-centered relationship between 'is' and 'ought' upon human beings. As rational, ethical beings, humans are the "focal point" of creation, of existence, and are thus distinct from all other extant creatures. Cohen helpfully elucidates this with the idea of spirit, explaining that both God and human beings are spirit, though not in such a way that their relationship is one of identity. When Cohen states, "spirit unites both members of the correlation,"[81] he means that human beings, as part of the process of becoming, receive their 'spirit' from the unique God who is being, the foundation of becoming. This derivation of spirit, however, is not a metaphysical relationship predicated upon causality, but is rather rooted in teleology, in the purpose of human beings—the link is ethical.

Cohen considers empirical human beings, human beings as they are given selves, as unformed and amoral, as corresponding to the 'is' in the relationship of 'is' and 'ought.' We see this when Cohen extends the notion of the correlation of 'spirit' to 'holy spirit.' Holiness, like spirit, binds God and human beings together, and yet it is distinct for each.[82] Holiness is ineluctably tied to morality.[83] God's holiness is nothing other than the unity of the Maimonidean 'attributes of action' (as Cohen interprets them), which enables God to serve as an ethical model for the creation of the Self out of the given self. Just as in his 'scientific' ethics, in his religious works Cohen remains dissatisfied with the given self of the particular subject. However, rather than deriving the task of the Self from the individual grounded in a state which is rooted in *Allheit* (conceived ethico-politically), now God (conceived through 'attributes of action') becomes the archetype for the infinite task of the construction and the teleological fulfillment of the moral Self. God, as the moral exemplar, grounds the Self in *Allheit*.

If, in this correlation, human beings are enjoined to perpetually emulate God, God in turn is conceived in strictly human terms, or to be more precise, God is conceived solely along the lines of human morality, which is the only sort of morality there is. This is what Cohen means in "Religion und Sittlichkeit," when he explains that the "essence of God is and remains the essence of human morality."[84] However, rather than completely reducing God to a functionary of ethics in the manner of Kant, Cohen remains within the horizons of scriptural universalism by crafting his account of God in language of unknowability. *"Outside of this interest in morality, the essence of God is unfathomable, that is, it is not an object of philosophical interest much less religious faith."*[85] God is perhaps not entirely reducible to morality, but as human beings, we cannot know God through anything but morality.

The result of this correlation is that morality and holiness, God and humanity, are thickly interwoven to such an extent that they are virtually inseparable even though they do not constitute an identity.[86] God's holiness exists for humanity as a task, and thus human beings are the medium in which God's holiness becomes manifest. "God accomplishes his holiness in man."[87] God's holiness is accomplished by means of human beings constructing Selves modeled upon God's moral attributes, which is inextricably bound up with moral action in the world. God's holiness, at least as it exists among human beings, is always a task, always the moral ideal. "Man, in the infinity of his moral tasks, in the infinitely distant view of his horizon, man in his moral absoluteness, detached from all the relativity of nature and history, this absolute man becomes the carrier and guarantor of the holy spirit."[88] In short, holiness is an ideal that demands to be realized. And human beings, as the partner in correlation with God, are the agents who are to bring about the realization of this order.[89]

Cohen's account of God, in the correlation between God and human beings, is much closer to Kant than to Mendelssohn. Mendelssohn remains indecisive about God, beholden to the rationally universal God of his natural theology as well as a version of the unfathomable God of scriptural universalism. Ultimately, Mendelssohn chooses the latter. Kant, on the other hand, subordinates God to the 'universal' morality of human beings (or better, of all finite rational beings) in such a way as to unilaterally subordinate the logic of scriptural universalism to what he takes to be that of rational universalism. God for Cohen is an idea and not a personality, but an idea which is inextricably bound up with human beings, and is particularly essential for their morality. Thus the correlation between God and the human being, with the holy spirit as its manifestation, must be understood as purely formal. It cannot be isolated in one party or another. It is merely "a function which signifies the correlation."[90] This logical function unifies God and human beings abstractly, such that God provides the grounds of human beings qua ethical beings, who exist as more than their given selves, who can construct themselves, having their Selves as infinite tasks.[91] In short, the correlation is as follows: God is the transcendental foundation of human beings as moral beings who are more than givenness, and human beings, to the degree they realize their moral Selves, provide the conditions whereby God is made manifest in the empirical world.

Cohen fruitfully distinguishes himself from Kant in that he is not only able to reconcile this rationalized notion of God with a specific Abrahamic-monotheistic tradition (Judaism), but he is also able to bring the universality of the God-idea into correlation with the particularity of the community in a way that preserves the momentum of the discursive structure of the monotheistic tradition, even as he alters its trajectory. That is, Cohen does not eviscerate scriptural universalism in the process of rooting it in rational universalism, but rather lets scriptural universalism serve as an essential supplement and partner to rational universalism. It is now imperative to investigate how Cohen, having successfully harmonized scriptural universalism with rational universalism, prioritizing the latter without eviscerating the former, proceeds to envision the unfolding of a monotheistic intolerance that is ethical.

8 | Rational Supererogation and the Suffering Servant

In the last chapter we discussed Cohen's basic methodology. We explored how Cohen's notion of correlation, particularly the correlation between God and human beings, serves as an especially fruitful framework for harmonizing particularity and universality, as well as scriptural universalism and rational universalism. Through the dialectical unfolding of the process of scriptural universalism in history (or at least the progression of its literary history), rational universalism comes more and more to the fore such that God is rationalized, Jews in their particularity become witnesses to totality, and the ideal of humanity (the moral order) as an ideal toward which all human beings should strive, is actualized. We will now continue to explore the other correlations which derive from the foundational correlation between God and human beings, and Judaism and humanity. However, it is first imperative to briefly reflect on the discursive structure of the elective-monotheistic worldview.

In traditionalist elective monotheisms, what Cohen refers to as the mythic level of monotheism, there is an unmediated encounter with God which results in writings that are held to be sacred, and treated as normative for the community and indeed for all of humanity. However, these teachings are only available to human beings through exposure to the revelation which the community itself possesses; human reason is insufficient to reach them on its own. These teachings not only disclose truths about metaphysical, cosmological, and world-historical realities, but their ultimate level of truth (what Jan Assmann calls their "emphatic concept of truth") pertains to the human *telos*.[1] This truth is the most foundational truth available to the human being because it discloses the human as such, i.e., who and how the human is created to be. There is no room for error here since, as Avishai Margalit points out, it is not simply that "errors have no value," but rather they carry a negative charge as *anti-truths*. Errors "become sins."[2]

In the wake of revelation, not only does a particular group receive special, privileged knowledge regarding the human *telos*, but this knowledge separates them from the Other even as this separation impels them toward the Other: it elects them. In short, by means of revelation, God elects the particular community in order for it to promulgate these teachings, spread this most profound notion of truth to the Other writ large, i.e., to the rest of the world, which remains mired in error. As a result of this error, however, the Other remains ambivalent. On the one hand, the Others are objects of pity in that they are those who have not received revelation and are therefore shrouded in darkness, lacking that knowledge which can make them whole. On the other hand, error is bound up with the active pursuit of and engagement in sin. And until the Others both receive the divine knowledge and accept it as true they remain not only outsiders of the community but also enemies of God, as those who actively inhibit God's plans. Only in the *eschaton* will all ambiguity be removed from the Other, but this requires that all otherness be stripped from the Other through either conversion or destruction.

It is to their credit that all three thinkers of the religion of reason trajectory recognize the central source of monotheistic intolerance in this ambivalence regarding the Other's lack of knowledge regarding the divine truth. Both Mendelssohn and Kant aim squarely at this ambivalence, either trying to ameliorate it by tinkering with the foundations of scriptural universalism (Mendelssohn) or undermining it altogether (Kant). Mendelssohn complicates scriptural universalism's notion of the Other, making it much more difficult to know whether or not the Other possesses the salvific truth concerning the universal human *telos*. Kant dissolves the tension between the particular and the universal by rooting the universal human *telos* in an *a priori* ground of practical reason rather than in revelation, thus undermining the dialectic of scriptural universalism altogether. Cohen differs from Mendelssohn and Kant in that he unabashedly embraces the 'emphatic concept of truth' inherent in the monotheistic worldview, as well as its notion of the Other as one who lives in error and thus sin, and therefore as one who obstructs God's plan.

Since he is privileging a developmental account of reason and a concomitant system of rational universalism in his readings of scriptural texts—or better, reading the scriptural texts in terms of their highest possibilities of reason (what Michael Zank calls a "hermeneutics of optimization"[3])— Cohen is able to trace out and secure ethical advancements within these documents, rather than reading them as if they are all of one piece, as is typical in (Jewish) scriptural universalism.[4] The idea of the unique God, which is disclosed in revelation, already contains the germs of subsequent moments including the final moment, the *eschaton*, which in Cohen's rationalized reading consists in universal harmony among all human beings.[5] The universal harmony of humanity, Cohen claims, involves recognition of the inherent value of all human beings and turns humanity itself into an ethical ideal.[6] This ideal, however, conflicts with other moments, such as the elevation of a particular community over others in election, even if this elevation is only for the promulgation of the ideas of God and humanity to the rest of the world. Thus, a dialectical process emerges in Cohen's religious thought through which a harmony must be achieved between the ethical content contained within the idea of God and the means by which this idea is to be brought to and established among the rest of the world. In short, as a form of *Ursprüngsdenken*, Cohen's elucidation of the discursive structure of the monotheistic worldview is such that each moment already contains the rational and ethical content of the whole, if only in latent or implicit form. The contradictions, in turn, serve as the impetus or catalyst that drives these rational and ethical elements to the surface and establishes their primacy.

JUDAISM AND THE INTOLERANCE OF THE MORAL ORDER

Cohen is adamant that Israel's significance is not limited to giving birth to the idea of the unique God. Rather the people of Israel, in all of their particularity, are to serve as the exemplar, the witness, to the universal idea of the unique God. This bearing witness constitutes at once the election and historical mission of the Jews. The Jews are elected insofar as they symbolize the universal idea of the unique God, and their mission consists in bearing witness to it. Thus, the correlation between particularity and universality in Israel continues. Cohen writes, "With regard to other peoples, therefore, Israel is not simply a people among a plurality of peoples. Because of its calling to profess the unique God and also to accomplish the historical work of the universal recognition of the unique God, Israel itself is distinguished as a unique people [*einzigen Volke*]."[7] The vocation of Israel secures its uniqueness, which is a special kind of particularity, among the pluralities of historical peoples qua relative communities vying for power in history. Israel is distinguished as unique, as distinct from all other particular communities, insofar as it points beyond history to the unique God, which alone is the true condition for totality.

However, this dialectical correlation between particularity and universality becomes complicated and contradictory in that "[o]nly knowledge
of [the unique] God establishes a unified community of men."[8] This claim
raises two difficulties, one being highly significant. The less significant difficulty is that if the idea of the unique God is the condition for the idea
of humanity as such, a united humanity with no divisions, then how is it
justified for the Jews as the keepers and witnesses to this idea to preserve
their distinct particularity? Is it not a contradiction for a particular people
to embody universal humanity and yet remain distinct from all Others?
Cohen deftly resolves this contradiction, because given that the world as it
is remains so fraught with difference, humanity remains only an ideal that
has certainly not yet been accomplished. Thus the particularity of the Jews
is able to symbolize the universality of humanity because this humanity is
not yet; it remains a future goal, and the Jews are to serve as the witnesses
in the present to a universal humanity that is to come.[9] Thus, this difficulty
is solved by Cohen's use of correlation.

The second difficulty, however, gets at the heart of Cohen's enterprise.
By arguing that 'only knowledge' of the unique God, of which the Jews are
symbols, generates the ideal of humanity—an ideal which is essential to
his ethics and all conceptions of proper living—Cohen decisively enters
into the intolerant orbit of the discursive structure of elective monotheisms. The difference between Cohen on the one hand, and Kant and even
Mendelssohn here, could not be sharper. Both Kant and Mendelssohn argue, albeit in different ways, that there is some sort of universal morality
which is more or less self-evident to the inherent rationality of human beings. To be sure, Mendelssohn is more skeptical of the capacity of human
beings to preserve the truths which undergird morality, and his conception of idolatry warrants a conservative view toward culture. Still, neither
Mendelssohn nor Kant makes being an adherent of an Abrahamic monotheism a necessary precondition for morality. However, it is precisely in
this sense that both thinkers fail to do justice to the self-understandings
of elective monotheisms. Elective monotheisms understand themselves as
not only entrusted with a task of world-historical importance, and thus being universally necessary for all of humanity without exception (even if this
necessity will not be recognized until the *eschaton*), but also as possessing
some sort of privileged knowledge that other traditions lack. That is, there
is an inherent religio-centrism within the self-conceptions of monotheistic religions, and thus, given their universal scope, intolerance toward the
cultural and religious views of the Other is inevitable.

Cohen recognizes this intolerance which is intrinsic to monotheistic
religions and nuances it by rendering it in terms of a contradiction which
arises between the Jews and the idea of humanity. On the one hand, with
their idea of the unique God, the Jews bequeath to the world the correlation

between God and human beings, which is inextricably linked to genuine ethics, where the difference between 'is' and 'ought' is preserved, in contrast to merely empirical or eudaemonistic conceptions of morality.[10] And the most significant fruit of this idea of the unique God in correlation with human beings is the universal idea of humanity, through which the inherent dignity of all human beings is recognized. The correlation between God and human beings is an ideal task which has its historical origin with the Jews (at least according to Cohen). This task is perpetual and yet demands to be fully realized, and thus the Jews are entrusted with the further task of firmly embedding this idea in history. To use monotheistic language, in giving birth to the idea of God the Jews are *elected* by its truth, and are as a result entrusted with the *historical mission* to bear witness to it.[11] On the other hand, to embed this idea in history, Jews must radically oppose and negate other conceptions of the divine as idolatry, and must work toward eliminating them.

The tension here is that the mission of the Jews (to spread monotheism) seems to implicitly involve a conflict with the fruit of the idea of the unique God (morality), in that monotheism demands the absolute destruction of polytheism, and thus the destruction of idolaters. Quite simply, monotheism absolutely "cannot permit any tolerance of polytheism. *Idolatry* has to be destroyed absolutely."[12] The deepest reason for this, Cohen argues, is that monotheism is firmly bound to the moral order and its ideality is bound up with and orients actuality, especially the ideal of humanity; whereas polytheism is bound up with empiricism, with existence as such, and in celebrating might and power it inhibits ethics on its most profound level. This tension emerges initially, and in its most troubling form, in those passages in the Hebrew Bible where the people of Israel are commanded by God to root out and destroy (i.e., kill) the idolaters in their midst, whether Jews or foreign peoples.[13]

But Cohen claims that within the Jewish literary sources it is soon recognized that this radical opposition to idolatry and polytheism (i.e., the historical mission of Judaism) is inconsistent with the idea which secures ethics and generates the ideal of humanity (i.e., the unique God) if this opposition is construed as a call to violence against idolaters, especially foreigners. Cohen argues that it is no coincidence that in the face of the demand to destroy idolatrous peoples, subsequent texts postulate contradictory demands, commanding love for the "Edomite" and even the "Egyptian." These texts insist upon the recognition that the Edomite and Egyptian are just as human as the Jew, that idolatry does not inexorably taint them or diminish their humanity.[14] The significance of this recognition can hardly be overestimated, as it thoroughly permeates Cohen's thought on monotheism. It is through this contradiction, Cohen claims, that the literary history demonstrates that Judaism is able "to correct its own teaching with respect to the strict commandment to destroy idol worship and idolatrous peoples."[15] In short, violence against the idolater becomes absolutely prohibited as a solution to the problem of polytheism.

As a result, while the Jews must remain true to the logic implicit in monotheism, that the "unique God 'should be called Lord over all the earth,' and all men and all peoples should know and worship him," they absolutely cannot embrace violence in carrying out the implications of this idea. Unlike Mendelssohn, who attempts to circumvent this problem by denying the very existence of polytheism, claiming that it is just culturally coded monotheism, or monotheism in a degraded form, Cohen insists that since polytheism is utterly contradictory to the unique God, the "plurality of gods should absolutely disappear from the earth."[16] Cohen remains true to the logic of monotheism, by insisting that one cannot escape the monotheistic demand to eradicate all polytheism.

In order to resolve any difficulties in Cohen's position regarding the prohibition to violence and hostility regarding the Other while nevertheless insisting on the radical truth of monotheism, it is helpful to turn to *Ethik des reinen Willens*. In this text, as in his later explicitly religious work, Cohen puts forward a highly Platonic reading of Judaic monotheism which stresses the redemptive power of knowledge.[17] Cohen's position accords with theorists of monotheism such as Margalit and Assmann, regarding the 'emphatic concept of truth' and the equation of error and sin in elective monotheism. However, Cohen rejects the notion that sin as such is an objection to humanity but rather, by means of a rational reconstruction of Ezekiel, he claims that sin is in fact "a rigorous means to *self-knowledge* and to the grounding [*Begründung*] of one's self." Sin, Cohen avers, works "to bring to light all hiding places of human frailty" (*alle Schlupwinkel der menschlichen Gebrechlichkeit*).[18] This frailty which causes our moral shortcomings, our inability to live up to the moral ideal, is rooted not so much in weakness of the human will as in lack of knowledge, lack of truth. Cohen follows Socrates in claiming that morality consists of "*knowledge*" (Wissen), and that "morality, as knowledge is *teachable* [lehrbar]."[19] Cohen (in)famously argues for the profound confluence between the Greek idealists (Socrates and Plato, but not Aristotle) and the Jewish monotheistic tradition on this point, although he claims superiority for the Jewish tradition because of its egalitarian impulse—all human beings, and not merely the intellectual elite, should pursue knowledge.[20]

How does Cohen reconcile this egalitarian impulse with the 'emphatic concept of truth' that is operative in the elective-monotheistic worldview? This is a complex question which ultimately involves a theodicy and a philosophy of history, which we are not yet prepared to discuss. However, the beginnings of an answer can be found in *Ethik des reinen Willens,* which forms a foundation upon which his religious writings will build. Since the ethical concept of the human being exists in the tension between actuality and the ideal, with the emphasis upon the perpetual striving after the ideal, no one is ever complete in the ethical sense, which means that no person is either fully good or bad. Rather, everyone is in the process of forming themselves.[21] Since ethical perfection is an impossibility, more ethically realized human beings develop the virtue of modesty (*Bescheidenheit*), which rejects judging oneself too favorably and especially the notion of condemning other people.[22] Most importantly, modesty "protects [one] from the full identification of the criticized action [*beurteilenden Handlung*] with the person [in question]." This refusal to render doer and deed identical protects one from "the calamity [*Unheil*] of condemnation."[23] Knowledge, moral knowledge, is itself redemptive for Cohen. Only it can bring one to atonement and freedom from a sinful past, preparing one morally for a new present and future. To be sure, Cohen thinks that criminals bear the guilt of their crime, but this can only be atoned for by criminals recognizing their own guilt and autonomously taking their punishment upon themselves. Only then will both the crime and criminal disappear in the transformation of the criminal by means of repentance.[24]

In *Religion of Reason Out of the Sources of Judaism,* Cohen argues that God as being (*Sein*) is nothing less than truth itself or Truth,[25] and thus exists as being in contrast to all actuality, all appearance, all becoming (*Werden*). Since the ideal orients the actual in ethics, and God is the foundation of the ideal, knowledge of God is imperative for ethics. That is, it is knowledge of God that properly grounds the subject in *Allheit.* Cohen explains, "Knowing God is loving God, and love of God is knowledge of God,"[26] and both "love of God and knowledge of God . . . are equivalent to love and knowledge of ethics; for ethics is the recognizable attribute of God."[27] In other words, one's relationship to God is construed purely in terms of ethical reason, and the construction of the ethical concept of the Self in light of the Maimonidean 'attributes of action.' If one lacks correct knowledge of God, one lacks the basis to sufficiently orient oneself ethically in actuality; one cannot strive after ideals that one does not *know.* Thus, all sin is ultimately *Shegagah,* or unintended sin, which Cohen concludes is ultimately a result of lack of knowledge.[28] Hence, the great danger of pluralities masquerading as totalities becomes evident; they distract and conceal the Truth, which alone founds ethics.

Cohen's importance to the religion of reason trajectory does not merely consist in his willingness to face the full implications of monotheism, but also in his elevation of those elements in the Jewish sources that render violence absolutely forbidden in the effort to root out and destroy polytheism. Almost a century before scholars of monotheistic intolerance and violence such as Martin Jaffee, Jan Assmann, Avishai Margalit, Regina Schwartz, and others, Cohen recognizes the tendency of monotheistic religions to translate their 'emphatic concept of truth' into hostility toward the Other and undercuts this hostility at its root. Since Cohen finds the center of gravity of the correlation between God and human beings to take place in ethics, any failure to recognize the humanity of the Other, any sort of hatred or violence, would be a contradiction with this correlation and therefore violate the foundations of monotheism. Thus, according to Cohen, the resolution to this contradiction requires that a way be found that Jews can oppose idolatry without violating ethics, without failing to recognize the humanity of the Other, even if she worships idols. Error and sin, although they are the root of all that prevents the actualization of the totality, nevertheless do not diminish the humanity of the one who errs and sins. While idolatry is to be opposed, the idolater must not be hated. Cohen insists, "All hatred is vain and wanton. All hatred is nothing but illusion."[29] Both sin and hatred are part of becoming and not being, part of unredeemed history which is to be overcome in the establishment of totality.

JUDAISM, CHRISTIANITY, AND MYTH

Since Cohen argues that the correlation between human beings themselves derives from the more primordial correlation between God and the human being, it is helpful to ask how the correlation between God and the human being engenders the correlation between human beings. However, in order to answer this, one more step backward is required, in that it is first necessary to understand what the ethical transfiguration of the idea of God that takes place in Cohen's correlation is itself competing with and replacing in its development. Myth is the primal layer, even in monotheistic religions, which must be overcome in order for the ethical transfiguration of the idea of God, and subsequently, the correlation between human beings, to emerge. And Cohen follows the practice common to Mendelssohn and Kant of employing a rival elective monotheism, Christianity and Judaism respectively, for rhetorical and heuristic purposes—namely, to reinforce and legitimize his own rationalized innovations.[30] For Cohen it is again Christianity, and by 'illustrating' how Christianity fails to overcome myth, and thus maintains a violent intolerance, Cohen is better able to elucidate how his version of Judaism overcomes myth and thus uproots the violence so often tied to monotheistic intolerance. It is this contrast which enables him to justify the innovations to tradition that he advocates.[31]

The most primordial and fundamental point of distinction between Judaism and Christianity regarding violence, according to Cohen, lies in their respective relationships to myth. Cohen claims that while Judaism decisively breaks with myth by means of the correlation between God and human beings, Christianity remains beholden to myth, at least in certain capacities. A central defining feature of myth, according to Cohen, is that it maintains an *"unmediated relationship between the human being and God"* (*unmittelbares Verhältnis zwischen Mensch und Gott*).[32] In myth, God exists as a person, as someone to whom one relates in an intersubjective mode. In one sense, then, God is a person to whom one relates in a manner like any other. And yet, at the same time, God is a person like no other, in that God is all-powerful and all-knowing, such that His will constitutes the good and the right.[33] As a result, in mythic worldviews and indeed in mythic monotheisms, one always encounters Others as mediated through one's personal relationship with the divine. This limits one to a tribal or communal chauvinism insofar as the Other's recognition of the divine (or lack thereof) is all-important in determining how one is to respond to her. In such a system, maintaining good relations with the divine is far more important than maintaining ethical responsibility for the Other. It is God-the-person who arbitrates what is right and wrong, and the Other is either actively helping to realize God's plan or actively thwarting it; there is no neutrality. God's honor and dignity are all-consuming, and thus human beings have no worth except insofar as God bestows it upon them. As Ludwig Feuerbach argues, for the monotheist nothing less is at stake in the encounter with the Other than the "honour of God."[34] The mythic-monotheist,[35] Feuerbach claims—and here Cohen would be in complete agreement—is forced to choose between her duty to God and her duty to other human beings. Which duties are more important? The answer is clear. According to Feuerbach, "By how much God is higher than man, by so much higher are duties to God than duties towards man."[36] Similarly, Cohen claims that mythic thinking inevitably causes hostilities between communities and fosters a kind of dichotomous thinking about humanity itself, leading Cohen to conclude: *"With [the idea of] humanity, myth has nothing in common."*[37]

Cohen does not argue that Christianity is straightforwardly mythic, but rather that unlike Judaism, Christianity has not entirely broken with myth. In short, aspects of myth live on in Christianity. Christianity, for Cohen, remains beholden to myth in two essential ways: It conceives of God as a person, which results in the dichotomy of faith and ethics; and it stresses the individual and the individual's relationship to God in salvation, rather than humanity as a whole. As a result, Cohen uses Christianity as the foil to his ideal of the 'religion of reason.'

The most striking mythical inheritance in Christianity is to be found in its notion of God. Whereas Judaism, in Cohen's view, engages in a steadfast war against anthropomorphism, Christianity conceives of a God "who at the same time is man."[38] This is problematic for Cohen not so much on strictly theological grounds as philosophical ones. By rendering God into a person, and even more, into a human being who actually exists in history rather than an ideal of reason, Christianity creates an opposition between ethics and religious faith. Cohen writes, "The God who at the same time is man, is not only and not exclusively the archetype of human beings [*Vorbild des Menschen*]. *Here therefore it is the essence of God [Wesen Gottes] which constitutes the peculiar content of faith.*"[39] That is, in sharp contrast to Cohen's Maimonidean-inflected Judaism which has no concern for God outside of God's ethical significance, this 'content of faith' pertains to an "extra-moral sphere," and takes recourse to dogmatic teachings over and above pure morality in determining the concept of the human being.[40] This reliance upon dogma highlights that Christianity is unable to subordinate scriptural universalism to the order of rational universalism. In fact, in Christianity rational universalism is unable to emerge since ethics, which is a sphere of human reason, is insufficient for salvation, and thus elements of faith and dogma, which transcend the bounds of human reason, are given priority. Or to put it another way, faith attempts to ground ethics in the teachings of particular religious documents rather than in universal, critical reason.[41]

In a manner strikingly similar to Kant's account of Judaism and the yoke of the Mosaic Law, Cohen points to the Christian requirement of faith as a species of pseudo-knowledge which compromises autonomy and undermines ethics. According to Cohen, myth is focused on the past, on the inevitability of fate rather than on freedom and the ethical, future-oriented, teleological striving for totality.[42] Ethics breaks with myth of necessity, in that it holds individuals responsible for their own deeds and refuses to justify the punishment of children for the guilt of their parents.[43] Christianity remains beholden to myth with its idea of original sin, which requires a notion of salvation that is to be distinguished from moral work.[44] Or as Cohen puts it, "*Christian* theology [*Gotteslehre*] is in its specific ground a teaching of salvation [*Erlösungslehre*]. The concept of the human being signifies to it the concept of *sin*. Salvation follows sin and guilt; indeed, original sin excludes freedom."[45] Original sin is a misunderstanding of the Hebraic concept of sin, which Cohen argues is the necessary condition for freedom, the necessary condition for ethics. Cohen is very critical of Kant's notion of freedom, grounded as it is in the noumenal self, which Cohen regards as a holdover of the antiquated metaphysics of rational psychology.[46] In contrast, Cohen conceives of freedom as a task, one rooted in a philosophy of law, which is itself rooted in the anticipated totality that is yet to be realized, the ideal.[47]

Ethics, whether 'scientific' in *Ethik des reinen Willens* or religio-critical in *Religion of Reason Out of the Sources of Judaism,* is grounded in totality, an ideal of perfect universality, where the ideal of humanity is fully realized.

In both texts, Cohen relies heavily on a notion of messianism rooted in the Jewish tradition, where the focus is on the redemption of humanity, which is entirely this-worldly and requires that all states and selves be grounded in totality—the fulfillment of the ideal in the actual. Christianity, on the other hand, translates "the Messiah through Christ" and thereby transfigures, or rather, distorts the proper understanding of the Messiah. The content of the mistranslation is that "Christ is the Redeemer of individuals," and only by saving all individuals can Christ save all humanity.[48] This focus on the individual, particularly on the supernatural fate of the individual after death, Cohen argues, inhibits Christianity's ability to recognize the ethical ideal of humanity, which requires access to genuine totality.

Since in Christianity scriptural universalism trumps rational universalism, and the 'extra-moral sphere' of faith trumps pure human morality, morality itself is now recast in terms of theological, doctrinal, and dogmatic knowledge. Thus in a rather polemical tone, Cohen states, "Now faith should possess a higher and entirely other sort of certainty than is possible for knowledge [*Wissen*]. Truly it is an entirely different sort of knowing which constitutes faith: it is the fate [*Schicksal*] of the individual, around which it all revolves." Cohen continues, claiming that Christian faith "remains fixed as an antipode [*Gegensatz*] against ethics as a member of a philosophical system."[49] Whereas Kant argues that Judaism as a result of its adherence to law is antithetical to philosophy and ethics, Cohen argues that it is the Christian notion of faith which in fact is the mythic, pre-rational anachronism (i.e., Christianity and not Judaism is the anachronistic holdover of scriptural universalism), and is therefore irreconcilable with philosophical morality.

This cleft between faith and knowledge results in a new teleological conception of the human being in Christianity, one grounded in dogmatic doctrines. As a result, faith and not ethics becomes the condition for the constitution of the 'Self' as a 'moral' project. Cohen writes, "The moral worth of human beings is not grounded in the power of one's own reason. Rather, one can receive it only from the outside, only God can confer it upon one."[50] This conferral takes place through a conception of revelation that is based on specific content, not the purely formal conditions for reason as Cohen conceives it for the 'religion of reason,' and as such, develops a notion of the ideal human being that is rooted thoroughly in a particular faith-tradition and only thenceforth in morality. Cohen argues that this notion of faith as content-bearing knowledge of the "divine essence" which takes a "determinate form and [an] unalterable content of knowledge of God," is "henceforth *elevated to the fundamental condition of human morality*." The result is not only a lack of rigor in ethics, but more importantly there is a corresponding "curtailment of *love for human beings* [*Menschenliebe*], for humanity in general [*Menschentums überhaupt*] . . . for in no other way is morality conceived, much less realized, than as this way of knowledge of God, of faith in the essence of God and of divine salvation."[51]

This 'curtailment of love for human beings' on the part of Christianity manifests itself in two ways. First, because the Christian notion of faith remains concerned with mythic (dogmatic) knowledge rather than rational (critical-ethical) knowledge, it remains primarily bound to the fate of the individual, whether in the next life she is to receive "eternal salvation" or "eternal damnation."[52] Second, as a result of this fate which is rooted in guilt (original sin) and which applies to all human beings unless they hold the correct doctrinal truth, Christianity justifies a policy of "world conquest."[53] In both cases there is no genuine universality, no access to totality, but only a plurality arrogating to itself such a status.

In contrast to the mythic monotheism of Christianity, the correlation between God and the human being, which determines God strictly in terms of human ethics, allows an entirely new and *direct* relationship to emerge between human beings. In "Religion und Sittlichkeit," Cohen argues that for the prophets—whom he claims are the true creators of genuine monotheism—rather than taking part in any sort of mediating relationship, "God withdraws" (*trat zurück*) in order to purify the "relation between human being and human being" (*Verhältnis zwischen Mensch und Mensch*). This withdrawal of God makes the concern for the other person more "urgent."[54] If God remained some infinitely important 'person' to whom we relate directly, as in myth, our relationships to everything else including other human beings, would be drastically subordinated.[55] Such a move would undermine the purity of ethics, which prioritizes autonomous obligations to human beings.[56] God is the founder of ethics and thus any sense of being an obstruction would be self-contradictory.

The correlation between human beings is an expansion and direct result of the correlation between God and human beings. The ethical transfiguration of God wrought by the prophets, which stands at the root of the correlation between God and human beings, opens the way for a new relationship between human beings. In order to understand the significance of this correlation we must briefly return to Cohen's discussions of myth. Mythic thought, which can only conceive of God as a person, is concerned with questions of causality, metaphysics, and cosmology. Thus, when confronted with the Other,[57] particularly the suffering of the Other, it asks questions of theodicy, and in order to justify God, it links this suffering inextricably to guilt, whether personal or inherited.[58] At best, the suffering of the Other is a theoretical problem, one that can be 'solved' through recourse to abstractions. One never encounters the Other in any sort of immediacy, particularly in regard to her suffering, but rather there is always room for ideological and conceptual frameworks to predispose one to indifference or hostility.[59]

Again, Christianity and Judaism differ in regard to their relationship with myth. Christianity finds the suffering of human beings to be rooted in guilt, and the release from suffering is tied to the Christological release from guilt. Since God has not been denuded of the mythic, extra-moral essence, the relationship between the individual and God remains primary, and thus the pure interpersonal relationship between human beings does not develop.[60] As a result of this individualistic focus, the suffering of the Other can never become one's primary focus. In addition, Cohen argues that Christianity takes recourse to the mythical balms of the otherworld to ease the burden that the view of degradation and suffering imposes upon one's conscience.[61] As a result of its ties to myth, Christianity serves as an obstacle to the correlation between human beings rather than a resource that supports it.

Judaism, on the contrary, having broken thoroughly with myth, is conducive to the correlation between human beings themselves. As a result of this break, for Judaism the suffering of the Other is not a theoretical question which entails one looking to God for justification. Rather, since human beings are the active agent in the correlation between God and human beings, one looks to humanity and not God in the face of human suffering. The suffering of the Other, particularly as it is objectively manifested in poverty, serves as a searing indictment of the failure to actualize the ideals of ethics. Those who suffer do not do so from their own guilt, nor do they suffer from death or other aspects pertaining to human finitude (which are ultimately metaphysical and particular in nature), but rather they suffer from the concrete failings of human beings to manifest the universal foundations of culture.[62] All of culture is indicted in poverty.[63]

It is precisely by means of taking the suffering of the Other seriously that the conditions emerge for the correlation between human beings. Poverty, the suffering of the Other, reveals that our culture has failed to bring about what ought to be from what is. Since the ethical conception of the Self is rooted in the ideal of totality, and poverty is a direct contradiction to totality, poverty serves as a constant reminder of one's own failure to achieve one's own ideal Self. Poverty is a purely social evil, and thus constitutes a distinctly separate problem for reason than the particular evils of illness and death, which are metaphysical, given their causal rather than teleological or purposive nature.[64]

Just by existing in and participating with an imperfect society, a society that allows poverty, this great inhumanity perpetrated against the Other, one is guilty. In the face of social suffering, a correlation between the guilty subject and the Other emerges, in which the subject is charged with a non-reciprocal, asymmetrical responsibility for the Other. A central force in the correlation between human beings is the role of the affect of pity.[65] Pity is not a mere passive reaction, for Cohen, but rather it is an active spur to moral responsibility; it transforms the Other from a mere *Nebenmensch* (next-person), a He or She, to a *Mitmensch* (fellow-person), a Thou who faces one.[66] The *Mitmensch* is the cornerstone of the correlation between human beings; it is the condition for community in that it prevents all indifference to the Other and demands a responsibility for the Other. It is the Thou, for whom one's relationship, one's responsibility, is rendered 'urgent.'

In light of this correlation, when one approaches the Other it is not with concerns about theodicy or with theoretical questions about her possible guilt, questions which look for explanations to make her intolerable condition more tolerable for the onlooker. Rather, one approaches the Other with a responsibility that is accompanied by the affects of both pity for her and personal guilt for one's own moral failures and the failings of a culture in which one is implicated. Cohen exclaims, "This is the new insight that true monotheism brings about: the poor man is your own flesh. You do not consist of your own body, nor is your wife, the object of your sexual love, the only flesh that is your flesh, but the poor man also is your flesh."[67] A sentence later, Cohen continues, "And the *Mitmensch* as the poor man brings God's love for man into the true light and the true understanding."[68] The poor person as *Mitmensch* reveals that the moral order, what ought to be, is yet to be enacted. God is the one who secures this moral order, and in the doctrine of messianism, God serves as an assurance that morality will prevail in history. However, God is not therefore primarily to be taken as a comfort, but rather as the conditions for the ethical pursuit in general, and more directly, as the ideal. God's meaning is found in the ever-present demand to actualize one's ideal ethical Self. But this Self has its own precondition in totality, in which it must concomitantly strive; in striving to properly ground itself, it is simultaneously striving to realize itself. In striving to realize the Self, the subject simultaneously strives to actualize the ideal, and in striving to actualize the ideal the subject strives to realize the Self.

In this manner, Cohen attempts to establish an asymmetrical or supererogatory ethics on rationalist grounds. The Self, an ideal which is to be striven after by all and is rooted in totality, is stymied by poverty and thus requires that one go above and beyond the law in order to facilitate its actualization, however incremental. To demand reciprocity, parity with the suffering Other, would involve losing sight of the ethical demand to actualize the ideal, in that it would inevitably lead back to asking theoretical questions about guilt and blame. Such questions involve a lapse into mythical thinking, into a search for origins which only detracts from the urgency of the Other's plight. Ethics has no interest in the past, in backward-looking questions of guilt (at least when it comes to the Other), but rather looks forward to teleological ends, to the realization of the ethical Self. Additionally, even those Others who are not directly suffering from poverty but who lack the truth are not living as they should, and thus suffering spiritually, which shows that they too are impoverished. It makes no sense to search for blame, since sin and immorality are rooted in ignorance which can only be rectified through teaching and by looking toward the future. Only a supererogatory ethics will suffice. In this manner, Cohen translates and incorporates the asymmetrical and supererogatory drives common to monotheistic, especially messianic, thinking into a rationalist idiom.

How is the subject to cope with the guilt that arises in the correlation with the Other? This brings to the fore another important contrast between Judaism and Christianity in Cohen's thought. For Cohen, guilt in Christianity is primordial and inherent, and freedom from sin is not acquired through ethical labor but is rather acquired from something entirely external to the power of human beings, namely grace.[69] In Judaism, however, sin is a point of mediation. Sin is the source of self-knowledge, and as such, "knowledge of sin in monotheism can only mean: to become free from sin."[70] Cohen's optimism about human nature appears in his view that sin serves as the condition for the possibility of freedom and ethics, in that sin is merely the occasion for freely turning away from sin, for rising above the guilt inherent in partaking in relative communities and their flawed, partial morals, and returning to God (t'shuvah).[71] Sin is the gateway from the particular (einzeln) person to ethical individual (Individuum) or Self, in that the "possibility of self-transformation makes the individual an I."[72] In this process of sinning and atoning, "one first becomes an individual who is not absolutely dependent upon the relations of the social plurality in which [one] is enmeshed."[73] In other words, in the act of t'shuvah, in the "capacity to turn away from [one's] previous way of life,"[74] from plurality, and reorient oneself toward totality, one gains autonomy.

Since all sin is error and vacillation—false knowledge of the unique God, and a lack of the proper foundation in totality that flows from it—the ethical implications of t'shuvah arise from a reorientation of one's foundations. Cohen argues that Christianity, lacking such autonomy, has God absolve the particular person of guilt. However, an autonomous individual "cannot be relieved of his consciousness of guilt."[75] Rather, in the act of t'shuvah, the human being creates a new heart and a new spirit and is thus freed from her old self, and consequently sin is not decisive but only a mediating concept. However, as Cohen is quick to point out, "The new heart and the new spirit are and remain *tasks*. The I, too, can be considered nothing other than a task."[76] Thus the call to atonement is an ethical task, to realize the ethical Self, and God remains only the condition. God is not a collaborator, much less an intercessor, who removes the task altogether, somehow mythically purifying the subject. Rather God demands that one sanctify oneself, create oneself anew, but God cannot and does not perform this task for one. By making God the primary agent in human atonement, Christianity undermines the process by which one becomes an ethical Self.

Christianity for Cohen is a religion rooted in myth and self-interest, thus serving as an ideal foil for the 'religion of reason,' which is rooted in reason and supererogatory ethics. Cohen reverses the terms of Kant's infamous account of Judaism, arguing that it is Christianity's notion of faith and Christianity's notion of grace that undermines autonomy and ethics.[77] Rather than conceiving of God as a person, a position that can only lead to a particularist ethic given that it requires knowledge of salvific doctrines derived from authoritative texts as preconditions for ethics, Cohen posits God as an ideal that undergirds ethics and gives it urgency. It is only by way of the 'Jewish' manner of thoroughly intertwining God with human ethics, in a formal/functional rather than dogmatic/theological manner, that the grounds for an ethics that recognizes the inherent dignity of all human beings regardless of their religious beliefs are secured.

THE SUFFERING SERVANT

The correlation between human beings, which Judaism enables to emerge, in fact, also affects the correlation between the particularity and universality of Israel. It affects this correlation regarding Israel in two interconnected ways, which enriches its complexity and further secures the extirpation of the violence implicit in monotheistic intolerance. The first way concerns laws pertaining to an idealized Jewish homeland, while the second bears upon the role of the Jews in history. Together, these interconnected influences on the correlation between human beings inform the historical mission of the Jews in bearing witness to the unique God of monotheism. In fact, the correlation between human beings is borne out in Cohen's rather unique take on the bearing-witness modality of the promulgation of the notion of truth in elective Judaism, which is rooted in the privileging of rational universalism, as he accounts for it, over scriptural universalism.

The first level in which the correlation between human beings influences the correlation between particularity and universality in Israel can be seen in the commands we discussed previously, to love the Edomite and the Egyptian. From the foundational notion of the unique God and its universality, Jewish literary works, particularly legal ones, extrapolate that it would be inconsistent for the universal God to love and care solely for the Jews, and thus, these works insist the contrary, that God must evince similar concerns and affections for all of humanity. Cohen reaches these positions by examining biblical laws about the Jewish homeland, and subsequent rabbinical laws which operate according to the ideal of a Jewish homeland, which in actuality, has long ceased to exist. In these laws the Other is a foreigner, a stranger, which in biblical and rabbinic thought is conceptually aligned with the poor person. Thus, rather than hatred or a feeling of supremacy, the Other is approached with pity, again understood as a lever to moral responsibility. As a result, the Other's rights are steadfastly maintained, as the ideal of humanity dominates. Even if she does not recognize the unique God, the Other benefits from its conceptual fruits. Thus, a rigorous universalism is preserved within the particularity of the Jewish homeland.

However, it is with the other side of the correlation that Cohen's real solution to the violence of monotheistic intolerance within the historical mission of Judaism becomes apparent. Whereas on the one hand, in Jewish law and its ideal notion of the Jewish state, the humanity of the Other is recognized, on the other hand, in actual history, Jews are the powerless ones whose rights and humanity are often not recognized. In their stateless existence the Other, in fact, has great power over the Jews. Cohen insists that the agony of statelessness, with the persecutions and endless sufferings that accompany it, are a necessary condition for Israel to play a universal role in world history.[78] That is, on the opposite side of the correlation, Judaism as a particularity demonstrates its universality, by serving as a symbol for the suffering of humanity, as the "prototype of human suffering in general," i.e., the "social analogue of poverty."[79] Israel's election is for the sake of highlighting the crisis of culture, that what ought to be has not been realized. The election of Israel, as a particular people, is not of a triumphant nation that conquers the Other, even if said conquest was to be done in order to bring truth to the Other. Rather, Israel suffers to draw attention to the unresolved social suffering in the world.[80] As such, "God does not love Israel more or differently from his love for men in general, nor needless to say, could God's love for Israel limit and impair his love for the human race. In Israel, God loves nothing other than the human race."[81]

Rather than taking a posture of conquest or aggressive proselytizing, which leads to a hostile relationship with the Other—which the recent scholarship on monotheism highlights, but again, which Cohen clearly foresees almost a century earlier—the mission of the Jews manifests itself in the posture of bearing witness, albeit idiosyncratically configured. In the split between those within the community and those outside of it, the humanity of the Other is never effaced. In fact, only by willingly taking suffering upon oneself, by serving as a "sacrificial victim who exposes himself to suffering because of his knowledge of the irreplaceable value of this suffering for the historical welfare of mankind,"[82] can the Jew oppose the idolatry of the Other without effacing the Other's humanity, i.e., without herself falling victim to idolatry. The violent posture which can be discerned in the methods of promulgating the 'truth' of monotheism, through conquest and forced conversion as well as aggressive proselytizing, causes suffering in the Other and thus is part and parcel of the order of history, of how the world has always been. The Jew, as the suffering servant, as the 'sacrificial victim' who willingly reverses the trajectory of suffering in order to testify to the unique God, opens up the dimension of the future, the order of the ideal, a bridge to totality, which is an order radically different from all that has hitherto existed in actuality. By willingly undergoing suffering, the Jew discloses an order higher than eudaemonism, that order which Cohen thinks has reigned throughout history, testifying instead to the "ethical concept of history" that refuses to recognize the equation of might with right.[83]

This notion of the suffering servant plays into Cohen's juxtaposition of Judaism and Christianity, especially in regard to the discovery of the individual in sin. As opposed to Christianity's spurious correlation of original sin and vicarious atonement, Cohen avers, Judaism stresses autonomy, in that "the correlation with God must not infringe upon the ethical essence of man."[84] In other words, the creation of a new ethico-religious Self only takes place through the autonomous act of penance, which is a perpetual process of self-sanctification. In order to maintain strict autonomy, an integral part of the creation of the universal, ethical Self as an infinite task undertaken by the particular, given self, is the willingness to recognize one's guilt and freely turn away from one's past through penance.

Penance involves punishment for one's past misdeeds. Cohen writes, "for man himself there is no other keystone of repentance but punishment." This punishment, however, "does not require any prison; for life itself is this prison of sin."[85] Rather, punishment is a positive force in that since Job, Cohen claims, suffering is recognized in the Jewish tradition as a "voluntary self-sacrifice."[86] In this manner, Cohen conjoins suffering as penance with the ethical task of the creation of the Self, which is possible only because he has already broken the mythic-metaphysical causal connection between suffering and guilt. Punishment, then, is not so much concerned with absolving the guilt of the past as purifying the subject for its future-oriented, teleological end, which is the Self.

Punishment as suffering does not derive its value from any sort of impulse toward asceticism, but rather in the recognition that suffering is "a force in God's plan of salvation," a "suffering for the sake of others."[87] In other words, everyone is a sinner, but the ethical person voluntarily accepts suffering and punishment not simply for penance, but because suffering as penance implies both suffering for the Other and the creation of the ethical Self. As Cohen explains, "Suffering is the characteristic feature of religion, and it is the task of monotheism that is symbolically expressed through the suffering of those who professed Jewish monotheism."[88] And he continues:

> Therefore, just as one acknowledges the punishment meted out by an earthly judge, so those who professed monotheism had to recognize and acknowledge suffering as God's providence, ordained for the purpose of their self-sanctification, their education to the maturity of the I in its correlation with God. Israel's suffering symbolically expresses the reconciliation of man with God.[89]

Suffering is a means to overcoming the eudaemonistic world, which fails to recognize the reality of the ideal moral order that has yet to be observed. Only by willingly embracing suffering do the Jews (conceived as an ideal, and not the empirical Jewish people) serve as a counter-testimony to the actual world in favor of the ideal, of what could be actual but is not yet, the establishment of the moral ideal in the actual, i.e., the reconciliation of human beings and God. As Andrea Poma points out, Cohen reconfigures the notion of theodicy by means of the "[i]dealisation of suffering," such that it is now the end of moral self-development, in that in freely taking suffering upon oneself one bears witness to the perversity and ethical corruption of the present, as well as to a higher ideal moral order that is yet to be realized.[90]

In fact, in an extensive commentary on the 'servant songs' from Deutero-Isaiah, Cohen explains how knowledge of the God of truth, of monotheism, leads the Jews to a supererogatory ethics that involves suffering for the Other. The servant of God, Cohen writes, is the one who has true knowledge of God, and is of necessity "set in opposition to the plurality of the peoples [Der Mehrheit der Menschen]."[91] The servant, in this case an idealization of the Jews (the constitution of which we will discuss briefly), willingly "exposes himself to suffering because of his knowledge of the irreplaceable value of this suffering for the historical welfare of mankind."[92] While the Jew views her suffering in terms of penance and thus self-sanctification, it is also supererogatory in that not only is it not expected of the Other, but rather serves as a "guilt-offering" for the Other.[93] To be sure, the guilt remains with the Other, at least until she atones, but the Jew suffers so that the Other will not have to. On the face of it, this notion seems problematic. The suffering of the Jews never stopped the persecution and gratuitous suffering of other groups. However, if we consider that in Cohen's idealization of suffering, by willingly embracing a life without security and filled with suffering, Cohen explains that the Jew objects both to the world of the 'is' and offers testimony to the Kingdom of God, the world of the 'ought,' by using her own precarious existence to gesture toward the transcendent moral order that can be realized but has not yet been. In other words, like God's servant in Deutero-Isaiah's 'servant songs,' the Jews are to serve as a counter-testimony to the *Realpolitik* of actuality. Cohen writes that it is "*in suffering for the peoples*" that Israel "*acquires the right to convert*" the Other.[94]

Cohen's anti-eudaemonist theodicy does not make suffering the final end, but rather a means to the true end, that of peace. Not military might and war but humility and peace are the true secrets of human existence. In this light, Cohen explains the development in the concept of the Messiah, its shift from a descendant of the warrior king, David, to the servant of God "seized by the distress of mankind in its entirety . . . as much without beauty, without the attractions of art, as he is without any signs of heroism." Humility is the great religious virtue of the suffering servant, who is "diseased and despised by men,"[95] and whose greatness consists in his opposition to all "superficial human reality as displayed in power, in splendor, in success, in dominion, in autocracy, in imperialism."[96] However, humility itself is rooted in a deeper, more fundamental virtue, which is peace. Peace is the profound trust and confidence in God, as the God of truth, which is also the trust that the blight of contemporary culture, poverty, inequality, and war will vanish before the ideal.

By proceeding in this manner Cohen elides the problem that philosopher Charles Taylor terms the "self-righteous reconstitution of the categorizations of violence," in his remarkable essay "Notes on the Sources of Violence: Perennial and Modern."[97] Taylor explains this paradoxical state as follows. "The goodness that inhabits our goal, or our vision of order, is somehow undone when it comes to struggling to realize it."[98] Elective monotheisms often exemplify this tendency toward the 'self-righteous reconstitution of the categorizations of violence' in that their foundations consist in a notion of a cosmic harmony that includes recognition of the inherent dignity of human beings as created in God's image. However, conquest and destruction of all those who fail to recognize this harmonious order (and thus become impediments to its realization) too often follows in the attempt to establish such a foundation. However, by constituting the bearing-witness modality of the promulgation of a rather robust (if highly Platonic) monotheistic 'emphatic concept of truth,' through the form of the suffering servant, Cohen remains within the ambit of the discursive structure of the elective monotheisms, while nevertheless successfully eliding the conditions that generate the self-righteous violence that Taylor speaks of so eloquently in his essay.

At this juncture, it will be helpful to contrast Cohen's account of bearing witness with that of Mendelssohn. The differences in regard to their notions of bearing witness are rooted in their respective conceptions of God, and the universalism, scriptural or rational, which they subsequently privilege as a result. The modality of bearing witness in Mendelssohn's thought rests upon notions of election and idolatry, which are in turn rooted in the ultimate supremacy of the logic of scriptural over rational universalism in his thought. That is, while Mendelssohn maintains a rational universalism in terms of natural theology, ultimately his notions of idolatry and election require recourse to the unfathomable God of scriptural universalism. Consequently, not merely the election of the Jews but also their mission to bear witness, what it means and how it works, remain mysteries to human reason.

Cohen, in sharp contrast, roots scriptural universalism in his account of rational universalism and the God of scriptural universalism gives way to the God of his rational universalism in his account of the development of Jewish literary history. Thus, the election of the Jews derives from the consequences of the idea of the unique God, which is an idea of reason that emerges within their national thought. Thus, their revelation and election contains nothing outside of the bounds of human reason; it consists solely in following through on the conceptual implications of this world-transforming idea.

The notion of God and the sort of universalism concomitant with it subsequently determine how Mendelssohn and Cohen conceive of the relationship of bearing witness to the Other. Mendelssohn's notion of God is ultimately the unfathomable God of scriptural universalism. Not only are God, the election of the Jews, and their mission beyond the ken of human reason, but the world of human affairs, history itself, is rendered more or less mysterious and impenetrable to human understanding, much less able to be improved by human action. As a result of his notion of God, Mendelssohn is deeply suspicious of all human efforts to achieve large-scale rational reformation, believing that idolatry will rule throughout the world until God determines otherwise, and God's hand cannot be forced.

For Mendelssohn, the ultimate concern in bearing witness lies not so much in responsibility for the Other as with an obligation to God. Cohen is critical of this aspect of Mendelssohn's thought, particularly as it manifests itself in terms of Halakhah. While Cohen correctly recognizes the messianic underpinnings of Mendelssohn's account of the Law, he thinks that it is one-sided, only stressing the importance of isolating the Jews, in preserving their distinctness, but failing to account for its positivity.[99] To be sure, Cohen fails to sufficiently acknowledge the degree to which Halakhah constitutes the uniqueness of the Jews insofar as it places them in an asymmetrical relationship with other peoples in Mendelssohn's framework. However, as a juxtaposition of their thought reveals, Cohen's critique hints at a deeper ethical problem with Mendelssohn's position, which he is able to solve.

Despite the fact that Mendelssohn makes great strides in freeing the Other from preconceptions of sin and error, his thought exhibits a certain indifference in regard to the Other. For one thing, Mendelssohn's gains regarding the Other pertain only to the specific Other who stands before one, as the election of the Jews is premised upon idolatry and therefore requires that a large number of Others, the majority of humanity perhaps, be idolatrous. To be sure, he does ameliorate this by rendering the determination of the identity of these idolatrous Others extraordinarily difficult to discern as the requisite idolaters are always in the background, so that the Other before one is always more or less a mystery. Nevertheless, the idolatrousness of the majority of human beings, Mendelssohn believes, is simply an aspect of the nature of the world that we live in, and he does not seem overly troubled by this situation. In addition, since Mendelssohn does not consider collective progress toward recovering the 'religion of reason' among the masses a viable possibility within history, but rather as an event limited to the *eschaton,* the obligation to the Other in bearing witness must be indirect in nature. That is, the Jews are obligated directly to God, they are duty-bound to God and must therefore keep their covenantal obligations to observe the Halakhah. One can surmise that this is problematic from Cohen's perspective, since Mendelssohn only explains (however dubiously) the manner in which the Halakhah helps the Jews retain the eternal truths of reason, but fails to offer an explanation as to how Halakhah can help the Other in terms of calling attention to these truths which are necessary for teleological fulfillment. Mendelssohn only adequately discusses the relationship between the Jew and the Other as mediated through Halakhic law in terms of separation. He never elucidates a convincing account, or much of any account for that matter, of how Jewish observance of Halakhah benefits the Other.

Mendelssohn's indifference to the Other makes sense in light of his belief that it will be an act of God, and not the work of human beings, that will cause an eschatological event of mass conversion to the 'religion of reason.' To be sure, the Jews have a central role to play in that they preserve these eternal truths in the face of a world ruled by idolatry. Nevertheless, while the Halakhah is tied into the eternal truths of reason, Mendelssohn never really explains how the Jews can serve as a 'light to nations,' i.e., how the Other benefits from the isolation of the Jews through Halakhah. Perhaps the reason for this is that ultimately, although the content of the revelation is tied into his notion of rational universalism—as the ceremonial law causes one to think about and ponder the eternal truths—his account of bearing witness is ultimately rooted in divine mystery. Perhaps human reason simply cannot fathom why God wants the Jews to observe the Halakhah and why it is important for the world. Revelation only tells us that it *is* important. Regardless, even according to Mendelssohn's own halting explanations that connect the Jews to the Other, when the Jews keep Halakhah, they are not necessarily doing this out of love for the Other, at least not directly, but rather out of trust in and loyalty to God.

There is no divergence between obligations to God and obligations to the Other in Cohen's conception of bearing witness. Rather, being obligated to God directly entails being responsible for the Other. Thus, one serves God directly by bearing witness out of responsibility for the Other. Since Cohen's reason is active, always unfolding, his notion of rational universalism is an ideal future in which the 'ought' becomes actualized in the 'is.' The 'ought,' or ideal morality, is itself inextricably linked to God. Morality, which is the outcome of the correlation of the human being and God, is the very site in which God is manifested. Since Cohen's monotheism is not predicated upon an unfathomable God in whose hands the decisive measures of redemption are to rest, the task of eradicating polytheism and idolatry, which are tantamount to immorality, is incumbent upon the Jews. This requires that the Jews forsake certain worldly advantages such as a homeland of their own and the security that affords, as well as the comforts of assimilation. On the contrary, by distinguishing themselves as suffering servants the Jews embrace the agonism in the heart of the monotheistic worldview in a non-violent manner. That is, in the act of bearing witness to the ideal of morality—to the new order of existence that the idea of the unique God entails—the Jews simultaneously critique the values of the 'pluralities of peoples.' However, in contrast to Mendelssohn, Cohen's position is predicated upon the comprehensibility of bearing witness to human reason, thus one does not reject the otherness of the Other on incomprehensible grounds. Rather, one's very witness and critique implies that the Other can also access the Truth, given that the Other too has the capacity to reason. And the idea of the unique God is an idea of reason, in fact, it is the ultimate idea of reason.

In order to further elucidate the differences between Mendelssohn's and Cohen's accounts of bearing witness, and to highlight the superiority of Cohen's position, it will be helpful to contrast their accounts with the critique of monotheistic martyrdom by a preeminent critic of monotheistic violence, Jan Assmann. While Cohen directly advocates martyrdom, Mendelssohn also acknowledges that persecution by the Other and social inequality is an inevitable result of their charge, the observance of Halakhah, which keeps the Jews distinct and inassimilable in any society. In *Die Mosaische Unterscheidung*, Assmann critiques the ethical potential of martyrdom, claiming that monotheistic martyrdom is part and parcel of the same violent intolerance that leads to murder and persecution of the Other.[100] He asserts that martyrdom "as a refusal, where one would rather die than accept forms of religion known to be false," is fundamentally tied to the problem of "monotheism and violence." According to Assmann, martyrdom is motivated by the same "hatred" of the Other as religious persecution. That is, for Assmann, martyrdom is not so much about bearing witness to the truth *for* the sake of the Other as it is about refusal and rejection of the religion and culture (i.e., the otherness) *of* the Other at all costs, even if that means one's own life. Thus, since hatred of the Other permeates and motivates martyrdom, according to Assmann, it is really only a question of a differential of power whether one is to "go from the suffering to the execution of violence."[101] To shift from suffering to persecution in the name of religion, then, requires no qualitative change, just an alteration of the direction of violence.[102]

Mendelssohn escapes the challenge of Assmann's critique insofar as he can claim that his account of election is rooted in an account of rational universalism, that his notion of revelation offers no *special* truths to the Jews and therefore does not offer any privilege for them over against other peoples. However, Mendelssohn's notion of bearing witness is tied to both the logic of rational universalism and the logic of scriptural universalism, and the latter is in fact privileged over the former. Second, Mendelssohn can claim that he sustains his rational universalism by limiting Halakhah to a sort of ceremonial law that only helps one remember the truths and rationally accounts for the election of the Jews. However, both responses betray that his commitment to rational universalism is only half-hearted, and that ultimately his allegiance lies with scriptural universalism. As a result, for Mendelssohn there is no reason comprehensible to human understanding why God elected the Jews and gave them the Halakhah, thus enabling them to preserve the eternal truths while other peoples must do without an equivalent aid. Therefore Mendelssohn must concede that according to his account the Jews are willing to suffer rather than convert and assimilate, at least in part, because they have special access to the truth that the Other does not have and are unwilling to relinquish their privileged inheritance. While Mendelssohn's innovations regarding the Other would certainly make it hard to allege that his account of revelation is rooted in hatred of the Other, it is nevertheless far from clear how the exclusion of the Other in his thought is not ultimately bound up with at least an indifference to the Other that is ethically problematic. Thus, Mendelssohn cannot escape Assmann's charge unscathed.

In sharp contrast, Cohen's account of bearing witness and martyrdom is immune to Assmann's critique. Essential to Cohen's success is not simply his subordination of scriptural universalism to rational universalism but also his insistence on human beings possessing the faculty of reason, and the rational core of revelation as preconditions to the modality of bearing witness. As we have mentioned, bearing witness as a modality of promulgation, for Cohen, is predicated upon the assumption that the Other has some capacity to recognize the validity of the correlations between God and human beings and between human beings themselves, as well as the moral order and the ideal of humanity that derives from them. Thus one suffers not because one has a privileged truth that the Other lacks, so that one seeks in suffering to preserve one's 'spiritual' advantage over the Other, but rather one suffers in order to draw the Other's attention to this truth, as she too can comprehend it and benefit from it.

Cohen secures the grounds for the possibility of bearing witness as a viable modality of promulgation in his very approach to elective monotheisms—one which is free from violence toward, and hatred of, the Other. Recall that Cohen understands revelation as the foundation of reason; it is not some specific truth with transcendent origins given to a particular community which then renders it radically distinct from all others. By following Kant both in regard to rendering God commensurate with reason, and in prioritizing the order of rational universalism over scriptural universalism, Cohen ensures the ethical foundations of witnessing by securing its universal foundations (i.e., accessibility through reason) over against the particular.

If Cohen follows Kant regarding the rationalization of God, he nevertheless distinguishes himself sharply from Kant regarding the relationship that this notion of God entails for a specific community. Kant can see no room in his rational universalism for a particular community to play a necessary role. For Kant, Christianity is only more advanced than other traditions in terms of rationalization; it is not qualitatively different. Cohen, however, takes a very different route. While Cohen no less than Kant accepts the primacy of rational universalism over scriptural universalism, he nevertheless secures a necessary and universal role for the particularity of Israel. That is, the rational necessity and universal significance of the particularity of Israel is secured in that Israel is ultimately "nothing other than the mere symbol for the desired unity of mankind,"[103] a unity whose fruition will not be achieved in actuality until the messianic era. By preserving this dynamic interchange between particularism and universalism, Cohen, unlike Kant, retains the integrity of scriptural universalism. Thus, in order to preserve this universal goal in all its purity, Israel must preserve its radical particularity. In this light the increase of ritual law, or Halakhah, under the rabbis, the 'building a fence around the Torah,' is to be understood as isolating the Jews and thus preserving the purity of the idea of the unique God throughout the vicissitudes of history.[104]

However, this one-sided particularity of the Jews for the sake of universality is not absolute. Ultimately, national limitations themselves are rendered superfluous, "and the 'people of Israel' becomes the 'remnant of Israel.'"[105] With this move, Cohen fulfills the logic of his task-oriented ethics and notion of religion. That is, rather than being privileged on the basis of belonging to a particular community and possessing salvific revelation that not only changes one's status in relation to God, but also gives one superiority over the Other, Cohen's account of Judaism presents this election as a perpetual task of infinite responsibility for the Other. In addition, not only are *not* all members of the empirical community part of this ideal 'remnant,' but those who are not empirically Jewish can belong to it. Judaism has long recognized the 'pious of the nations of the world' as possessing a religious status in Judaism, as 'honorary Jews,' and thus they too "have their fully entitled share in this messianic suffering."[106] In short, whereas Mendelssohn's scripturally universal commitments inhibit his conception of bearing witness from addressing the Other-who-lacks-truth until the *eschaton,* Cohen's innovative conception enables his notion of bearing witness to directly engage the Other *within history,* potentially guiding the Other toward the 'religion of reason' (and not toward empirical Judaism per se). While Cohen's account of bearing witness is active, refraining from 'waiting for God' and rather steering the Other in history, it is not proselytizing, at least not in any traditional sense. Rather, Cohen puts forward a form of religious inclusivism which is centered around ethical idealism, such that anyone recognizing the true totality is part of the 'righteous remnant' even if they are not empirically Jewish. The Other is not passively awaiting the good graces of the Jewish community to recognize them as 'honorary Jews,' but rather for Cohen the Other makes herself a Jew (qua 'righteous of the nations') through her active participation in the task of redeeming the world.

Cohen, unlike the other thinkers of the religion of reason trajectory, successfully reconstitutes the worldview of the elective monotheisms, or at least Judaism, in such a way that he extirpates the violence implicit in its structural intolerance. Cohen's humane intolerance is ethically responsible in regard to the Other. That is, Cohen succeeds in fundamentally altering the trajectory of monotheistic intolerance, rooting the messianic redemption of humanity and a supererogatory ethics in it. It is not an intolerance that denies the humanity of the Other, but rather recognizes the humanity of the Other to such a degree that the monotheist is willing to suffer to show the Other the truth, even when the Other persecutes and does violence against her.

Conclusion: Revelation, Reason, and the Legacy of the Enlightenment

Our contemporary world-historical situation is characterized by the increased interaction of cultural and social communities with contradictory and often mutually exclusive worldviews. The plurality of worldviews and ways of life is of course not new, but this interaction between different cultures and communities is becoming an increasingly regular experience. The refusal to recognize the epistemic, social, and political challenges of religious and cultural diversity by resorting to fundamentalist religious communities which eschew or vilify difference is one common response to this new historical situation. The appeal of Hick's and Habermas's quest for symmetrical relations—relations which are rooted in mutual respect and recognition between citizens, between self and Other—is seen most starkly in light of this regressive threat. However, we must ask ourselves whether this is the only or indeed the best way to respond to our current theological-political situation.

The one-sided emphasis on symmetrical relations with the Other, as manifested in the modern values of tolerance and pluralism, threatens the core of the discursive structure of the monotheistic worldview, which is rooted in the asymmetrical and agonistic relationship with the Other. It is important to recognize that the particular strand of the Kantian legacy taken up by Hick and Habermas decisively privileges the universal over the particular, i.e., transcendental theories of religious pluralism or communicative rationality over specific religious traditions and communities.

As a result of this prioritization of the universal, their philosophies are unable to allow for the tense and dynamic relationship between particularity and universality that is inherent in the discursive structure of the elective monotheisms. Indeed, as I argued in chapter 1, these attempts to reach the conditions for the possibility of tolerance and/or pluralism essentially preclude any possible reconciliation of the monotheistic religions with the fruits of modern philosophy. And for the most part, Jewish and Christian philosophers of religion have lost sight of and essentially forsaken this dialectic, comfortably subordinating the particular to the universal.[1]

Perhaps, then, it should not be surprising that for some time there has been a growing discontent with the universalist, egalitarian legacy of the Enlightenment and with philosophy of religion in general. In the last few decades there has been a proliferation of traditionalist Jewish and Christian theologians who elaborate political theologies that prioritize revelation and the sensibilities of robust particular communities, and who reject the Kantian-Enlightenment legacy as filtered through thinkers such as Hick and Habermas. With their skepticism of 'universal reason,' these recent thinkers prioritize the practices and values of particular traditions, rejecting or severely curtailing the scope of the authority of 'secular' reason. By prioritizing revelation and tradition, these thinkers pose a significant challenge to the continuing relevance of the philosophy of religion as a discipline, at least as it has been conceived in modernity.

For example, the traditionalist Jewish political theologian David Novak insists that the "Torah can never and, therefore, must never be justified by the world or anything in it."[2] Philosophy is subordinate to theology, and theology is grounded in the 'fact' of revelation, or more specifically, that God elected Israel (the religious community, not the nation-state) and gave her the Torah. Positions which proceed philosophically—which use human reason to reconfigure Torah, for whatever reason—"reduce the Torah to the world," and thus fall into mere "apologetics."[3] To Novak's mind, no matter how subtle the thought of Mendelssohn and Cohen (and Novak is a particularly sophisticated reader of Cohen), their methodology ultimately compromises God's transcendence and freedom and is thus insufficiently Jewish. Indeed, Novak is quite explicit that modern Jewish thought, at least when it is understood as the endeavor to synthesize reason and revelation—or better, to account for the universal status of Judaism's particularity using philosophical reason—must be overcome so that "the classical sources, the Bible and the rabbinic writings, may once again speak with their full power and richness to the Jewish people in the world, and even to the world itself."[4]

Modern Jewish thought should be theology, should begin with the 'fact' of revelation, and should rely on Jewish sources. Novak gives philosophy a subservient role, as the handmaiden to theology. Thus Novak objects to Cohen reconstituting the Jewish tradition using his Neo-Kantian hermeneutic, such that the covenant between God and the Jews becomes something to be constituted by the ideal of the Jewish people through the ethical action of bearing witness, rather than something received from on high. In other words, where Cohen rationally reconstructs the religion of reason from *out of the sources of Judaism,* i.e., culling the highest ethical meaning from its texts, Novak begins with privileging Jewish tradition and its understanding of election, God, and revelation. In this manner, Novak hopes to forestall the problems and challenges raised by modernity. To be sure, Novak has worked tirelessly to elucidate theological frameworks in which relationships between Jews and other cultures and religions can be understood. However, he never questions his foundational privileging of Jewish tradition, which he takes to be a prerequisite of genuine Jewish theology.

Since the modern world is inherently pluralistic, it is simply no longer defensible to unconditionally privilege the sources of one's own religious tradition. In the wake of globalization, decolonialization, and multiculturalism, we cannot help but ask: On what basis are we justified in assuming that the particular tradition we happen to belong to, as opposed to the myriad of others, has some sort of theological privilege? One can read Kenneth Seeskin's critique of Novak's methodology in this vein. Seeskin asserts that Novak's treatment of revelation and election as irreducible 'facts,' and therefore as foundational, "presupposes a vast body of theological doctrine before its significance can be grasped, let alone accepted."[5] In short, it is hard to see how Novak escapes the charge of arbitrariness.

Hick and Habermas are surely correct when they argue that any attempt to elide the epistemic challenges of diversity and modernity will face significant problems. And is not Novak's approach such an attempt? Here, however, Novak's position—which is nothing if not rigorous—holds up at least equally well as Hick's and Habermas's to the challenges they raise, and his thought reveals the shortcomings of their thought at least as well as theirs highlights his. In the face of plurality, Hick and Habermas insist that all religious traditions recognize that they are equally valid—or better, equally invalid—in that every tradition is essentially particular. And, as I have elaborated in chapter 1, such a view is incommensurable with the basic structure of the monotheistic worldview. Novak can indeed sustain this dynamic between the particular and the universal, which Hick and Habermas cannot, but he cannot do so in a way that sustains its intelligibility, i.e., he takes recourse to the mystery of election. Of course, this raises all sorts of philosophical questions, in that every other religious tradition can do the same. However, this suits Novak just fine, as he is content to wait until the *eschaton* for validation.[6] Indeed, he thinks that society would be much improved on a pragmatic level if people would embrace traditionalist accounts of their respective faith-traditions, with the secular sphere then serving as a neutral zone in which religious cultures interact.[7]

However, unlike Novak, many of us are neither willing nor able to avoid the power of Habermas's claim that in modern societies "religious doctrine has to accommodate itself to the unavoidable competition with other forms of faith, and other claims to truth. It no longer moves in a self-contained universe directed, so to speak, by its own absolute truth."[8] For many of us, such a return to traditionalist iterations of particular faith traditions is simply no longer tenable. It is not enough to posit the 'fact' of revelation as one's methodological starting point. Once the question of plurality is even raised, one can never go back—at least not in the same way. And it is not at all clear why we should want to.

What is so promising about the religion of reason trajectory for the present, particularly as it culminates in the work of Cohen, is that it fills the breach between traditionalist theologies such as Novak's and liberal and secularist philosophies such as Hick's and Habermas's. While Mendelssohn ultimately succumbs to scriptural universalism, Cohen's rational universalism seeks to provide a compelling account of the Jewish worldview, and more importantly to account for the universal significance of the particularity of Judaism by rationalizing the *sources of Judaism*. Rather than taking things such as revelation, election, and world-historic mission as 'facts' of Jewish existence as a result of divine fiat, Cohen reconfigures the Jewish tradition and its sources, and the tense dialectic between particularity and universality in the process becomes a perpetual task of reason which is extracted from the sources of Judaism. Not only does this render fundamentalism impossible, but in doing so Cohen creates the conditions for the possibility of bearing witness to the Other.

The ultimate outcome of the religion of reason trajectory—and here its project could be appropriated by any of the Abrahamic traditions—is to rationalize the sources of a particular tradition in order to make it intellectually sustainable and make a case for its universal validity. Of course, such a task is a perpetual one. However, if one privileges one's tradition simply because it is one's tradition, the Other can do the same. In other words, there is a certain inescapable arbitrariness in one's foundations. Indeed, it is because this sense of arbitrariness has so often gone unacknowledged in theology that Hick and Habermas can so easily, and not altogether without justification, insist on the particularity of each specific community, thereby undermining the dialectic between particularity and universality. Only if one's tradition is reconfigured—its sources rationalized and reconstructed—can one do justice to the problem of pluralism *and* address the problem of arbitrariness. While one may begin in arbitrariness, i.e., the fact that one belongs to this tradition and not another, one must then work to show that one's particularity has universal significance through rational reconstruction. In this way one preserves the dialectic of particularity and universality in a specific tradition.

We must not overlook the significance of the backlash against the values of tolerance and pluralism. Indeed, the discourse of tolerance and pluralism—in which the symmetrical relationship with the Other is taken as an unconditional good—must be critically interrogated. It has not helped contemporary discourse in philosophy of religion and theology; if anything, it has harmed. It is precisely here that the religion of reason trajectory has much to offer current conversations. Mendelssohn and particularly Cohen represent a viable alternative to religious liberals and secularists like Hick and Habermas, and as such they also present an important counterpoint to traditionalist theologians who are eager to have done with Enlightenment thinking and any strong conception of 'philosophy of religion.' The thinkers of the religion of reason trajectory, and most clearly Cohen, reveal that Enlightenment rationalism possesses resources to absorb the agonistic, intolerant structure of elective monotheisms while denuding it of violence. That is, they show why the agonism at the heart of the monotheistic worldview can be embraced by a rationalist position, with rigor and integrity, while ethics and concern for the Other remain paramount.

NOTES

1. Monotheism, Tolerance, and Pluralism

1. I employ the term 'Other' to denote a person who is different from oneself in regard to culture and especially religion, such that an encounter with her merits a response involving toleration and/or pluralism. It is important to be clear that by such phrases as 'the otherness of the Other' I primarily mean religious difference, which should be distinguished from the notion of alterity as it is commonly understood in current discussions in Continental philosophy—not that such notions are unrelated, but the two conceptions of 'the Other' are not interchangeable.

2. As will become evident, I follow Martin Jaffee's argument in "One God, One Revelation, One People: On the symbolic Structure of Elective Monotheism," *Journal of American Academy of Religion* 69, no. 4 (December 2001): 753–775, that "Judaism, Christianity, and Islam are equally rich, historical embodiments of a single structure of discourse that underlies the historically developed symbol systems specific to each community" (757). This will be discussed in more detail in the section on monotheism below.

3. As will become apparent shortly, while the term 'intolerance' maintains a negative valence in common parlance, I use it here in a very specific sense that is intended to be free of any pejorative resonance. Indeed, I deliberately use this term as a way of calling attention to certain assumptions in the discourse surrounding tolerance and pluralism, which I will illuminate shortly.

4. For an important account of the ideological assumptions of early German biblical criticism and theology see Susannah Heschel, *Abraham Geiger and the Jewish Jesus* (Chicago: University of Chicago Press, 1998). For a recent account of early Christianity that explodes such universalist presumptions, see Denise Buell, *Why This New Race: Ethnic Reasoning in Early Christianity* (New York: Columbia University Press, 2005).

5. While some scholars such as Nick Fotion and Gerard Elfstrom, in their book *Toleration* (Tuscaloosa: University of Alabama Press, 1992), subtly differentiate between 'tolerance' and 'toleration' (10), it is also common to use these terms interchangeably, as is the case in the collection edited by David Heyd, *Toleration: An Elusive Virtue* (Princeton, N.J.: Princeton University Press, 1996), 17 n. 1. In the present work, I will use the terms interchangeably. And I should clarify that when I speak of a certain blindness or uncritical character of the discourse surrounding tolerance and pluralism, I certainly do not include the philosophers I am discussing in this section. If anything they help us to see what these principles entail. Rather, my critique is aimed more squarely at liberal and secularist discussions (inside and outside the academy) which champion these principles without giving careful consideration to their costs.

6. There is a ubiquitous trope in the scholarly literatures on tolerance termed 'the paradox of toleration.' This phrase refers to the paradoxical nature of tolerance when it is viewed as a moral good. If viewed as a moral virtue, tolerance is that virtue which can only be practiced by suppressing other moral virtues, i.e.,

those which would entail expressing disapproval of what one considers to be non-virtuous behavior in the Other. For a clear account of the 'paradox of toleration,' see Susan Mendus, *Toleration and the Limits of Liberalism* (Atlantic Highlands, N.J.: Humanities Press, 1989), 19.

7. To be sure, I am talking about what philosophers would call cases of 'strong' tolerance, where moral disapproval is involved, as opposed to cases of 'weak' tolerance, where the concerns involve matters of cultural etiquette or subjective preference rather than issues possessing moral overtones. However, the distinction between what constitutes a situation requiring 'weak' or 'strong' tolerance is not always easy to assess, given that cultural and religious norms possess moral overtones. I will simply skirt this murky issue by asserting that only cases of strong tolerance are relevant for this project. Therefore whenever I say 'tolerance,' strong tolerance is implied.

8. Thomas Scanlon, "The Difficulty of Tolerance," in *Tolerance: An Elusive Virtue*, ed. David Heyd, 226.

9. See Jay Newman, *Foundations of Religious Tolerance* (Toronto: University of Toronto Press, 1989), 8–9; Fotion and Elfstrom, *Toleration*, 61.

10. Perez Zagorin, *How the Idea of Religious Toleration Came to the West* (Princeton, N.J.: Princeton University Press, 2003), 6.

11. To be sure, Zagorin answers this question in the form of an in-depth historical reconstruction of the emergence of the idea of religious freedom/tolerance (the two are inextricably bound up for him) from the intense religious wars and debates that rocked Europe in the sixteenth and seventeenth centuries.

12. For a nice account of tolerance-as-respect, see Amy Gutman and Dennis Thompson, *Democracy and Disagreement: Why Moral Disagreement Cannot Be Avoided in Politics, and What Should be Done About it* (Cambridge, Mass.: Belknap Press, 1996).

13. See David O. Wong, *Moral Relativity* (Berkeley: University of California Press, 1984), 180.

14. This definition of pluralism admittedly fails to encompass the range of accounts of pluralism—from Jean-François Lyotard's 'postmodern condition' and the collapse of meta-narratives, to William Connolly's immanentist pluralism of agonistic respect, to Isaiah Berlin's ontologically grounded value-pluralism. To be sure, it is erroneous to claim that Wong's terminology in *Moral Relativity* adequately describes them all. While it would be an important and worthwhile venture to trace out the important epistemological and indeed ontological affinities and disparities between these 'pluralisms' and the account I offer above, such a task is unnecessary here, since the monotheistic worldview is uniformly opposed to all of them.

15. Scholarly works on this topic include the following: Jan Assmann, *Moses the Egyptian* (Cambridge, Mass.: Harvard University Press, 1997), and Assmann's even more important work, *Die Mosaische Unterscheidung: Oder der Preis des Monotheismus* (Munich: Carl Hanser Verlag, 2003); Jaffee, "One God, One Revelation, One People," 753–775; Moshe Halbertal and Avishai Margalit, *Idolatry*, trans. Naomi Goldblum (Cambridge, Mass.: Harvard University Press, 1992); Avishai Margalit, "The Ring," in *Tolerance: An Elusive Virtue*, ed. David Heyd, 147–157; and Regina Schwartz, *The Curse of Cain: The Violent Legacy of Monotheism* (Chicago: University of Chicago Press, 1997).

16. Unlike so much of the recent literature on monotheisms, some of which I draw on here, this model is in no way intended as a critique. I am merely trying to

identify ways in which the structure of monotheistic religions conflicts with the modern values of tolerance and pluralism, in order to understand the nature of the challenge confronting modern religious thought in the West.

17. Jaffee, "One God, One Revelation, One People," 753–775.

18. Ibid., 759. I will use the terms 'Abrahamic monotheism,' and 'elective monotheism' interchangeably in the present work.

19. Jaffee, "One God, One Revelation, One People," 757.

20. It is important to point out that most empirically existing iterations of the elective monotheisms are not driven purely by the logic of scriptural universalism. Nevertheless this aspect of these religions, this logic, is present, even if it is not the only logic which motivates empirically existing individuals and communities.

21. I am making certain surface (not substantive) changes to Jaffee's schema in "One God, One Revelation, One People." First, Jaffee actually configures these moments into two intersecting planes, one vertical and one linear. While this is quite valuable in the context of his essay, as it demonstrates how this generic structure (761) manifests itself in Judaism, Christianity, and Islam respectively (763), for our purposes it is not necessary. Second, Jaffee's notion of 'Self-Disclosure' on the vertical plane is what I will generally term 'revelation'; what Jaffee terms 'Recipient community' in his schema, I will generally refer to as 'election'; and what Jaffee terms historical drama, I will variously term 'history' or 'historical mission.'

22. Jaffee, "One God, One Revelation, One People," 761.

23. Assmann, *Die Mosaische Unterscheidung*, 14.

24. Ibid., 13–14.

25. Ibid., 14.

26. Assmann offers some insights into the nature of this truth, such that it is grounded in transcendence as opposed to immanence, but he mostly remains on a historical-cultural level in his investigations. However, these are not sufficient for our purposes.

27. See chap. 6, "The Ethics of Belief," in Halbertal and Margalit, *Idolatry*, 163–179.

28. Ibid., 171. See also Alisdair MacIntyre on internal and external goods and their relationship to the human *telos*, in *After Virtue*, 2d ed. (Notre Dame: University of Notre Dame Press, 1984), 187–203.

29. Halbertal and Margalit, *Idolatry*, 171.

30. Schwartz, *The Curse of Cain*, 16.

31. Lenn Goodman, *The God of Abraham* (New York and Oxford: Oxford University Press, 1996).

32. Erich Zenger, "Was ist der Preis des Monotheismus?" republished in Jan Assmann, *Die Mosaische Unterscheidung: oder der Preis des Monotheismus* (Munich: Carl Hanser Verlag, 2003), 209–220.

33. Jürgen Werbick, "Absolutististischer Eingottglaube?—Befreiende Vielfalte des Polytheismus?" in *Ist Der Glaube Feind Der Freiheit? Die Neue Debatte Um Den Monotheismus*, ed. Thomas Söding (Freiburg: Herder, 2003), 143–175.

34. Jaffee, "One God, One Revelation, One People," 774.

35. In the emerging debate over monotheism and tolerance, the critics of monotheism—many of whom I am using in this section—are no less guilty than its advocates of not respecting the ambiguity of monotheism's relationship to universality and particularity. If the advocates fail to appreciate the significance of the particularist nature of monotheistic religions, the critics fail to appreciate the resources within monotheistic religions for ameliorating this antagonistic energy

through recourse to the universality of God. To be sure, however, monotheistic fundamentalists are perhaps even guiltier than the critics of monotheism, in failing to recognize the capacity within their own religions for mitigating this hostile energy.

36. There are some features of traditional monotheistic religions which mitigate, or at least can potentially mitigate the hostility of the exclusivity of such notions of identity. We can see a prime example of this in regard to a certain feature of the purity codes in the Hebrew Bible, a corpus shared in some form or other by the three Abrahamic-monotheistic traditions. In regard to the purity codes of the Hebrew Bible, there are specific priestly rites that pertain to purity codes which must be respected in regard to the Temple in general, and specific places within the Temple (the Holy of Holies is only to be entered by the high priest), that other Israelites need not obey. To be sure, if a lay-Israelite becomes impure he or she must obey the rules to become pure, so that his or her impurity does not affect the Temple (Jacob Milgrom, "Priestly ('P') Source," *The Anchor Bible Dictionary*, vol. 5 [New York: Doubleday, 1992], 455). However, what is promising, from a perspective of tolerance, is that there are also certain ritual laws of purity, less stringent of course, that apply to humanity as a whole, which are contained under the universal prohibition of shedding blood in Genesis 9 (Milgrom, "Priestly ('P') Source," 456–457). At least in this instance, then, one can make a case for the Israelites offering a form of tolerance for Others, in that the Other is accepted as Other (at least to some degree), i.e., as not being subject to the same codes and rules as the monotheistic community.

37. Margalit, "The Ring," 156.

38. See Assmann, *Die Mosaische Unterscheidung,* 29.

39. Jaffee, "One God, One Revelation, One People," 762.

40. Assmann, *Die Mosaische Unterscheidung,* 66.

41. Jaffee, "One God, One Revelation, One People," 760–761.

42. Ibid., 773.

43. Wilfred Cantwell Smith attempts to undercut Jewish and Christian discussions of idolatry when he claims that: "One cannot perceive the non-divinity of Krishna, or of the Qur'ān. (That these are not forms of God for oneself one may know. Whether they are or are not for other people one has to ascertain by investigation.) To believe that other groups are *not* divine is a purely doctrinal construct. To hold that Buddhist, or post-Biblical Jewish, life is not the locus of God's salvific activity, fully comparable to God's activity in Christian life, is a sheer man-made hypothesis" ("Idolatry," in *The Myth of Christian Uniqueness: Toward a Pluralistic Theology of Religions,* ed. John Hick and Paul F. Knitter [Eugene, Ore.: Wipf and Stock, 1987], 60). Cantwell Smith, who equates the agonistic tendency of elective monotheisms toward the Other with chauvinism, fails to take into account not only the teleological nature of scriptural universalism but also its fundamental premise that only the revealed texts given to a *particular* community can lead to the fulfillment of the universal human *telos.*

44. Jaffee, "One God, One Revelation, One People," 761.

45. To be sure, there are modes of proselytizing that do not rely on power imbalances and therefore are not violent. But where to draw the line on what sort of 'benefits for conversion' amount to 'coercive incentives' is a difficult question. As a way of avoiding this thorny issue, I will stipulate that we are not concerned here with non-violent forms of proselytizing.

46. The issue of Jewish conversion in Germany is very problematic, given that

Jews were characterized as both a racial and religious group. Thus, there were very serious debates about whether Jews really could become a Christians, whether their 'Jewishness' could be 'overcome.' Indeed, the tragic history of the Jews of Europe is bound up with this debate. However, I cannot go into this important issue here. What is more relevant for our purposes is that when I say both Mendelssohn and Cohen faced aggressive proselytizing, I mean they faced social disadvantages as a result of their refusal to convert.

47. Mendelssohn lived before there was any talk of Zionism, and Cohen was an ardent anti-Zionist. I am deliberately bracketing the highly contentious issue of Zionism and the questions of its religious status and relationship to Judaism in general.

48. Jaffee, "One God, One Revelation, One People," 768–769.

49. For a strong defense of Hick's pluralism, see Sumner B. Twiss's article, "The Philosophy of Religious Pluralism: A Critical Appraisal of Hick and His Critics," in *The Philosophical Challenge of Religious Diversity*, ed. Philip L. Quinn and Kevin Meeker (New York: Oxford University Press, 2000), 67–99.

50. For philosophical critiques of Hick's religious pluralism, see Keith Ward, "Truth and Diversity of Religions," in Quinn and Meeker, eds., *The Philosophical Challenge of Religious Diversity*, 109–125; Paul Griffiths and Delma Lewis, "On Grading Religions, Seeking Truth, and Being Nice to People—A Reply to Professor Hick," *Religious Studies* 19 (1983): 75–80; Peter Byrne, "John Hick's Philosophy of Religions," *Scottish Journal of Theology* 35 (1982): 289–301; and George A. Netland, "Professor Hick on Religious Pluralism," *Religious Studies* 22 (1986): 249–261.

51. For Hick's implicit monotheistic bias see Ward, "Truth and Diversity of Religions," 117.

52. John Hick, *God Has Many Names* (Philadelphia: Westminster Press, 1980), 42.

53. Ibid., 52.

54. Hick, *Problems of Religious Pluralism* (New York: St. Martin's Press, 1985), 42.

55. Hick, *God Has Many Names*, 102–103.

56. Hick, *Problems of Religious Pluralism*, 36.

57. Ibid., 36–37.

58. Halbertal and Margalit, *Idolatry*, 171.

59. Hick, *Problems in Religious Pluralism*, 44.

60. Ward, "Truth and Diversity of Religions," 111. Incidentally, in his excellent study *Habermas and Theology* (Cambridge: Cambridge University Press, 2006), Nicholas Adams points out that Habermas operates "with a generalised notion of 'religion'" and that he "implicitly . . . claim[s] that all religions are, equally, instances of religion" (14).

61. Hick, *God Has Many Names*, 42. For a potentially devastating critique of Hick on precisely this point, see Ward, "Truth and Diversity of Religion," esp. 113–117.

62. Hick, *God Has Many Names*, 75.

63. Gavin D'Costa, ed., *Christian Uniqueness Reconsidered: The Myth of a Pluralistic Theology of Religions* (Maryknoll, N.Y.: Orbis Books, 1990); Joseph Cardinal Ratzinger, *Truth and Tolerance: Christian Belief and World Religions* (San Francisco: Ignatius Press, 2004).

64. The notion of *telos* which is operative in Habermas's thought is collective, pertaining to the development of the communicative capacities of human beings

on a societal level, whereas the notion of *telos* which is operative in the elective monotheisms and the religion of reason trajectory pertains to individual human beings.

65. Jürgen Habermas, *Theory of Communicative Action*, vol. 1: *Reason and the Rationalization of Society*, trans. Thomas McCarthy (Boston: Beacon Press, 1984), 119.

66. Habermas, "A Genealogical Analysis of the Cognitive Content of Morality," in *The Inclusion of the Other*, ed. Ciaran Cronin and Pablo De Greiff (Cambridge, Mass.: Massachusetts Institute of Technology Press, 1996), 33–46.

67. Habermas, *The Philosophical Discourses of Modernity: Twelve Lectures*, trans. Frederick G. Lawrence (Cambridge, Mass.: Massachusetts Institute of Technology Press, 1990), 314.

68. Adams, *Habermas and Theology*, 4.

69. Habermas, "The Unity of Reason and the Diversity of Its Voices," in *Postmetaphysical Thinking: Philosophical Essays*, trans. William Mark Hohengarten (Cambridge, Mass.: Massachusetts Institute of Technology Press, 1992), 140–141.

70. Habermas, "Transcendence from Within, Transcendence in this World," in *Religion and Rationality: Essays on Reason, God, and Modernity*, ed. Eduardo Mendieta (Cambridge, Mass.: Massachusetts Institute of Technology Press, 2002), 67–94. For an analysis and critique of this point, see William J. Meyer, "Private Faith or Public Religion? An Assessment of Habermas's Changing View of Religion," *Journal of Religion* 75 (1995): 371–391.

71. Habermas, *The Philosophical Discourses of Modernity*, 315.

72. See for instance, Habermas, "The Unity of Reason and the Diversity of Its Voices," *Postmetaphysical Thinking*, 145. Habermas has been repeatedly criticized for his use of tradition/religion in this regard. For a good account of the criticisms, see Adams, *Habermas and Theology*, 43, 218, 219.

73. Habermas, "Themes in Postmetaphysical Thinking," *Postmetaphysical Thinking*, 51.

74. See for example, Habermas, "Faith and Knowledge," in *The Future of Human Nature* (Cambridge: Polity, 2003), 101–115; Habermas, *Religion and Rationality: Essays on Reason, God and Modernity*, ed. Eduardo Mendieta; and Giovanna Borradori, *Philosophy in a Time of Terror: Dialogues with Jürgen Habermas and Jacques Derrida* (Chicago: University of Chicago Press, 2003). Also see Habermas, "On the Relation Between the Secular State and Religion," in *The Frankfurt School on Religion*, ed. Eduardo Mendieta, trans. Matthias Fritsch (New York: Routledge, 2005), 339–350; and "Religion and the Public Sphere," *European Journal of Philosophy* 14, no. 1 (2006): 1–25.

75. The epistemic conditions of modernity apply to all modern institutions, and do not apply simply to the institution of religion. For a helpful discussion of the epistemic conditions of modernity see Donald Jay Rothberg, "Rationality and Religion in Habermas's Recent Work: Some Remarks Between Critical Theory and the Phenomenology of Religion," *Philosophy and Social Criticism* 11 (Summer 1986): 222–223.

76. Habermas, "A Conversation About God and the World: Interview with Eduardo Mendieta," *Religion and Rationality*, 150.

77. For a helpful critique of the manner in which Habermas lumps the religious together with the metaphysical, at least in regard to monotheistic religions, see Adams, *Habermas and Theology*, 175–177.

78. Habermas, *Theory of Communicative Action*, vol. 1, 214.

79. Habermas, *Theory of Communicative Action*, vol. 2: *Lifeworld and System: A Critique of Functionalist Reason*, trans. Thomas McCarthy (Boston: Beacon Press, 1989), 133.

80. Adams's critique of Habermas's account of rationalization, namely that this account is a founding narrative but that Habermas provides nothing in the way of argument to validate it (*Habermas and Theology*, 66–92) is doubtlessly correct. Nevertheless, despite his failure to provide sustainable arguments, Habermas's account of rationalization has certainly captured something important about the inability, or perhaps better, unwillingness, of monotheistic religions to create conditions of symmetry with the Other.

81. Habermas, *Theory of Communicative Action*, vol. 2, 107.

82. Ibid., 108–109.

83. Habermas, "Transcendence from Within, Transcendence in this World," 75–76; see Meyer, "Private Faith or Public Religion?" 377–378.

84. It is to his credit that Habermas appears to recognize this problem and is struggling to come to grips with religion in the 'post-secular' society in a number of recent writings.

85. Habermas, in Borradori, *Philosophy in a Time of Terror*, 31.

86. Habermas, "A Conversation About God and the World," 151.

87. For the history surrounding the emergence of modern conceptions of tolerance (and to a lesser degree, pluralism), see Zagorin's study, *How the Idea of Religious Tolerance Came to the West*.

88. Jean-Jacques Rousseau, "On the Social Contract," in *Rousseau: The Social Contract and Other Later Political Writings*, ed. Victor Gourevitch (Cambridge: Cambridge University Press, 1997), 39–152.

89. Ibid., 151.

90. Ibid., 147.

91. Ibid., 151.

92. On religious intolerance as a virtue, see Zagorin, *How the Idea of Religious Toleration Came to the West*, 16.

93. John Locke, *Two Treatises of Government and A Letter Concerning Toleration*, ed. Ian Shapiro (New Haven, Conn.: Yale University Press, 2003), 211–256.

94. J. B. Schneewind argues that in the "Letter Concerning Toleration," Locke goes so far as to create a new "comprehensive view" in the place of warring Christianities. See Schneewind, "Bayle, Locke, and the Concept of Toleration," *Philosophy, Religion, and the Question of Intolerance*, ed. Mehdi Amin Razavi and David Ambuel (Albany: State University of New York Press, 1997), 11.

95. Locke's bias against Catholicism is inconsistent with the logic of his position.

96. Locke, "Letter Concerning Toleration," 218.

97. Ibid., 219. While such a division may exist in certain forms of Protestantism, it is certainly foreign to Catholicism, Islam, and Judaism. However, if one examines the ominous history of intra-Christian warfare, one is inclined to doubt that this division is indigenous to most, if any, forms of Protestantism.

98. Ibid., 218.

2. LEARNING FROM THE PAST

1. J. B. Schneewind, *The Invention of Autonomy: A History of Modern Moral Philosophy* (Cambridge: Cambridge University Press, 1998), 8.

2. This Jewish strand of the Enlightenment evident in Mendelssohn and his

inheritor Cohen is especially promising because it resists the prominent trend in Enlightenment thinking to subsume particularity into universality. Since the 'universality' championed by so many Enlightenment thinkers was tacitly Christian (even if in a secular or atheistic guise), it demanded that Jews had to forsake their particularity (their Jewishness) if they were to enter society. It makes sense then that Jewish thinkers associated with the Enlightenment would be more appreciative of particularity than their gentile contemporaries.

3. There has been a rediscovery of the 'religious' dimension of Kant's thought in recent years with a number of works by noted scholars. I will make use of many of these in my chapters on Kant.

4. In order to facilitate clarity, I will use scare quotes to distinguish between the religion of reason trajectory (no scare quotes) and the category which these thinkers apply to religion in general, i.e., the 'religion of reason' (scare quotes). I should also remark here that the title of the present work consciously uses the indeterminate 'a' rather than the more definitive 'the' before 'religion of reason.' This choice of words hopes to reflect the title of Cohen's posthumous work, *Religion of Reason Out of the Sources of Judaism*. (Hermann Cohen, *Religion der Vernunft aus den Quellen des Judentums*, 2d ed. (Frankfurt: M. Kauffmann, 1929); *Religion of Reason Out of the Sources of Judaism*, trans. Simon Kaplan (Atlanta: Scholars Press: 1995). I will abbreviate the German title as *RdV*.) Cohen deliberately omits the word 'the' before 'religion of reason' as this might imply that the 'religion of reason' is a product of one empirical tradition when it is rather an ideal of reason and thus a measure and ideal for all religious traditions. (See Steven S. Schwarzschild, "The Title of Hermann Cohen's 'Religion of Reason Out of the Sources of Judaism,'" in Cohen, *Religion of Reason*, 7–8.) While I will argue in chapter 7 that Cohen is somewhat disingenuous on this point, the idea that other monotheisms can adopt this model is worth preserving—indeed, this idea is central to my entire argument. However, in terms of the actual discussions of the thinkers themselves, I will frequently use the wording *the* 'religion of reason.' This is because the thinkers in question claim that there is one universal religion implicit in, or commensurate with, human reason; it does not imply that any one empirical religious tradition is somehow identical with *the* 'religion of reason.'

5. G. E. M. Anscombe, "Modern Moral Philosophy," *Ethics, Religion and Politics: Collected Philosophical Papers*, vol. 3 (Oxford: Blackwell, 1981), 26–43.

6. In Anscombe's "Modern Moral Philosophy," Enlightenment figures such as Hume and Kant and nineteenth-century philosophers such as Bentham and Mill play important roles, but she considers later thinkers such as Sidgwick and Moore as well. On this note it is important to consider Alisdair MacIntyre's remarkable reworking of this essay, in his chapter "Why the Enlightenment Project of Justifying Morality Had to Fail," *After Virtue*, 2d ed., 36–50.

7. Anscombe, "Modern Moral Philosophy," 30.

8. Ibid., 29–30.

9. To be sure there is a teleology operative in Habermas's thought, but it takes place on the level of society rather than on the level of the individual. The teleology operative in the elective monotheisms primarily pertains to the individual. In the elective monotheisms, there is certainly a social process through which the particular community imbued with universal significance by means of receiving revelation from the universal God promulgates this message to the rest of the world, but this process is not teleological in the sense that its dynamic is largely driven by external forces (God and the Other).

10. Actually, Anscombe treats Kant as a characteristically modern thinker. However, she considerably underestimates his theistic commitments.

11. Although by using this term, I do not wish to obscure the fact that since Mendelssohn, Kant, and Cohen each maintain different conceptions of reason they also conceive of rational universalism differently.

12. I am using mathematics as an example here because it was widely used during the Enlightenment, but it should be pointed out that while all three thinkers might agree on mathematics as a helpful model of rational universalism, they would disagree as to the specifics of why it functions in this way. This gets at their specific disagreements over what constitutes rationality, which we will discuss shortly.

13. While the notion of revelation that is operative in rabbinic Judaism understands itself as an ongoing process of discovery rather than as fixed and static, it is nevertheless rooted in the Sinai event.

14. Habermas, "A Genealogical Analysis of the Cognitive Content of Morality," 39.

15. Leo Strauss, *Philosophy and Law: Contributions to the Understanding of Maimonides and His Predecessors,* trans. Eve Adler (Albany: State University of New York Press, 1995), 24; my italics.

16. Moses Mendelssohn, *Jerusalem or on Religious Power and Judaism,* trans. Allan Arkush (Hanover, N.H.: Brandeis University Press, 1983), 126; "Jerusalem: oder über religiöse Macht und Judentum," in Mendelssohn's *Gesammelte Schriften Jubiläumsausgabe (JubA)*, vol. 8 (Berlin: Friedrich Fromann Verlag (Günther Holzboog), 1983). Henceforth I will refer to this German edition of *Jerusalem* as *JubA* 8.

17. As we will see, Mendelssohn is quite prepared to discuss why these 'self-evident' truths constitutive of rationality are, in fact, not recognized by everyone.

18. Despite the fact that Mendelssohn always sought to avoid religious controversy, as a result of his being the first Jewish public figure in Prussia, Christian theologians such as Johann Caspar Lavater and Friedrich Heinrich Jacobi repeatedly sought to draw him out as a Jew. He was repeatedly challenged to publicly refute Christianity or convert. Such challenges forced Mendelssohn to virtually abandon the natural theology for which he was so famous and take up the defense of the Jews. For an excellent account of this aspect of Mendelssohn's life, see Alexander Altmann's magisterial *Moses Mendelssohn: A Biographical Study* (London: Vallentine Mitchell, 1973), 194–346, 421–637.

19. Mendelssohn, "Gegenbetrachtungen über Bonnets Palingenesie," *Moses Mendelssohn: Gesammelte Schriften Jubiläumsausgabe,* vol. 7 (Berlin: Friedrich Frommann Verlag (Günther Holzboog), 1971), 67–107.

20. Mendelssohn, "Sache Gottes: oder die gerettete Vorsehung," *Moses Mendelssohn: Gesammelte Schriften Jubiläumsausgabe,* vol. 3.2 (Berlin: Friedrich Frommann Verlag [Günther Holzboog], 1971), 221–260.

21. Immanuel Kant, *Critique of Practical Reason,* trans. Werner S. Pluhar (Indianapolis: Hackett, 2002); *Kritik der praktischen Vernunft,* in *Ak.,* vol. 5. Henceforth I will refer to the German edition of this text as *KpV.*

22. Immanuel Kant, *Religion Within the Limits of Reason Alone,* trans. Theodore M. Greene and Hoyte H. Hudson (London: Harper Torchbooks, 1960); *Die Religion innerhalb der Grenzen der bloßen Vernunft,* in *Ak.,* vol. 6. Henceforth I will refer to the German edition of this work as *RGV.*

23. As we will see in chapter 3, Kant does not consider scriptural universal-

ism to be genuinely universal given that it lacks the rational universality which he considers a prerequisite for universality.

24. Hermann Cohen, *Ethik des reinen Willens,* in *Werke,* vol. 7, repr. of 2d ed. (Hildesheim: Georg Olms Verlag , 1981).

25. Hermann Cohen, *Ethics of Maimonides,* trans. Almut Sh. Bruckstein (Madison: University of Wisconsin Press, 2002); "Charakteristik der Ethik Maimunis," in Cohen's *Jüdische Schriften,* vol. 3 (New York: Arno Press, 1980), 221–289. Henceforth I will refer to this as *CEM.*

26. Hermann Cohen, "Religion und Sittlichkeit," in Cohen's *Jüdische Schriften,* vol. 3 (New York: Arno Press, 1980), 98–168.

27. As we will see, Cohen is by no means a simple foundationalist, in that his post-metaphysical thought is precisely a perpetual 'laying of foundations.'

28. In chapter 7, I will explore the methodology of '*Ursprüngslogik*' and 'correlation' that Cohen pioneered as founder of the Marburg School of Neo-Kantianism.

3. MENDELSSOHN AND THE REPUDIATION OF DIVINE TYRANNY

1. In his recent book *The Jewish Social Contract: An Essay in Political Theology* (Princeton, N.J.: Princeton University Press, 2005), David Novak continues this legacy of critiquing the tenability of Mendelssohn's thought, in this case for ceding too much to the secular state and for leaving insufficient space for a robust account of Jewish life. Novak argues that "Jews need to overcome Mendelssohn rather than retrieve him" (187). Novak's account, like so many others, is too quick to attribute assimilationist tendencies to Mendelssohn or at least his thought.

2. While Mendelssohn himself uses the designation 'natural religion' more frequently than 'religion of reason,' we will use the latter designation more frequently for the purposes of underscoring his continuity with the other thinkers considered here.

3. Mendelssohn's relationship to the principles of tolerance and pluralism is a bit tricky. While Mendelssohn's social philosophy (book 1 of *Jerusalem*) maintains a notion of tolerance-as-respect and his philosophy of religion is an anti-imperialist, cultural egalitarianism that many contemporary scholars read as a form of pluralism (as will become clear, I do not), his account of Judaism maintains a non-violent and non-political intolerance. As the present chapter develops, we will see the contours and tensions which develop in his thought.

4. In recent years, the only scholar who considers it worth noting is Arnold Eisen, who mentions it in his important essay, "Divine Legislation as 'Ceremonial Script': Mendelssohn on the Commandments," in *AJS Review: The Journal of the Association for Jewish Studies* XV (Fall 1990): 247, 255, 256. However, since the primary purpose of Eisen's article lies with Mendelssohn's account of Halakhah, the ambiguous status of the Other is not extensively thematized in this essay.

5. The classical expressions of this argument in Mendelssohn scholarship can be seen in Altmann's *Moses Mendelssohn,* 546–547; Fritz Bamberger's "Mendelssohn's Concept of Judaism," in *Studies in Jewish Thought: An Anthology of German Jewish Scholarship,* ed. and trans. Alfred Jospe (Detroit: Wayne State Press, 1981), 343–360; as well as Julius Guttmann's "Mendelssohn's *Jerusalem* and Spinoza's *Theologico-Political Treatise,*" also in *Studies in Jewish Thought,* 373–377. More recent scholarly accounts that continue to aver this incongruity can be seen in Michael Morgan, "Mendelssohn's Defense of Reason in Jerusalem," *Judaism* 38 (Fall 1989): 457–459; David Sorkin, *Moses Mendelssohn and the Religious Enlightenment* (Berkeley: University of California Press, 1996), 134, 141, 142; and

"Moses Mendelssohn's Biblical Exegesis," in *Moses Mendelssohn im Spannungsfeld der Aufklärung,* ed. Michael Albrecht and Eva J. Engel (Stuttgart-Bad Cannstatt: Frommann-Holzboog), 271–273; and Kenneth Seeskin, *Autonomy in Jewish Philosophy* (Cambridge: Cambridge University Press, 2001), 142–144.

6. Allan Arkush, *Moses Mendelssohn and the Enlightenment* (Albany: State University of New York Press, 1994), 219.

7. This is a major theme in Willi Goetschel's account of Mendelssohn in *Spinoza's Modernity: Mendelssohn, Lessing, Heine* (Madison: University of Wisconsin Press, 2004).

8. Steven D. Kepnes, "Moses Mendelssohn's Philosophy of Jewish Liturgy: A Post-Liberal Assessment," *Modern Theology* (April 2004): 186–212.

9. Micah Gottlieb's "Mendelssohn's Metaphysical Defense of Religious Pluralism," *The Journal of Religion* 86, no. 2 (2006): 205–225 explicitly identifies Mendelssohn as a pluralist.

10. This view is explicitly elucidated by Arkush in *Moses Mendelssohn and the Enlightenment,* 167–239, but if pushed, it seems that the other scholars who stress Mendelssohn's cultural egalitarianism would have to take recourse to such a position. There is much in Mendelssohn's writing that would support such a claim, as his discussions of the election of the Jews arise, at least ostensibly, to refute Christian calls for Jewish conversion. For good discussions of the context in which Mendelssohn writes his polemical Jewish works, see Altmann, *Moses Mendelssohn,* 194–263, 638–759; Jeffrey S. Librett, *The Rhetoric of Cultural Dialogue: Jews and Germans from Moses Mendelssohn to Richard Wagner and Beyond* (Stanford: Stanford University Press, 2000), 44–99; and Jonathan M. Hess, *Germans, Jews and the Claims of Modernity* (New Haven, Conn.: Yale University Press, 2002), 1–90.

11. Hereafter, I will refer to this text as *Jerusalem.*

12. Hereafter, I will refer to this text as "Gegenbetrachtungen."

13. Hereafter, I will refer to this text as "Sache Gottes."

14. Moses Mendelssohn, *Phaedon: or the Death of Socrates,* trans. Charles Cullen (Bristol: Thoemmes Continuum, 2004); "Phaedon: oder über Unsterblichkeit der Seele in drey Gesprächen," in Mendelssohn's *Gesammelte Schriften Jubiläumsausgabe,* vol. 3.1 (Berlin: Friedrich Fromann Verlag (Günther Holzboog), 1971).

15. Schneewind, *The Invention of Autonomy.* To be sure, Schneewind only mentions Mendelssohn once in a footnote in *The Invention of Autonomy.* Nevertheless, the text provides a plethora of information about Mendelssohn's interlocutors and is therefore invaluable for our purposes.

16. Schneewind, *The Invention of Autonomy,* 4, 8, 9, 158.

17. Ibid., 25.

18. Ibid., 8, 9, 17, 18, 251.

19. Ibid., 535.

20. Ibid., 535–536.

21. Ibid., 536.

22. Ibid., 540.

23. Ibid., 536.

24. Ibid., 537, 542, 543.

25. Ibid., 537.

26. Ibid., 540.

27. Ibid., 536–537.

28. I suspect that a major reason that Mendelssohn's thought has fallen into

obscurity, or at least by and large into the domain of historians rather than contemporary philosophers, is that it adheres to the 'Pythagoras story' which, not
without reason, is ultimately eclipsed by the 'Socrates story'. Schneewind locates
the death-stroke of the Pythagoras story with the publication of *Geschichte der
Moralphilosophie*, by the Kantian historian of philosophy Carl Friedrich Stäudlin,
in 1822 (cited on pages 542–543 of Schneewind's *The Invention of Autonomy*).

29. In fact, as we will see, the respective allegiances to these stories is a point
of distinction between Mendelssohn, Kant, and Cohen, in that Mendelssohn adheres firmly to the Pythagoras story, Kant holds to a hybrid which incorporates
elements of both the Pythagoras and Socrates stories (Schneewind, *The Invention
of Autonomy*, 544–546), and Cohen unabashedly holds to the Socrates story.

30. Mendelssohn, "Phaedon," *JubA* 3.1, 102–103.

31. Divine tyranny was a common charge that intellectuals would level
against the voluntarist notion of God; see Schneewind, *The Invention of Autonomy*,
239, 510.

32. Mendelssohn, "Sache Gottes," 221, §2.

33. Ibid., 230, §40.

34. Ibid., *ad passim*.

35. As Schneewind points out, Leibniz's theodicy (of which Mendelssohn's is a
variation) takes place on an *a priori* level of reasoning (*The Invention of Autonomy*,
240), which means that God is transformed from a God who acts in history and
must be borne witness to, to a God that can only be comprehended through philosophical investigation into the transcendental conditions of existence as such.
Interestingly enough, theodicy, as we will see, is a major theme of all three thinkers of the religion of reason trajectory, and for all three it takes place on an *a priori*
basis. However, while Schneewind's contention about the non-historicality of the
God of the Leibnizian theodicy may have merit, to the degree that Mendelssohn
incorporates scriptural universalism into his thought (which, as we will see, he
does), God takes an active role in history—which is a source of great tension in
Mendelssohn's thought. Additionally, history plays an active role for both Kant
and Cohen, who maintain robustly *a priori* or transcendental theodicies that are
not altogether unrelated to Leibniz's. On this point, see Andrea Poma, "Authentic
and Historical Theodicy in Kant and Cohen," *Yearning for Form and Other Essays
on Hermann Cohen's Thought* (Dordrecht: Springer, 2006), 43–60.

36. Mendelssohn, "Sache Gottes," 251, §78.

37. It might be helpful to clarify Mendelssohn's account of 'inner perfection'
from Kant's better known 'regulative ideal,' to which it bears a remarkable similarity, at least on certain levels. In fact, the difference between Mendelssohn's doctrine of 'inner perfection' and Kant's 'regulative ideals of morality' is in regard
to form rather than content. That is, Mendelssohn believes he can demonstrate
the necessity of the doctrine of inner perfection using metaphysical argumentation such that it can be known with theoretical, metaphysical certitude. In the
Critique of Practical Reason, Kant also offers an account of human perfection as an
infinite process requiring immortality. However, he rejects that one can prove the
immortality of the soul using theoretical reason. Rather, immortality of the soul
is something that human beings must postulate in terms of practical reason. In
other words, for morality to have rational coherence, human beings must assume
that there is an afterlife in which our 'selves' continue and keep progressing toward
higher levels of virtue. Kant believes this postulate is warranted inductively on
the grounds of the moral law's status as a fact of reason. Nevertheless, for Kant as

opposed to Mendelssohn, this knowledge always remains a postulate, a qualified hypothesis, and not a metaphysical or 'scientific' fact.

38. Mendelssohn, "Sache Gottes," 251, §78.

39. Ibid., 255, §81. To be sure, Mendelssohn explains that this ban on sacrificing rational beings for the greater good is meant in a long-term sense. That is, in the temporal world there is injustice and degradation suffered by rational beings that cannot be justified within this-worldly limits. This is precisely where Mendelssohn, given his *a priori* reasoning regarding God, finds the rational necessity for the immortality of the soul.

40. Mendelssohn frequently uses felicity and eternal felicity, *'Glückseligkeit'* and *'ewige Glückseligkeit'* interchangeably.

41. Mendelssohn, "Sache Gottes," 251, §78.

42. Ibid., 240, §60. For Leibniz's philosophical justification of eternal damnation for innumerable sinners, see G. W. Leibniz, *Theodicy: Essays on the Goodness of God, the Freedom of Man, and the Origin of Evil*, ed. Austin Farrer, trans. E. M. Haggard (New Haven, Conn.: Yale University Press, 1952), 126, 134.

43. To be sure, the human *telos* for Mendelssohn is the infinite striving after human perfection, so strictly speaking one never actually *reaches* or *fulfills* it; the *telos* itself consists in infinite striving, and not in any state of actualization of finality of fulfillment.

44. See Hess, *Germans, Jews and the Claims of Modernity*, 100, 119.

45. Mendelssohn, *Jerusalem*, 126; *JubA* 8, 191.

46. Mendelssohn, letter to Karl-Wilhelm, hereditary prince of Braunschweig-Wolfenbuettel, exact date unknown, sometime after 1770, in *Moses Mendelsssohn: Selections from His Writings*, ed. and trans. Eva Jospe (New York: Viking Press, 1975), 116.

47. For discussions of Mendelssohn's interaction with the philosophy and philosophical theologies prevalent in the Berlin of his day, see Altmann, *Moses Mendelssohn*, 25–194, and Arkush, *Moses Mendelssohn and the Enlightenment*, 37–67.

48. Actually, as we will see, it is not the concept of idolatry alone that enables Mendelssohn to remain within the sphere of elective monotheisms, but rather the connection between idolatry and election—idolatry proves to be the necessary condition for God's election of the Jews.

49. Mendelssohn's recourse to idolatry fits with the 'Pythagoras story' of the history of morality described by Schneewind in *The Invention of Autonomy*. In this story, which argues that God originally provided all human beings with basic moral truths, it becomes imperative to answer the important question of how these truths were lost in the first place and hence from where the need for moral philosophy derives (537). Whereas Christian thinkers tend to use the idea of original sin to answer this question, Mendelssohn takes recourse to the notion of idolatry, but in both cases the Pythagoras "schema . . . leaves a role for reason while not making revelation superfluous" (540).

50. In "Divine Legislation as 'Ceremonial Script': Mendelssohn on the Commandments," Arnold Eisen perspicaciously notes that however problematic Mendelssohn's account of idolatry may be, it nevertheless remains the very cornerstone of his account of Judaism (248). Matt Erlin's essay, "Reluctant Modernism: Moses Mendelssohn's Philosophy of History," in the *Journal of the History of Ideas* 63 (January 2002): 83–104, helpfully elucidates that the long-derided notion of idolatry in Mendelssohn is in fact heavily misunderstood due to its intimate con-

nection with Mendelssohn's extremely complex and hitherto largely unexplored philosophy of history.

51. For the definitive account of Mendelssohn's life, including the numerous controversies in which he became embroiled as a result of his historically unprecedented status as both a public intellectual and a Jew in the Europe of his day, see Altmann's magisterial and voluminous, *Moses Mendelssohn*. For two excellent recent discussions of the conceptual anti-Judaism with which Mendelssohn struggled, see Librett, *The Rhetoric of Cultural Dialogue: Jews and Germans from Moses Mendelssohn to Richard Wagner and Beyond*, 44–99 and Hess, *Germans, Jews and the Claims of Modernity*, 1–136.

52. Hess, *Germans, Jews and the Claims of Modernity*, 128.

53. Despite appearances to the contrary, it would be inappropriate to say that Mendelssohn advocates pluralism given that his metaphysical conception of the universe does not really allow for a plurality of diverse but more or less equally plausible worldviews. In fact, since Mendelssohn roots all religions in the 'religion of reason,' which is predicated upon specific eternal truths of a metaphysical variety available to all human beings, pluralism as we conceive it seems to not really be an option. To be sure, he allows for a plurality of cultural, symbolic, and linguistic forms of expression for these truths but beneath these superficial differences is a deep homogeneity that would hardly qualify as pluralism, at least by contemporary standards. Incidentally, Mendelssohn's conception of the deep continuity between religions in regard to their theoretical contents despite their surface differences is very much in keeping with the Enlightenment's conception of religion (see Ernst Cassirer, *The Philosophy of the Enlightenment*, trans. Fritz C. A. Koelln and James P. Pettegrove [Princeton, N.J.: Princeton University Press, 1951], 139).

54. This is not to claim that Mendelssohn's discussions of Christianity are fair and balanced. My argument is merely that his discussions of Christianity are productive for understanding his reconfiguration of the moments of the discursive structure of Judaism.

55. Mendelssohn is not the first Jewish thinker to argue that Judaism is more rational than Christianity, and to present a vision of Judaism as rooted in natural theology over against a Christianity which is viewed as possessing an erroneous metaphysical scheme. Maimonides can be seen as an important forerunner of this approach.

56. Hess in *Germans, Jews and the Claims of Modernity*, and Adam Sutcliffe, in *Judaism and Enlightenment* (Cambridge: Cambridge University Press, 2003) have persuasively shown that the relationship between Judaism and Christianity in regard to reason and modernity is far more complex than Christianity being simply taken as more rational than Judaism. Rather, as Sutcliffe points out, "In much Enlightenment thought, the vital conceptual space of that which is most deeply antithetical to reason—Enlightenment's defining 'Other'—was occupied above all by the Jew" (*Judaism and the Enlightenment*, 5).

57. For a compelling discussion of Mendelssohn's own rhetorical attempt to treat Jesus as a Jew, see Hess, *Germans, Jews and the Claims of Modernity*, 91–136.

58. Mendelssohn, "Gegenbetrachtungen," 90, 91.

59. Mendelssohn, "Sache Gottes," 221, §2.

60. Mendelssohn, "On Evidence in the Metaphysical Sciences," in *Moses Mendelssohn: Philosophical Writings*, ed. and trans. Daniel O. Dahlstrom (Cambridge: Cambridge University Press, 1997), 297–298.

61. Mendelssohn, "Sache Gottes," *ad passim*.

62. Ibid., 259, §84.

63. Ibid., 250, §77.

64. Mendelssohn, letter to Lavater, Berlin, 15 January 1771, in *Moses Mendelssohn: Selections from his Writings*, 127.

65. Mendelssohn, "Gegenbetrachtungen," 73.

66. Mendelssohn, "Sache Gottes," 259, §84; "Gegenbetrachtungen," 96.

67. Mendelssohn, "Sache Gottes," 240, §60.

68. Ibid., 240, §60.

69. Ibid., 250, §77.

70. Ibid., 250, §77

71. See Hess, *Germans, Jews and the Claims of Modernity*, 95–96, 100, 104, 119, 125–126, and 128; cf. Goetschel, *Spinoza's Modernity: Mendelssohn, Lessing, and Heine*, 126.

72. Mendelssohn, *Jerusalem*, 94; *JubA* 8, 161. There is a remarkably similar passage in the earlier work, "Gegenbetrachtungen," 73.

73. Mendelssohn, "Gegenbetrachtungen," 73.

74. Ibid., 73.

75. See for example, Mendelssohn's Letter to "a Jewish friend," that is later quoted by Lessing in his reply to Michaelis, in September 1754, included in *Moses Mendelssohn: Selections from his Writings*, 93–94; cf. Hess, *Germans, Jews and the Claims of Modernity*, 1–90.

76. To be sure, the problem of idolatry is somewhat mollified for Mendelssohn in that his natural theology prevents the eternal damnation of idolaters, who, as a result of their deficient understandings of the eternal truths (i.e., their idolatries), are out of kilter with the universal human *telos*. Eternal punishment, Mendelssohn claims, would indicate a less than perfect God, as these human beings are capable of striving—and in fact, are still moving, albeit in a stunted manner—toward their own teleological fulfillment. Mendelssohn does think such individuals will be 'punished' by God in the afterlife, but this punishment is not eternal damnation, but rather a temporary punishment for the purposes of setting the sinner right in regard to her own teleological development.

77. For an excellent discussion of Mendelssohn's account of history, particularly his rejection of a progressive notion of history, see Erlin, "Reluctant Modernism: Moses Mendelssohn's Philosophy of History," 83–104.

78. Mendelssohn, "Gegenbetrachtungen," 75.

79. I use the masculine pronoun for God for the following reason: In his account of Judaism and the revelation of the Law, Mendelssohn returns to a scripturally universal conception of religion which no longer conceives of God primarily in the abstract, gender-neutral metaphysical terms of his natural theology but more in the biblical conceptions, which are gendered and predominantly (if not exclusively) male.

80. Mendelssohn, *Jerusalem*, 93–94, 126; *JubA* 8, 160–161, 191.

81. These laws are developed primarily in the Babylonian Talmud, in the tractate *Avodah Tzarah*. For an extended treatment of these laws and their historical reception and development in Jewish thought, see Novak, *The Image of the Non-Jew in Judaism: An Historical and Constructive Study of the Noahide Laws* (New York: Edwin Mellon Press, 1984).

82. Moses Maimonides, *Mishneh Torah*, "Hilkhot Sefer Shofetim 8:11," included in *A Maimonides Reader*, trans. Isadore Twersky (Springfield, N.J.: Behrman House, 1972), 21. See Eugene Korn's excellent article, "Gentiles, the World to Come,

and Judaism: The Odyssey of a Rabbinic Text," *Modern Judaism* 14 (October 1994): 265–287, for a sustained discussion of the long and ambiguous reception history of this text by Maimonides. Korn explores not only the problems relating to variant editions with very different wording, but also how this text, in its important reception history, has been used to justify both pluralism and Jewish exclusivism. In Mendelssohn's day, this authoritative text was seen by Halakhic authorities to be indicative of the exclusivist position. I would like to thank Kenneth Seeskin for bringing this article to my attention.

83. See Guttmann, "Mendelssohn's *Jerusalem* and Spinoza's *Theologico-Political Treatise*," 367–368; Arkush, *Moses Mendelssohn and the Enlightenment*, 199–203 offers a recent discussion of this matter, and includes a helpful history of the scholarly disputes over it.

84. See Novak, *The Image of the Non-Jew in Judaism*, 376. However, if Korn's thesis is correct in "Gentiles, the World to Come, and Judaism," then Mendelssohn's position, in fact, is potentially not all that different from that of Maimonides in this matter. For a contrary view, see Schwarzschild, "Do Noachites Have to Believe in Revelation? (A Passage in Dispute between Maimonides, Spinoza, Mendelssohn, and Hermann Cohen) A Contribution to a Jewish View of Natural Law," in *The Pursuit of the Ideal: Jewish Writings of Steven Schwarzschild*, ed. Menachem Kellner (Albany: State University of New York Press, 1990), 29–60.

85. Mendelssohn, *Jerusalem*, 94; *JubA* 8, 165.

86. Ibid., 113–115; *JubA* 8, 179–181.

87. Mendelssohn, "Gegenbetrachtungen," 75.

88. Mendelssohn, *Jerusalem*, 97; *JubA* 8, 164.

89. See note 5, above.

90. To be sure, to the extent that Mendelssohn claims to be using reason to defend his account of Judaism, his argument fails by that standard. Thus, critics like Morgan in "Mendelssohn's Defense of Reason in Jerusalem," 457–459 are justified in pointing out where it deviates from reason.

91. Mendelssohn's account of the Halakhah has been an area of some interest to scholars. Important recent accounts of this aspect of Mendelssohn's thought can be seen in Eisen's "Divine Legislation as 'Ceremonial Script'" and Morgan's "History and Modern Jewish Thought: Spinoza and Mendelssohn on the Ritual Law," *Judaism* 30 (1981): 467–478. For an important critique of Eisen's position, namely, that it does not sufficiently take into account the importance of adequate knowledge of the eternal truths advocated in Mendelssohn's writings in natural theology, see Arkush, *Moses Mendelssohn and the Enlightenment*, 212–219. See also the classic position of Altmann, *Moses Mendelssohn*, 539–552.

92. Mendelssohn, *Jerusalem*, 99; *JubA* 8, 166.

93. Mendelssohn, "Gegenbetrachtungen," 89–90.

94. Mendelssohn, letter to Karl-Wilhelm, hereditary prince of Braunschweig-Wolfenbuettel, exact date unknown, letter after 1770, provided in *Moses Mendelssohn: Selections from his Writings*, 118.

95. Mendelssohn, "Gegenbetrachtungen," 98.

96. Mendelssohn, *Jerusalem*, 115; *JubA* 8, 181.

97. Altmann has described Mendelssohn's surmise about the origins of idolatry in abuses related to writing as "the least substantiated of all theories he ever advanced" (*Moses Mendelssohn: A Biographical Study*, 546). However, perhaps part of the reason Mendelssohn does not feel the need to give much attention to the argument of idolatry is simply that the notion of some sort of religious calamity

causing the degradation of the originary reason among the peoples of the world is an extremely familiar trope in the Pythagoras story of the history of moral philosophy, a tradition in which Mendelssohn's thought clearly belongs.

98. Mendelssohn, *Jerusalem*, 102–103; *JubA* 8, 169.

99. Ibid., 118; *JubA* 8, 183.

100. This sense of mission, present and future, which pervades Mendelssohn's thought (at least on a subterranean level) about the Jews and the enduring relevance of Halakhah, is altogether lacking in Novak's account of Mendelssohn in *The Jewish Social Contract,* where for example he makes such claims as: "Yet for Mendelssohn, it would seem, the keeping of the commandments of the Torah is a matter of gratitude for what God did as '[p]atron and Friend by covenant of their ancestors'" (181). While not technically incorrect, this misses the larger framework of Mendelssohn's account.

101. Mendelssohn, *Jerusalem*, 120; *JubA* 8, 185.

102. Mendelssohn, letter to Herz Homberg, in *Moses Mendelssohn: Gesammelte Schriften Jubiläumsausgabe,* vol. 7 (Berlin: Friedrich Frommann Verlag (Günther Holzboog), 1971), 134.

103. Mendelssohn, "Gegenbetrachtungen," 98.

104. For a brief discussion of the messianic dimension to Mendelssohn's account of the Halakhah, see Altmann, "Moses Mendelssohn's Concept of Judaism Reexamined," 246–247.

105. Mendelssohn, "Gegenbetrachtungen," 98.

106. Mendelssohn, letter to Karl-Wilhelm, hereditary prince of Braunschweig-Wolfenbuettel, exact date unknown, letter after 1770, in *Moses Mendelssohn: Selections from his Writings,* 118.

107. Arkush is apparently satisfied with this response as a tenable position, *Moses Mendelssohn and the Enlightenment,* 218–219.

108. Altmann, *Moses Mendelssohn,* 547.

4. Monotheism and the Indiscernible Other

1. Mendelssohn, *Jerusalem*, 138; *JubA* 8, 202.

2. Ibid., 113; *JubA* 8, 179.

3. Ibid., 115; *JubA* 8, 181.

4. Ibid., 114; *JubA* 8, 180.

5. Ibid., 97; *JubA* 8, 163–164. However, it is important to point out that this room for individuals in Mendelssohn's thought is different from Kant's famous account of Enlightenment which rejects all "self-incurred immaturity"; see Kant, "An Answer to the Question: What is Enlightenment," in *Perpetual Peace and Other Essays,* trans. and ed. Ted Humphreys (Indianapolis: Hackett Publishing, 1983), 41. For Mendelssohn, independence of the individual does not require a complete break with culture—i.e., *individual* autonomy—but rather more and less refined relationships to a tradition.

6. In accordance with his Pythagoras-story commitments, Mendelssohn argues that one only requires a modest knowledge of the eternal truths to be in accordance with one's *telos.* He is not impressed with claims about the development or increased complexity of reason with the procession of history. Mendelssohn's reply to arguments about the 'rational' development of human beings is that intellectual sophistication brings new problems. While the religious beliefs of "the man who lives simply" are not sophisticated, and perhaps not conceptually adequate to the full complexity of the eternal truths, to his benefit the simple man "has not

yet devised the objections which so greatly confuse the sophist," not to mention the more complex problems raised by skeptics like Hume (*Jerusalem*, 95; *JubA* 8, 161–162). In short, greater sophistication is not necessarily to be identified with religious or moral progress, although it is by no means necessarily opposed to it.

7. Here it is very important to keep our terms straight. 'Idolater' for Mendelssohn is one who has a deficient understanding of the eternal truths, and thus is not an adherent of the 'religion of reason.' That is, his notion of an idolater is anyone who lacks an adequate conception of the eternal truths. Thus, while Mendelssohn is more egalitarian than the traditionalist Jewish view, his notion of idolatry is actually significantly more demanding. For the rabbis, the Noahide laws require only a minimum of knowledge and observance of a small set of prohibited behaviors by non-Jews in order to be considered non-idolatrous. The disparity between Mendelssohn and the traditionalists stems from the fact that Mendelssohn thinks that non-Jews possess the same capacities for knowledge of the eternal truths, whereas traditionalist Jews think that non-Jews will always be lacking (at least until the Messiah comes) to some degree in truth because they lack the Torah.

8. Mendelssohn is, therefore, introducing a sort of limit regarding knowledge about the status of the Other which has interesting resonances and dissonances with the communal notion of tolerance rooted in "epistemological modesty" put forward recently by Adam Seligman; see his *Modest Claims: Dialogues and Essays on Tolerance and Tradition* (Notre Dame: University of Notre Dame Press, 2004), 12.

9. This is a significant theme throughout the third dialogue of *Phaedon*.

10. Mendelssohn, *Jerusalem*, 58; *JubA* 8, 126.

11. Mendelssohn, letter to Lavater, Berlin, 12 December 1769, in *Moses Mendelssohn: Selections from his Writings*, 132–139.

12. Incidentally, this is where the source which I quote frequently, "Gegenbetrachtungen über Bonnets Palingenesie," arises. Given the social climate of the time, Mendelssohn wisely decides neither to publish this work nor to share it with Lavater.

13. See Altmann, *Moses Mendelssohn*, 194–264, 553–759.

14. Mendelssohn, letter to Lavater, Berlin, 12 December 1769, in *Moses Mendelssohn: Selections from his Writings*, 136.

15. Mendelssohn, *Phaedon*, vii, 15; *JubA* 3.1, 15.

16. Mendelssohn, letter to Lavater, Berlin, 12 December 1769, in *Moses Mendelssohn: Selections from his Writings*, 137.

17. Ibid., 137; my italics.

18. Ibid., 137.

19. Mendelssohn, *Jerusalem*, 63; *JubA* 8, 131.

20. Ibid., 62–63; *JubA* 8, 130–131. Notice that Mendelssohn neglects to mention religious fanaticism in this passage. This omission does not indicate, however, that it is no longer a concern. Rather, Mendelssohn addresses this issue, in terms of an erroneous conception of God, elsewhere in *Jerusalem*.

21. As Hess points out, for Mendelssohn, "Judaism as a politics belongs to the irretrievable past" (*Germans, Jews and the Claims of Modernity*, 108).

22. Fritz Bamberger, "Moses Mendelssohn's Concept of Judaism," 354.

23. Mendelssohn, *Jerusalem*, 117–118; *JubA* 8, 183–184.

24. Ibid., 118; *JubA* 8, 183–184.

25. Even Mendelssohn's method of discussing and defending the revelation

at Sinai differs significantly from his rational universalism by falling back into a highly traditionalist, scripturally universalist logic. On the medievalist nature of Mendelssohn's arguments here, see David Sorkin's "Moses Mendelssohn's Biblical Exegesis," *Moses Mendelssohn im Spannungsfeld der Aufklärung*, ed. Michael Albrecht and Eva J. Engel (Stuttgart-Bad Cannstatt: Frommann-Holzboog, 2000), 265–273. For a view more skeptical of Mendelssohn's motives see Arkush, *Moses Mendelssohn and the Enlightenment*, 261–274.

26. Mendelssohn, "Gegenbetrachtungen," 75.

27. See Morgan, "Mendelssohn's Defense of Reason in *Jerusalem*," 459.

28. For a vigorous defense of universalism in Jewish philosophy against recent, particularist trends, see Seeskin, *Jewish Philosophy in a Secular Age* (Albany: State University of New York Press, 1990).

29. Mendelssohn, *Jerusalem*, 134–139; *JubA* 8, 199–204.

5. RADICAL EVIL AND THE MIRE OF UNSOCIAL SOCIABILITY

1. Philip J. Rossi, *The Social Authority of Reason: Kant's Critique, Radical Evil, and The Destiny of Humankind* (Albany: State University of New York Press, 2005), 3. Other scholars stress the social dimension of Kant's account of rationality, such as Onora O'Neill, *Constructions of Reason: Explorations of Kant's Practical Philosophy* (New York: Cambridge University Press, 1989); and Sharon Anderson-Gold, *Unnecessary Evil: History and Moral Progress in the Philosophy of Immanuel Kant* (Albany: State University of New York Press, 2001).

2. Kant claims that the *Critique of Pure Reason* brings reason to a stage of "matured judgment" for the first time, such that it attains "self-knowledge" (trans. Norman Kemp Smith (Boston: Macmillan, 1929), 9, A xii). As a result, reason no longer "comes into conflict with itself" (10, A xiii), i.e., no longer makes claims and rulings that fail to adhere to "its own eternal and unalterable laws" (9, A xii).

3. As we will see in Kant's thought, given the nature of radical evil, the other person who more or less shares my religious and cultural beliefs and practices may nevertheless be just as troubling to me as the Other, from the vantage point of toleration.

4. In his book *Kant and the Problem of God* (Oxford: Blackwell, 1999), Gordon Michalson uses the terminology of 'transcendence' and 'immanence' to characterize the shift in Kant's later thinking about God. While I frequently disagree with Michalson's reading of Kant, I nevertheless find his use of these terms in regard to Kant's account of God quite useful, and will utilize them as well.

5. Fackenheim, "Kant and Radical Evil," in *The God Within: Kant, Schelling, and Historicity*, ed. John Burbidge (Toronto: University of Toronto Press, 1996), 31.

6. Kant, *Religion within the Limits of Reason Alone*, 35; *Die Religion innerhalb der Grenzen der bloßen Vernunft* (hereafter *RGV*), 40.

7. Ibid., 35–38; *RGV*, 41–43.

8. For a brief discussion of the reception history of the notion of radical evil, see Fackenheim, "Kant and Radical Evil," 20–21. Philip Quinn, in "Original Sin, Radical Evil, and Moral Identity," *Faith and Philosophy* 1 (April 1984): 188–202, fruitfully argues that Kant's notion of radical evil is in fact a rationalization of the Christian doctrine of radical evil. However, it is important to point out that, while Quinn looks upon Kant's account of radical evil as a rationalization of original sin with favor, he is much less well disposed toward Kant's attempts to resolve it (197–201). I do not make as fine a distinction between Kant's notion of radical evil and his attempt to solve it as Quinn does, but consider them as both inextricably

bound up with one another and thus will talk of them both as part of Kant's notion of 'radical evil'; cf. Denis Savage, "Kant's Rejection of Divine Revelation and His Theory of Radical Evil," in *Kant's Philosophy of Religion Reconsidered*, ed. Philip J. Rossi and Michael Wreen (Bloomington: Indiana University Press, 1991), 54–76.

9. See chapter 3, pages 57–60, above.

10. The text in which original sin is discussed in most detail by Mendelssohn, "Sache Gottes," was written in 1784 for Mendelssohn's son and never meant to be published. It was only published posthumously and the details of its emergence remain murky given missing information from the original publication of *Moses Mendelssohns Gesammelte Schriften*, vol. 2 (Leipzig: F. A. Brockhau, 1843–1845), 441. On this point, see Strauss's introductory essay to "Sache Gottes," in *Moses Mendelssohn: Gesammelte Schriften Jubiläumsausgabe*, vol. 3.2 (Berlin: Friedrich Frommann Verlag, 1971), xcvi–cx. I would like to thank Martin Yaffe for generously sharing his working translation of Strauss's essay with me, which brought this information to my attention.

11. Kant, *Religion Within the Limits of Reason Alone*, 29; *RGV*, 34. For a detailed account of the process through which Kant reaches his conclusions, see Anderson-Gold, *Unnecessary Evil: History and Moral Progress in the Philosophy of Immanuel Kant*, 40; cf. Savage, "Kant's Rejection of Divine Revelation and His Theory of Radical Evil," 68.

12. Kant, "Idea for a Universal History with a Cosmopolitan Intent," in *Perpetual Peace and Other Essays*, trans. Ted Humphrey (Indianapolis: Hackett Publishing, 1983), 31–32; "Idee zu einer allgemeinen Geschichte in weltbürgerlicher Absicht," in *Ak.*, vol. 8 (hereafter *IG*), 20. It is an essential component of the arguments of Philip Rossi in *The Social Authority of Reason* and of Sharon Anderson-Gold in *Unnecessary Evil*, that radical evil is inextricably bound up with Kant's concept of 'unsocial sociability' which he develops in his 'political essays' such as "Idea for a Universal History with a Cosmopolitan Intent," and "Perpetual Peace," as well as in the *Critique of Judgment*. Kant elucidates the dialectic of unsocial sociability as a facet of nature through which the very conditions necessary for reason itself emerge. While we will discuss unsocial sociability in much greater length below, for now it is enough to know that this term characterizes the inherently social, yet amoral nature of human beings which stymies their innate desire for happiness and yet, as a result, fosters a dynamic which is conducive to historical progress.

13. See Quinn, "Original Sin, Radical Evil, and Moral Identity," 191–197, for an elegant exegesis of Kant's account of radical evil.

14. Kant, *Religion within the Limits of Reason Alone*, 22; *RGV*, 27–28.

15. Ibid., 22; *RGV*, 27. With his discussion of the 'predisposition to humanity' Kant is clearly interweaving *Religion* with his works on politics. On this point, see Anderson-Gold, *Unnecessary Evil*, 35–37.

16. Fackenheim, "Kant on Radical Evil," 27.

17. Kant, *Religion within the Limits of Reason Alone*, 40; *RGV*, 44.

18. Ibid., 27; *RGV*, 32.

19. Ibid., 32; *RGV*, 37.

20. Leslie A. Mulholland, "Freedom and Providence in Kant's Account of Religion: The Problem of Expiation," in *Kant's Philosophy of Religion Reconsidered*, ed. Rossi and Wreen, 84.

21. Kant, *Religion within the Limits of Reason Alone*, 32; *RGV*, 37.

22. Ibid., 32, 43; *RGV*, 31–32, 47. For powerful critiques of the possibility of a person reforming by herself her own supreme maxim, her own basic disposi-

tion, see Mulholland, "Freedom and Providence in Kant's Account of Religion: The Problem of Expiation," 87–91; and Quinn, "Original Sin, Radical Evil and Moral Identity," 197–201.

23. Kant, *Religion within the Limits of Reason Alone,* 32; *RGV,* 37.

24. Ibid., 32; *RGV,* 37.

25. Ibid., 39; *RGV,* 44.

26. Ibid., 38; *RGV,* 43.

27. Ibid., 47; *RGV,* 52.

28. Ibid., 134; *RGV,* 143.

29. Ibid., 3; *RGV,* 4.

30. Ibid., 5; *RGV,* 6.

31. Regarding Kant's claim that 'the moral law leads to religion,' Yirmiahu Yovel insists that "in spite of the traditional terminology of the discussion, the 'God' here attained has no theological meaning" (*Kant and the Philosophy of History* [Princeton, N.J.: Princeton University Press, 1980], 92–93). Presumably, Yovel means by this that Kant's notion of God no longer retains any traces of the mysterious and active God of scriptural universalism.

32. On this point, see Joseph Runzo, "Kant on Reason and Justified Belief in God," in *Kant's Philosophy of Religion Reconsidered,* ed. Rossi and Wreen, 22–39.

33. As Schneewind points out, Kant's "astonishing claim is that God and we can share membership in a single moral community only if we all equally legislate the law we are to obey. The mature Kant does not hesitate to make an explicit comparison between human agents and God" (*The Invention of Autonomy,* 512).

34. However, as Allen W. Wood reminds us, we should not think of these religions as simply 'aids' which individuals knowingly employ to evade the duties of their conscience, but rather that "ecclesiastical faiths have devised highly effective means of inculcating 'pious terror' into people and powerful means of playing on the human propensity to a 'servile faith in divine worship'" ("Kant's Deism," in *Kant's Philosophy of Religion Reconsidered,* ed. Rossi and Wreen, 6). Regardless, fear is an inclination and thus is categorically different than duty. Therefore however different fear may be from inclinations such as lust, they both nevertheless pertain to that which is sensible rather than to the rational/moral capacities of the self.

35. I agree with Quinn's account of the 'religion of reason,' which is to be ultimately freed from the shell of all ecclesiastical faith ("Kantian Philosophical Ecclesiology," *Faith and Philosophy* 17, no. 4 (October 2000): 517–520), rather than with Stephen Palmquist, who suggests that Christianity is essentially identical with the 'religion of reason' in Kant ("'The Kingdom of God is at Hand!' (Did Kant Really Say That?)," *History of Philosophy of Quarterly* 11, no. 4 (October 1994): 426–427).

36. Kant, *Religion within the Limits of Reason Alone,* 66, 107; *RGV,* 72, 116.

37. Ibid., 109; *RGV,* 119.

38. Ibid., 162; *RGV,* 174.

39. Ibid., 179; *RGV,* 191.

40. We will discuss this aspect of Kant's thought, which he calls 'conscience,' especially as it bears upon tolerance, in the next chapter.

41. Ibid., 43; *RGV,* 47.

42. Ibid., 43; *RGV,* 47.

43. Ibid., 40; *RGV,* 44–45.

44. Michalson, in "Moral Regeneration and Divine Aid in Kant," *Religious*

Studies (September 1989), 263–264, trenchantly points out, "We might say, then, that this turn to narrative in Kant's account of both the fall and moral regeneration marks the limits of the critical philosophy's ability to account for its own content. At the same time, however, Kant puts this seemingly negative result to positive use. The fact that these moral transformations are finally inscrutable and conceptually inexplicable yields Kant a cleverly employed argumentative dividend." As I mentioned in note 22 of the present chapter, both Quinn and Mulholland raise problems for Kant's argument regarding the change from a corrupt maxim to a fundamentally good one. While the problems raised by these two philosophers are not negligible, I will not address them here. Our concern is not so much with the success or failure of this particular argument as with how this argument relates to Kant's larger project, especially concerning monotheism and tolerance.

45. Kant, *Religion within the Limits of Reason Alone*, 46; *RGV*, 51.

46. The postulates are not illicit metaphysical arguments of theoretical reason, according to Kant, because he believes to have uncovered them as transcendental conditions of the moral law, which is a 'fact' of practical reason. God and immortality play a vital role in ensuring the rational structure and coherence of morality in a world that exceeds the powers of the finite moral agent. Belief in God, then, insofar as the moral proof is concerned, is by no means a matter of disinterested speculation but is rather, in the words of Allen Wood, a practically necessary "response to the dialectical perplexities which threaten practical reason" (*Kant's Moral Religion* [Ithaca, N.Y.: Cornell University Press, 1970], 166). Thus, I disagree with Lewis White Beck when he famously argues that the necessity of the possibility of the highest good and therefore the rational acceptability of the postulates that Kant derives from it are based on a mistake. They are spurious, Beck maintains, in that they are concessions to human weakness rather than genuine needs of practical reason as such, and therefore their supposition is without any rational necessity (*A Commentary on Kant's Critique of Practical Reason* [Chicago: University of Chicago Press, 1960], 244–246). Beck fails to account for the need for coherence between the right and the good, which, in Kant's system, only the postulate of God and immortality can provide. This reconciliation of the right and the good, of virtue and happiness, exceeds any naturalistic interpretation and requires a genuine metaphysical component, albeit one that can only be thought along practical grounds rather than known through theoretical ones. Interestingly, this reconciliation of the right and the good, whose necessity Beck questions, is precisely a point of critique that Cohen levels against Kant's religious thought, which slips, he claims, into amoral eudaemonism with its concern for happiness.

47. Kant, *Critique of Practical Reason*, trans. Werner S. Pluhar (Indianapolis: Hackett, 2002), 155–166; *Kritik der praktischen Vernunft*, in *Ak.*, vol. 5 (hereafter *KpV*). Michalson trenchantly notes the similarity of this argument to the postulates of God and immortality, in "Moral Regeneration and Divine Aid in Kant," 265–266, although he does not discuss whether or how it modifies them.

48. For a careful investigation of the developments in Kant's thought regarding the highest good as the object of morality, with which I mostly agree, see Rossi's excellent article, "The Final End of All Things: The Highest Good as the Unity of Nature and Freedom," in *Kant's Philosophy of Religion Reconsidered*, ed. Rossi and Wreen, 132–164.

49. Kant, *Critique of Practical Reason*, 155; *KpV*, 122.

50. For Kant's account of the regulative ideal of reason, see *Critique of Pure Reason*, 485; A 567–568/B 595–596.

51. Kant, *Critique of Practical Reason*, 155; *KpV*, 122.

52. On this point, see also Rossi, "The Final End of All Things: The Highest Good as the Unity of Nature and Freedom"; Michalson, *Kant and the Problem of God;* and Sharon Anderson-Gold, *Unnecessary Evil.*

53. Yovel, *Kant and the Philosophy of History*, 98–99.

54. However, given that Kant sustains a notion of immortality in the *Religion*, even if he does not place much emphasis upon it, I do not see any reason to suppose that this earlier notion of the highest good is unable to coexist with his later, immanent model. I therefore disagree with Paul Guyer, *Kant on Freedom, Law, and Happiness* (New York: Cambridge University Press, 2000), 351–352; Michalson, "God and Kant's Ethical Commonwealth," *The Thomist* 65 (2001), 79; and *Kant and the Problem of God*, 121; and Rossi, "The Final End of All Things," 151; who argue that the postulate of immortality becomes essentially irrelevant to Kant's thought by *Religion Within the Limits of Reason Alone.*

55. Kant writes, "Granted that some supernatural cooperation may be necessary to his becoming good, or to his becoming better, yet whether this cooperation consists merely in the abatement of hindrances or indeed in positive assistance, man must first make himself worthy to receive it, and must *lay hold* of this aid" (*Religion Within the Limits of Reason Alone*, 40; *RGV*, 44).

56. Kant's account of radical evil then brings about a sort of reflexivity and decentration that is by no means foreign to the elective monotheisms, especially in regard to the sense of being judged by God. In fact, this development in Kant's thought gives the lie to Fackenheim's attempt to show the incommensurability of Kant's thought with Judaism on precisely these grounds. Fackenheim writes, "For Kant, the oneness of the human with the divine will is assured once virtue is achieved. For prophets and rabbis, such oneness is very far from assured even for the virtuous man, and indeed, in one sense, for him least of all. For in the minds of the prophets and rabbis, there is an endless gulf between God who is God and man who is only human" ("Kant and Judaism," *Commentary* (December 1963), 466). Clearly, in this article, Fackenheim, who is otherwise a superb interpreter of Kant, has not taken radical evil sufficiently into account, where the gap between God and the human being is precisely the achievement of virtue, about which one can never possess any sort of assurance.

57. Mulholland, "Freedom and Providence in Kant's Account of Religion," 79. While I agree with Mulholland up to the point quoted, I part ways when she claims on the same page that this notion of grace serves as a source of encouragement in terms of progress of virtue and happiness. As will soon be evident, I think Kant's notion of grace helps facilitate a notion of the self whose moral status is indeterminate, at least from the self's own vantage point, a position that is conducive to that form of tolerance grounded in respect for the otherness of the Other and mutuality with the Other in processes of reasoning and community-formation.

58. Anderson-Gold, *Unnecessary Evil*, 41.

59. Ibid., 40.

60. Anderson-Gold is referring here to Kant's rigorism, i.e., that one's disposition is either good or evil. There is no moral middle ground for Kant.

61. Ibid., 41.

62. For two summaries of Kant's theoretical philosophy of history, see Allen D. Rosen, *Kant's Theory of Justice* (Ithaca, N.Y.: Cornell University Press, 1993), 71–81; and Howard Williams, *Kant's Political Philosophy* (New York: St. Martin's Press, 1983).

63. Anderson-Gold, *Unnecessary Evil*, 31.

64. Kant, *Critique of Practical Reason*, 38; *KpV*, 25.

65. Kant, *Critique of Judgment*, trans. Werner S. Pluhar (Indianapolis: Hackett, 1987), 318; *Kritik der Urteilskraft*, in *Ak.*, vol. 5, 430.

66. It is by no means coincidental that Kant uses the same terminology regarding war and the process of founding a secure and legal peace which highlights the process of reason bringing itself into accord with itself in the *Critique of Pure Reason* again in the *Religion within the Limits of Reason Alone*. Kant, having provided the conditions by which to bring theoretical reason into accord with itself and thus to end the ceaseless wars of metaphysical systems whose foundations presume too much and thus fail to meet the criteria of rationality in the first *Critique*, now focuses on endless religious conflict with a very similar methodology. That is, in the *Religion within the Limits of Reason Alone*, Kant uses the notions of war and a legitimate rational and legal order in the search for a new secure basis, a new 'foundation' as it were, by which to bring peace and harmony to religion. There are two major reasons why Kant fixes his attention to religion. The first reason is that religion is plagued by interminable wars of its own, albeit ones whose implications are primarily political rather than intellectual, which involves physical violence and political stagnation. The second reason, which offers additional justification to the first reason, is that religion in Kant's estimation is the primary driving institution in the development of human history (see Yovel, *Kant and the Philosophy of History*, 201), and thus to elaborate the conditions for establishing a rational order in regard to religion, an order which Kant claims is latent in all forms of religion (*Religion Within the Limits of Reason Alone*, 102; *RGV*, 110–111), is a vital step in achieving the immanent sense of the highest good, namely the ethical commonwealth in this world. However, it is beyond the purposes of this chapter to explore the deep interconnection of Kant's notion of critical reason and its relationship to radical evil.

67. For an excellent account of the lack of necessity in revealed religions, read the through the lens of Kant's account of necessity in *Critique of Pure Reason*, see Savage, "Kant's Rejection of Divine Revelation and His Theory of Radical Evil," esp. 58–64.

68. Kant, *Religion within the Limits of Reason Alone*, 99–100; *RGV*, 109–110.

69. See for instance Kant, *Foundations in the Metaphysics of Morals*, trans. Lewis White Beck (Upper Saddle River, N.J.: Prentice-Hall, 1997), 48; *Grundlegung zur Metaphysik der Sitten*, in *Ak.*, vol. 4. Henceforth I will refer to the German edition of this text as *G*.

70. Kant, *Foundations in the Metaphysics of Morals*, 52; *G*, 435.

71. Ibid., 50; *G*, 433.

72. Rossi, *The Social Authority of Reason*, 31; cf. Anderson-Gold, *Unnecessary Evil*, 28–31. Rossi additionally points out the importance of the kingdom of ends in Kant's formulation of the concept of autonomy, which he claims puts the lie to discussions of Kantian autonomy that focus exclusively or even primarily on the individual. It is precisely "this connection between one's rationally legislative power and other rationally legislative agents," Rossi claims, "that Kant seeks to capture in his image of 'a Kingdom of ends'" (*The Social Authority of Reason*, 31).

73. On this point, see Quinn, "Kantian Philosophical Ecclesiology," 515–516.

74. Kant, *Religion within the Limits of Reason Alone*, 94; *RGV*, 103.

75. Yovel helpfully points out that Kant also considers human beings to have an innate religiosity or "religious consciousness" which will lead them astray by predisposing them to superstitious religions if it is not properly brought under the

guidance of reason. However, as Yovel notes, Kant thinks that this same religiosity can serve as a powerful instrument to support and buttress morality, if it is nurtured by reason (*Kant and the Philosophy of History*, 210).

76. Kant, *Religion within the Limits of Reason Alone*, 114 n.; *RGV*, 129.

77. Ibid., 94; *RGV*, 103.

78. Kant, unlike Habermas, believes in universal morality that is ascertainable to reason—or better, is quite simply an *a priori* 'fact of reason.'

79. Kant, *Religion within the Limits of Reason Alone*, 94; *RGV*, 103.

80. O'Neill, *Constructions of Reason*, 17. In his essay, "Kant's Deism," Wood claims that Kant's argument about the insufficient universality of what I have termed scriptural universalism is seriously flawed. Wood speculates that Kant claims that historical faiths are restricted to one people and cannot comprise a world religion most likely because they are not rational. Wood charges Kant with being swayed here by the logic of his own system rather than the empirical events of history. Wood points out that whereas his 'religion of reason,' supposedly accessible to all human beings and thus capable of genuine universality, at best only had a tiny following, religions predicated upon revelation like Islam and Christianity are genuinely international ("Kant's Deism," 13–14). However, while Wood's observation is doubtlessly correct on one level, one must not lose sight of the deeper point that Kant's argument is about the conditions for rational discourse and the problems of communication associated with religions premised upon scriptural universalism. As if directly addressing Wood's challenge in regard to Christianity and Islam, O'Neill usefully points out, "Whatever means of communication are available, communications may fail to be public if they do not meet standards for being interpretable by others. No amount of publicity can make a message that is interpretable either by no others or only by some others into a fully public use of reason" (*Constructions of Reason*, 33). And thus, while Kant's 'religion of reason' may not have had the reach of Islam or Christianity, it is nevertheless thoroughly universal according to Kant's own standards in a way that neither Islam nor Christianity is. As O'Neill points out, "Communications that presuppose no external authority are, even if they aim at and reach only a small audience, fit to be public uses of reason" (34).

81. I am purposefully using the masculine pronoun to highlight the anthropomorphic tendencies of the notion of God in historical religions. This will contrast with the gender-neutral notion of God in Kant's 'religion of reason.'

82. Kant, *Religion within the Limits of Reason Alone*, 160; *RGV*, 172.

83. Ibid., 105; *RGV*, 115.

84. Ibid., 100; *RGV*, 109.

85. Anderson-Gold and Rossi offer helpful ways of thinking about how moral reasoning is itself corrupted in radical evil. Anderson-Gold points out that in the world mired in radical evil, human beings still desire the rational aim of equality. However, in the dialectic of unsocial sociability this desire for equality is corrupted such that it takes the form of being merely concerned with acquiring worth in the eyes of others/Others and thus is without any recognition of the other as an end in herself (*Unnecessary Evil*, 36). According to Rossi, as a result of radical evil, one almost inevitably makes "an exemption in one's own favor in the face of the universal demand of a moral law that bears the stamp of one's own self-governing reason" (*The Social Authority of Reason*, 52). Thus, both Anderson-Gold and Rossi point out the one-sidedness of corrupted reason, its inability to foster a genuine symmetry or mutuality between the self and the other/Other.

86. Rossi, *The Social Authority of Reason*, 146.

87. Kant, "Perpetual Peace: A Philosophical Sketch," in *Perpetual Peace and Other Essays*, trans. and ed. Ted Humphreys (Indianapolis: Hackett Publishing, 1983), 111; "Zum ewigen Frieden: Ein philosophischer Entwurf," in *Ak.*, vol. 8, 349. Henceforth I will refer to the German text as *F*.

88. In his essay, "On the Common Saying: That May be Correct in Theory, but it is of no use in Practice," Kant offers an extended critique of Mendelssohn's decidedly anti-teleological vision of the human race. (See *Immanuel Kant: Practical Philosophy*, trans. and ed. Mary J. Gregor [Cambridge: Cambridge University Press, 1996], 278–309; "Über den Gemeinspruch: Das mag in der Theorie richtig sein, taugt aber nicht für die Praxis," in *Ak.*, vol. 8, 273–313. Henceforth I will refer to the German edition of this text as *TP*.) If we recall, Mendelssohn maintains a teleological conception of the human individual but rejects the idea of humanity as a whole progressing toward its *telos*. Kant's critique is facile when it suggests that Mendelssohn's position leads to a surfeit of punishment that is contrary to a wise God (306; *TP*, 307). What Kant fails to see here is that Mendelssohn reconciles this problem of suffering with a transcendent solution in terms of the afterlife. While Kant also uses a notion of the immortality of the soul as a postulate of practical reason, he combines this more transcendent approach to the problem of evil with an immanent one where the world is improved and made ethical in time. Mendelssohn, however, only accepts the transcendent notion of God and transcendent solutions for what Kant would term 'the highest good,' but he does not for that reason render his notion of God's perfection or wisdom problematic. Moreover, from a contemporary vantage point, Kant makes his case more problematic when he attempts to take recourse to empirical evidence "to show that in our age, as compared with previous ages, the human race as a whole has actually made considerable moral progress" (307; *TP*, 309), or at least to make this appear more likely. However, Kant is on much firmer ground when he stresses that the belief in a teleological improvement is necessary as a practical postulate lest one be threatened with moral despair (306; *TP*, 307). Here Kant cuts to the heart of the dispute between him and Mendelssohn, i.e., whether this world can be improved by human beings and if so whether it is therefore incumbent upon human beings to transform the natural and social world in light of morality. Kant clearly thinks it is both possible and necessary for human beings to proceed with the assumption that they can and must improve the world whereas Mendelssohn is much more pessimistic about the capacity of human beings to effect change on their world and as a result relies much more heavily on an active God.

89. Kant, "Idea for a Universal History with a Cosmopolitan Intent," 33; *IG*, 22.

90. To be sure, it is a paradoxical feature of Kant's historical-political writings that the conditions necessary to engender reason among humanity, namely conflict and war, are conditions which are themselves absolutely incommensurable with reason itself. On this point see Wood, *Kant's Ethical Thought* (Cambridge: Cambridge University Press, 1999), 294.

91. Although the question of how one would know that history itself is progressing is a complex one for Kant, given that it is a presupposition rooted in practical not theoretical reason. On this question see Anderson-Gold, *Unnecessary Evil*, 1–24.

92. Kant, "Perpetual Peace," 124; *F*, 366. On this point see George Armstrong Kelley, "The Structure of Legality in Kant," *The Journal of Politics* 31, no. 2 (May 1969): 513–517; Rosen, *Kant's Theory of Justice*, 75–76, 88–89; and Williams, *Kant's Political Philosophy*, 60.

93. Kant, "Perpetual Peace," 135; *F,* 380.
94. Anderson-Gold, *Unnecessary Evil,* 37.
95. Rossi, *The Social Authority of Reason,* 102.

6. KANT AND THE RELIGION OF TOLERANCE

1. See Yovel, *Kant and the Philosophy of History,* 7, 13, 110; Rossi, *The Social Authority of Reason,* 6, 7.
2. Rossi, *The Social Authority of Reason,* 12–13.
3. Ibid., 13.
4. For a fascinating take on the role of history in Kant's thought, particularly as manifested in his essay "An Answer to the Question: What Is Enlightenment?" see Michel Foucault's "What Is Enlightenment," in *Foucault Reader,* ed. Paul Rabinow (New York: Pantheon, 1984), 32–50. Foucault claims that "this little text is located in a sense at the crossroads of critical reflection and reflection on history." Foucault goes on to suggest that this is perhaps "the first time that a philosopher has connected . . . closely and from the inside, the significance of his work with respect to knowledge, a reflection on history and a particular analysis of the specific moment at which he is writing" (38).
5. Kant, "An Answer to the Question: What Is Enlightenment?" 44; "Beantwortung der Frage: Was ist Aufklärung?" in *Ak.,* vol. 8., 40. Henceforth I will abbreviate this German text as *A.*
6. Ibid., 45; *A,* 40.
7. In *Kant and the Philosophy of History,* 153–154, Yovel convincingly argues that for Kant the Enlightenment is a dialectical turning point in history, such that the realization of rationality will henceforth begin to emerge in history itself; cf. Wood, "Kant's Deism," 6.
8. Kant, "An Answer to the Question: What Is Enlightenment?" 44–45; *A,* 40–41.
9. Kant, *Religion Within the Limits of Reason Alone,* 122; *RGV,* 131.
10. *Pace* Stephen Palmquist's "'The Kingdom of God is At Hand!' (Did Kant Really Say That?)," Kant thinks Christianity's place in the 'religion of reason' is not one of identity but more like a vanguard.
11. Kant, *Religion Within the Limits of Reason Alone,* 145–155; *RGV,* 155–157. Wood argues that Kant lists the contingency and lack of necessity of revelation as his primary objection "for the sake of tact" ("Kant's Deism," 14). That is, Wood suspects that Kant in fact finds the content of revelation more problematic, but hides his concern beneath this critique of revelation's historicity. While Wood is doubtlessly correct that there is much regarding the content of the beliefs of revealed religions, including Christianity, that Kant finds highly problematic, I think one cannot stress Kant's concerns about the lack of necessity and universality (i.e., contingency, particularity, and historicity) enough. That is, the problems Kant has with the content of revealed religions are inextricably bound up with the lack of necessity and universality in the form of these religions; content and form are inseparable for Kant.
12. Kant, *Religion Within the Limits of Reason Alone,* 78; *RGV,* 83.
13. Ibid., 74; *RGV,* 80.
14. Schneewind, *The Invention of Autonomy,* 546.
15. Kant, *Religion Within the Limits of Reason Alone,* 131; *RGV,* 140.
16. See Schneewind, *The Invention of Autonomy,* 544–546.
17. Ibid., 548.

18. Kant presents a practical argument for this moral interpretation of Christianity. Kant claims, from the perspective of practical reason, that Jesus' divinity should be rejected because if Jesus is divine, then human beings cannot treat him as a regulative ideal of morality (*Religion Within the Limits of Reason Alone*, 57; *RGV*, 64). In all matters relating to the supernatural, Kant never disputes the possibility of their historical truth. Rather, he undermines the value of historical events altogether, regardless of whether they possess miraculous qualities or not, stressing their inherent contingency and particularity. In comparison to the limitations (no necessity or universality) of contingent and particular historical events surrounding Jesus, however wondrous, the rational teachings of Jesus are universally and necessarily true, and thus far more significant.

19. Kant, *Religion Within the Limits of Reason Alone*, 56; *RGV*, 62.

20. This is not to claim that his works did not have direct or indirect effects for or on empirically existing Jews.

21. For a discussion of the relationship between Judaism and the Enlightenment in Germany, see Hess, *Germans, Jews and the Claims of Modernity*, and for a broader look at the European Enlightenment context, see Sutcliffe, *Judaism and the Enlightenment*.

22. Hess, *Germans, Jews and the Claims of Modernity*, 6.

23. See ibid., 137–168.

24. To be sure, legalism and scriptural universalism differ in that Kant stresses that legalism's heteronomy derives primarily from concerns about temporal rewards and punishments administered by God, whereas our notion of scriptural universalism is more preoccupied with the mission entrusted to it by a God. However, legalism resembles scriptural universalism, as both are rooted in the revelation of a God that is all-powerful and who rewards and punishes. That is, for both legalism and scriptural universalism the revelation of this all-powerful God, rather than autonomous moral reason, determines the actions of adherents of these different 'logics.' In addition, Kant thinks that practitioners of 'religions of mere worship' are motivated by the desire for happiness rather than moral duty, and thus are virtually identical to adherents of legalism, except they may have a notion of the afterlife and may or may not think physical coercion is advisable in the here and now. However, from the standpoint of Kant's morality, they are easily conflated, and Kant frequently does so.

25. Given Kant's Christian chauvinism, I use this term deliberately. Kant also (deliberately?) presents a truncated and impoverished notion of the philosophical resources in the Hebrew Bible or Old Testament, at least in his account of Judaism.

26. Kant, *Religion within the Limits of Reason Alone*, 116–118; *RGV*, 125–127.

27. To refer back to the Enlightenment discourse on Judaism, we see that like many of his contemporaries, a key aspect of Kant's *Religion within the Limits of Reason Alone* is to show "how Christianity *transcended* its concrete historical origins," a project whose "typical corollary . . . was a vision of Judaism as the historical religion *par excellence*, a religion that made little sense outside the historical framework that originally gave rise to it" (Hess, *Germans, Jews and the Claims of Modernity*, 12). Although for Kant Judaism is not, technically speaking, a genuine religion.

28. Kant, *Religion within the Limits of Reason Alone*, 117; *RGV*, 127.

29. Ibid., 118; *RGV*, 127.

30. Ibid., 116–118; *RGV*, 126–127.

31. Ibid., 116; *RGV*, 125.

32. Ibid., 117; *RGV*, 127.

33. Schneewind, *The Invention of Autonomy*, 530.

34. Or perhaps the turn to teleological accounts of history, such as Kant's, Lessing's, and (to some degree) Cohen's, are concomitant with a disappearance of the active God of scriptural universalism. While this is a fascinating and important question, it cannot be investigated here.

35. Kant, *Critique of Practical Reason*, 185; *KpV*, 147.

36. Ibid., 186; *KpV*, 147.

37. Kant, *Religion within the Limits of Reason Alone*, 74; *RGV*, 79. See also "On the Common Saying: That May be Correct in Theory, but it is of no use in Practice," 304; *TP*, 306.

38. Kant, *Religion within the Limits of Reason Alone*, 74; *RGV*, 80.

39. For a sophisticated contemporary Jewish response to the view that legality, especially in a religious context, is incommensurable with autonomy, see Seeskin, *Autonomy and Jewish Philosophy*.

40. Kant, *Religion Within the Limits of Reason Alone*, 25; *RGV*, 30.

41. Ibid., 26; *RGV*, 30.

42. Ibid., 26; *RGV*, 31.

43. Ibid., 116; *RGV*, 125.

44. Ibid., 37; *RGV*, 42.

45. Ibid., 116; *RGV*, 126.

46. Ibid., 116–117; *RGV*, 126.

47. Williams, *Kant's Political Philosophy*, 60.

48. On this point see Williams, *Kant's Political Philosophy*, 57–62, 68; Rosen, *Kant's Theory of Justice*, 88–92.

49. Williams, *Kant's Political Philosophy*, 68; cf. Rosen, *Kant's Theory of Justice*, 59–60.

50. Kant, *Religion Within the Limits of Reason Alone*, 92; *RGV*, 100.

51. I use the term 'non-politics' to characterize the ethical commonwealth because it is an ordering of human beings, a community, that functions without the use of coercion or external legislation—and thus differs fundamentally from 'politics' as discussed in Kant's political writings. We will discuss its peculiarity in the conclusion of this chapter.

52. It is hard to talk in concrete terms about the ethical commonwealth. As Rossi points out, Kant "leaves unspecified what he envisions to be the final concrete form that the ethical commonwealth will take with the notable exception that it will assure perpetual peace" (*The Social Authority of Reason*, 60).

53. Kant, *Religion Within the Limits of Reason Alone*, 89; *RGV*, 97.

54. In fact, Kant claims, in contrast to his earlier, more individualistic focus regarding the highest good, that "the highest moral good"—i.e., the actualization of the ethical commonwealth—"cannot be achieved merely by the exertions of the single individual towards his own moral perfection, but requires rather a union of such individuals into a whole towards the same goal—into a system of well-disposed men in which and through whose unity alone the highest moral good can come to pass" (*Religion Within the Limits of Reason Alone*, 89; *RGV*, 97–98).

55. On this point, see Quinn, "Kantian Philosophical Ecclesiology," *Faith and Philosophy* 17, no. 4 (October 2000): 515; and Rossi, *The Social Authority of Reason*, 61–64.

56. Kant, *Religion Within the Limits of Reason Alone*, 140; *RGV*, 153.

57. Rossi, *The Social Authority of Reason*, 62.

58. Kant, *Religion Within the Limits of Reason Alone*, 89; *RGV*, 98.

59. See Kant, "On the Common Saying: That May be Correct in Theory, but it is of no use in Practice," 304; *TP*, 306.

60. Kant, *Religion Within the Limits of Reason Alone*, 90–91; *RGV*, 98–100.

61. Ibid., 90; *RGV*, 99.

62. Anderson-Gold, *Unnecessary Evil*, 50.

63. Ibid., 49.

64. Anderson-Gold stresses that only a "[s]hared moral faith," according to which "God as Absolute Person, through whose continuous presence the moral law abides while our commitments waver, who is the necessary object of this moral faith," serves as the condition of the ethical community (*Unnecessary Evil*, 51).

65. I thus follow Anderson-Gold and disagree with Yovel and Michalson, who argue that there is no genuine content to Kant's discussion of God in the ethical commonwealth. Yovel suggests when Kant speaks of the 'moral author of the world' or of God as 'the highest law-giver,' we should look beyond the traditional theological language and realize the term 'God' has been drained of all theological meaning. 'God' is simply a term for that 'something' which enables human beings to have confidence that they can actually remake nature in the image of reason (*Kant and the Philosophy of History*, 92–93). And in regard to the process of the "propagation and enlargement" of the ethical commonwealth, God lacks any philosophical import as "the sole function of this idea . . . is to encourage human action" (*Kant and the Philosophy of History*, 111–112). Michalson, who traces what he takes to be the diminishment of God's autonomy and transcendence in Kant's work, finds that Kant's use of God in terms of the ethical commonwealth actually provides no new information, and in fact, does not really concern God at all. Michalson writes, "Kant's invocation of God's name in the course of speaking of the law-giver of the ethical commonwealth simply turns out to be a way of distinguishing between 'public' and 'inner' laws" ("God and Kant's Ethical Commonwealth," 82). For Michalson, God here is merely a device for discussing the ethical commonwealth as a government of sorts, without having to resort to heteronomy. These positions are problematic in that they fail to sufficiently take into account the manner in which radical evil as a fundamentally social phenomenon requires a notion of God to relate both with individuals and humanity as a whole, and to serve a vital function (as we will see) in the very possibility of discourse with the Other, and thus in the very possibility of the ethical commonwealth.

66. Kant, *Religion Within the Limits of Reason Alone*, 117; *RGV*, 127.

67. Ibid., 117–118; *RGV*, 127.

68. Ibid., 118; *RGV*, 127.

69. Goodman, *The God of Abraham*, 13.

70. Ibid., 28.

71. See Goodman's *God of Abraham*, chapter 1, "The Logic of Monotheism," 3–36.

72. Kant, *Religion Within the Limits of Reason Alone*, 121; *RGV*, 130.

73. Rossi, *The Social Authority of Reason*, 151.

74. Ibid., 152.

75. Kant, *Religion Within the Limits of Reason Alone*, 116; *RGV*, 125.

76. Ibid., 112; *RGV*, 122.

77. Ibid., 112–113; *RGV*, 122.

78. Ibid., 173; *RGV*, 185–186.

79. Ibid., 174; *RGV*, 186.

80. Ibid., 175; *RGV*, 187.

81. Ibid., 177; *RGV*, 189.

82. By difference here, I mean substantial differences meriting 'strong tolerance' or an attitude of pluralism. I am not referring to the inevitable differences which inhere in particular individuals, such as those pertaining to taste, and so on.

83. O'Neill, "Vindicating Reason," *The Cambridge Companion to Kant,* ed. Paul Guyer (Cambridge: Cambridge University Press, 1992), 292.

84. O'Neill, "Vindicating Reason," 293; cf. *Constructions of Reason,* 23–24.

85. In "Kantian Philosophical Ecclesiology," Quinn suggests that Kant is of two minds regarding the ethical commonwealth (517). On the one hand, Quinn argues, the ethical commonwealth is a regulative ideal and thus never to be actualized, and on the other, it is indeed to be realized by human beings in history. While I agree that Kant is not always consistent on this point, I nevertheless follow Rossi who stresses that Kant ultimately prioritizes the latter option—the realization of the ethical commonwealth "both can and must be made actual by the exercise of practical reason" (*The Social Authority of Reason,* 61)—against Yovel, who reads Kant as holding fast to the former option (*Kant and the Philosophy of History,* 6, 72, 73, 79, 80).

86. See Schneewind, *The Invention of Autonomy,* 543–548.

87. See MacIntyre, *After Virtue,* 36–61.

88. Quinn, "Kantian Philosophical Ecclesiology," 526.

89. Ibid., 525.

90. Joseph Runzo writes, "Kant assumes that there is a universally valid basic conception of God which is trans-historically and cross-culturally comprehensible by anyone who honestly pursues rational thought. This seems highly doubtful, especially for us in the twentieth [or now, twenty-first] century with our pluralist understanding of the great world religions as well as the recognition of the enormous variety of world-views in general, nonreligious as well as religious. If anything, we have better grounds for supposing that not all rational people will come to hold the same pure concept of the divine" ("Kant on Reason and Justified Belief in God," in *Kant's Philosophy of Religion Reconsidered,* 34).

91. Rossi, *The Social Authority of Reason,* 60.

92. Ibid., 101.

93. Ibid., 103.

94. Ibid., 103.

95. Ibid., 116.

96. Ibid., 117.

97. While I will only discuss Habermas in this light, it is clear that contemporary Kantians like O'Neill and Rawls should also be read in this light.

98. Kant, *Critique of Pure Reason,* 602; *KrV,* A 752/B 780.

99. Habermas, "A Genealogical Analysis of the Cognitive Content of Morality," 41.

100. See Habermas, "Excursus on Leveling the Genre Distinction between Philosophy and Literature," *The Philosophical Discourses of Modernity,* 185–210. For a critique of Habermas, which argues that he relies on the 'narrative' of secularism, see W. J. Meyer, "Private Faith or Public Religion? An Assessment of Habermas's Changing View of Religion," 371–391; and Meyer's review of Habermas,

"Postmetaphysical Thinking: Philosophical Essays," in *Journal of Religion* 73, no. 4 (October 1993): 646–647.

101. As Adams points out, "The public sphere needs to be the locus of peaceable unity," although this unity is procedural and not contentful in nature, and thus contains "heated conflict, rival claims and unresolved differences" (*Habermas and Theology*, 2).

102. Habermas, "A Genealogical Analysis of the Cognitive Content of Morality," 39.

103. Ibid., 10.

104. Rossi, *The Social Authority of Reason*, 16.

105. See ibid., 60.

106. Habermas, "A Genealogical Analysis of the Cognitive Content of Morality," 39.

107. For instance, see Nicholas Wolterstorff's critique of Rawls in Robert Audi and Nicholas Wolterstorff, *Religion and the Public Sphere* (New York: Rowman and Littlefield, 1997), and Habermas's response to them in "Religion in the Public sphere," *European Journal of Philosophy* 14, no. 1 (2006): 1–25. Jeffrey Stout proposes an interesting solution to the impasse between religious conservatives and liberal proceduralists like Rawls (and Habermas) by relying on American traditions of democracy in his book *Democracy and Tradition* (Princeton, N.J.: Princeton University Press, 2004).

7. Cohen and the Monotheism of Correlation

1. A condensed and much earlier version of chapters 7 and 8 has appeared as an article titled "Hermann Cohen and the Humane Intolerance of Ethical Monotheism," in *Jewish Studies Quarterly* 15, no. 2 (2008): 148–173.

2. I will use the terms 'moral' and 'ethical' interchangeably, despite the common practice in contemporary moral philosophy to associate 'ethics' with the good and 'morals' with the right. While the distinction between morality and ethics is an important one, and one which is not foreign to Cohen's thought, to bring it into consideration in these pages would take us too far afield.

3. For a marvelous account of the distinct but intertwined role of religion and ethics, see Andrea Poma, "Religion of Reason and Judaism in Hermann Cohen," in *Yearning for Form and Other Essays on Hermann Cohen's Thought* (Dordrecht: Springer, 2006), 111–128; this is also a theme explored in great depth throughout Michael Zank's *The Idea of Atonement in the Philosophy of Hermann Cohen* (Providence, R.I.: Brown Judaic Studies, 2000).

4. Without going into a detailed discussion of the relationship between religion and ethics, where Cohen claims that religion is an *Eigenart* or peculiarity of ethics, I will follow Andrea Poma, who argues that Cohen's religious writings remain within the realm of critical idealism but are no longer within the stricter limits of Cohen's 'scientific' idealism. (See Andrea Poma, "Correlation in Hermann Cohen's Philosophy of Religion: A Method and More Than a Method," *Yearning For Form and Other Essays on Hermann Cohen's Thought*, 75; and *The Critical Philosophy of Hermann Cohen*, trans. John Denton (Albany: State University of New York Press, 1997), 157–170.) Thus, while Cohen's religious thought is also intimately bound up with ethics, as we will see, it is occasionally necessary to differentiate between the two methods of thinking about the human being as a moral agent. To differentiate them accordingly, I will speak of the ethics of Cohen's system of philosophy (i.e., *Ethik des reinen Willens*) as his 'scientific' ethics, and the ethics of Cohen's religious thought as his 'religio-critical' ethics.

5. See Leo Strauss, "Introductory Essay," in Hermann Cohen, *Religion of Reason Out of the Sources of Judaism*, 2d ed., trans. Simon Kaplan (Atlanta: Scholars Press, 1995), xxv.

6. On this point see Robert Gibbs, "'Preface' to Hermann Cohen's *Ethics*," in *Journal of Jewish Thought and Philosophy* (2006): 13.

7. For a defense of Cohen, especially in regard to the notion of alterity, from the critiques of phenomenologists like Heidegger but also from Jewish thinkers of dialogue such as Buber and Rosenzweig, as well as Levinas who bridges both categories (as a phenomenologist in the tradition of the Jewish thinkers of dialogue), see Reinier Munk, "Alterität im Denken Hermann Cohens," in *Sinn, Geltung, Wert: Neukantianische Motive in der modernen Kulturphilosophie*, ed. Christian Krijnen and Ernst Wolfgang Orth (Würzburg: Königshausen und Neumann, 1998), 109–117; cf. Poma, *The Critical Philosophy of Hermann Cohen*, trans. John Denton (Albany: State University of New York Press, 1997), ix–xi; Helmut Holzhey, "Gott und Seele: zum Verhältnis von Metaphysikkritik und Religionsphilosophie bei Hermann Cohen," in *Hermann Cohen's Philosophy of Religion*, ed. Stéphane Moses and Hartwig Wiedebach (Hildesheim: Georg Olms Verlag, 1997), 89–90; Edith Wyschogrod, "The Moral Self: Levinas and Hermann Cohen," in *Crossover Queries: Dwelling with Negatives, Embodying Philosophy's Others* (New York: Fordham University Press, 2006), 405–422; Munk, "The Self and the Other in Cohen's Ethics and Works on Religion," in *Hermann Cohen's Philosophy of Religion*, 174–176; Dieter Adelmann, "Ursprüngliche Differenz: Zwischen Einzigkeit und Einheit im Denken von Hermann Cohen," *Archivio di Filosofia* 71 (2003): 28, 37; and Martin Kavka, *Jewish Messianism and the History of Philosophy* (New York: Cambridge University Press, 2004), 105.

8. As remarked in chapter 1, the religion of reason trajectory is deeply rooted in European philosophy and the European Enlightenment, and I do not presume to assess the extent to which it might translate to Islam. I do, however, suggest that Cohen's conception of ethical intolerance at least deserves the attention of Islamic philosophers and theologians.

9. As Zank points out, "Cohen proceeds to interpret Kant's transcendental method as one step in the age old conversation of philosophy that begins with Plato and in which we must participate actively and creatively in order not to fall beneath the level of cultural sophistication that we are called upon to inherit. It is therefore misleading to call Cohen a neo-Kantian and not also a neo-Platonist, neo-Leibnizian, or neo-Maimonidean" (*The Idea of Atonement in the Philosophy of Hermann Cohen*, 213). For a less sympathetic account of Cohen's interpretations of Kant, see Klaus Köhnke, *The Rise of Neo-Kantianism: German Academic Philosophy between Idealism and Positivism*, trans. R. J. Hollingdale (New York: Cambridge University Press, 1991), 178ff.

10. Kant, *Critique of Pure Reason*, 485; *KrV*, A 567–568/B 595–596.

11. Cohen, *Ethik des reinen Willens*, 227; cf. Poma, *The Critical Philosophy of Hermann Cohen*, 37–72.

12. Dieter Adelmann, "Ursprüngliche Differenz: Zwischen Einzigkeit und Einheit im Denken von Hermann Cohen," 26.

13. See Martin Kavka, *Jewish Messianism and the History of Philosophy*, 105; Robert Gibbs, "Hermann Cohen's Messianism: The History of the Future," in *"Religion der Vernunft aus den Quellen des Judentums," Tradition und Ursprüngsdenken in Hermann Cohens Spätwerk*, ed. Helmut Holzhey, Gabriel Motzkin, and Hartwig Wiedebach (Hildesheim: Georg Olms Verlag, 2000), 334–335, 338–339, 341.

14. On this point see Reiner Wiehl, "Identity and Correlation in Cohen's

System," *Hermann Cohen's Critical Idealism,* ed. Munk (Dordrecht: Springer, 2005), 91.

15. Cohen, *Ethik des reinen Willens,* 85. Zank argues that this terminology of 'laying of the foundations' highlights the profoundly anti-metaphysical, anti-essentialist nature of Cohen's thought (*The Idea of Atonement in the Philosophy of Hermann Cohen,* 250–251).

16. See Holzhey, "Gott und Seele," 103; and Holzhey, "Cohen and the Marburg School in Context," 17–18.

17. Again, Cohen is by no means solely drawing on Kant for his philosophy of science. His other influences, which are perhaps equally significant to Kant in this process, include Leibniz and Plato. See Poma, *The Critical Philosophy of Hermann Cohen,* 21–48, and for a detailed account of the changing role of Plato in Cohen's thought, see Poma, "Plato's Idea of the Good in its Different Interpretations by Cohen and Natorp," *Yearning for Form and Other Essays on Hermann Cohen's Thought,* 21–42.

18. Hermann Cohen, *Logik der reinen Erkenntnis,* in *Werke,* vol. 7, repr. of 2d ed. (Hildesheim: Georg Olms Verlag , 1981).

19. Ibid., 62; cited in Munk, "The Self and the Other in Cohen's Ethics and Works on Religion," 167. The translation is my own.

20. Kavka, *Jewish Messianism and the History of Philosophy,* 105; cf. Munk, "Alterität im Denken Hermann Cohens," 115.

21. In his article "Ursprüngliche Differenz: Zwischen Einzigkeit und Einheit im Denken von Hermann Cohen," Adelmann helpfully elucidates the difference between philosophical and religious thought, as two related but distinct sorts of '*Denken.*' Philosophy is concerned with "*Einheit,*" which presupposes the "*Umwandlebarkeit von allem . . . nämlich indem vorausgesetzt wird, dass es 'vom Denken in eine Einheit verwandelt' werden kann: d.i. die Instabilität von 'allem' bildet die elementare Voraussetzung der Philosophie*" (27). Hence, its preoccupation with the 'Ideal,' and the need of the future in its epistemological methodology. However, the "'*Sein des Einzigen'; oder eben 'das einzige Sein,'*" i.e., God, exists in radical contrast to the 'All' in that it is fundamentally unchangeable (28). Thus, the full complexity of thinking involves "*Denken zwischen Philosophie und Religion*" (30).

22. Hermann Cohen, *Ethik des reinen Willens,* vol. 7 of *Werke,* repr. of 2d ed. (Hildesheim: Georg Olms Verlag, 1981).

23. Cohen, *Ethik des reinen Willens,* 441.

24. Ibid., 89. On the significance of the term "*Einklang,*" see Peter A. Schmid, *Ethik als Hermeneutik. Systematische Untersuchung zu Hermann Cohens Recht- und Tugendlehre* (Würzburg: Königshausen & Neumann, 1995), 220–221.

25. Cohen, *Ethik des reinen Willens,* 450. It should be noted, as Zank trenchantly points out, that Cohen's "project of critical idealism would . . . be insufficiently characterized as a logic of the sciences. Rather, its full pathos and appeal rests on the combination of efforts in logic and ethics." As Zank continues: "Within the context of his logic, Cohen not only attempts the exposition of the implications of the new concept of reality for mathematics and physics but also aspires to demonstrate its fertility for the foundation of the humanities, i.e. for morality (Sittlichkeit) and ethics" (*The Idea of Atonement in the Philosophy of Hermann Cohen,* 241).

26. Cohen, *Ethik des reinen Willens,* 446.

27. Ibid., 463.

28. Cohen certainly does not deny the role of psychological and biologi-

cal drives, and although he wrote prior to Heidegger and Levinas, his position would necessarily not deny their insights. Indeed, for Cohen's efforts to incorporate physiology into his ethics, see Hartwig Wiedebach, "Physiology of the Pure Will: Concepts of Moral Energy in Hermann Cohen's Ethics," in *Hermann Cohen's Ethics*, ed. Robert Gibbs (Leiden: Brill, 2006), 85–104. But for example, for Cohen, Heidegger's account of *Da-sein* (were one to conceive of it, to Heidegger's chagrin, as a philosophical anthropology) would at best only be the subjects' particularity from which the universal Self must be projected. As for Levinas and a juxtaposition of his position with Cohen's, see Wyschogrod, "The Moral Self," 405–422.

29. Holzhey, "Ethik als Lehre vom Menschen: Eine Einführung in Hermann Cohens *Ethik des Reinen Willens*," *Journal of Jewish Thought and Philosophy* (2006): 29.

30. Holzhey, "Cohen and the Marburg School in Context," 22.

31. Cohen, *Ethik des reinen Willens*, 3–7. 'Plurality' here designates *Mehrheit* and 'totality' designates *Allheit*. Regarding the latter term see note 34, below; and on these terms see Holzhey, "Ethik Als Lehre Vom Menschen," 22–23.

32. I shall henceforth use 'given self' to designate *Einzelheit* when it refers to an individual and 'particular' when it refers to a specific community, and 'individual' or 'Self' to designate *Individuum*.

33. I use the word 'totality' with some reluctance. While it has been the standard translation for Cohen's term *Allheit*, I am hesitant to use it since Levinas and the range of post-structuralist thinkers have made this term into a pejorative. However, Cohen's sense of *Allheit* is quite distinct from a reading of the Hegelian, totalizing manner of philosophy that the post-structuralists critique. Rather, with Cohen the 'totality' is an ideal of a unified humanity, which in *Ethik des reinen Willens* takes place through a cosmopolitan, legal confederation of states that is always to-come. This vision, even as early as the *Ethik*, is closely associated with messianic vision of the Hebrew prophets, especially what Cohen takes to be their leaning toward socialism, although in this ostensibly 'secular' work Cohen is sure to methodologically purify and subordinate the religious and theological elements to the ethico-political. (On this see Munk, "On the Idea of God in Cohen's *Ethik*," *Journal of Jewish Thought and Philosophy* 13 (2006): 105–114.) In his later religious writings—as opposed to religious writings that are contemporary with *Ethik des reinen Willens*—*Allheit* or 'totality' is linked even more explicitly with the Hebrew prophets, while the role of the state recedes and the stateless Jews qua 'suffering servant' come to play a more prominent role, as we will see, in guiding society to founding itself in *Allheit* with the advent of the Messianic age.

34. Cohen, *Ethik des reinen Willens*, 56–64, 77–78.

35. Ibid., 235.

36. Ibid., 82, 486.

37. 'Religion' is a term that has a normative, idealistic, and therefore universal valence as opposed to the beliefs and practices of particular and thus relative religious communities, insofar as they are only pluralities without connection to the totality.

38. Cohen, *Religion of Reason Out of the Sources of Judaism*, 7; *RdV*, 8–9.

39. For a thorough account of the debate, beginning with Rosenzweig's famous and influential misreading of Cohen's *Religion of Reason Out of the Sources of Judaism*, see Poma, *The Critical Philosophy of Hermann Cohen*, 157–169, and the invaluable and extensive endnotes at 302–309.

40. It should be noted that my own account here follows by and large the

position articulated by Poma in *The Critical Philosophy of Hermann Cohen*, and especially his recent *Yearning for Form*, regarding the larger relationship between ethics and religion.

41. Cohen, "Religion und Sittlichkeit," 154.

42. Cohen, *Ethik des reinen Willens*, 214–216, 401–407.

43. See Munk, "On the Idea of God in Cohen's Ethik," *Journal of Jewish Thought and Philosophy* 13 (2006): 113.

44. Cohen, "Religion und Sittlichkeit," 154–155; cf. *Ethik des reinen Willens*, 49, 53, 61–62, 64, 77–78, 333–337.

45. In "Religion und Sittlichkeit," 106–107, Cohen puts this quite nicely: "*Das Sittliche betrifft die* unmittelbaren Verhältnisse der Menschen untereinander, und damit auch des Menschen zu sich selbst." (Cohen's emphasis from "*unmittelbaren.*")

46. Cohen, *Religion of Reason Out of the Sources of Judaism*, 13–23; *RdV*, 15–27.

47. Action (*Handlung*) is a central feature of the methodology of Cohen's *Ethik des reinen Willens*, where he writes: "*Nicht darum darf es der Ethik zu tun sein, was man glauben dürfe, um hoffen und wünschen, oder gar um fürchten und zagen zu können; sondern darum allein darf es sich handeln, was ich zu tun habe, auf dass mein Tun und Treiben den Wert einer menschlichen Handlung erlange. Der Begriff der Handlung besteht in der Einheit der Handlung. Die Einheit der Handlung begründet die Einheit des Menschen. In der Einheit der Handlung vollzieht sich und besteht die Einheit des Menschen*" (81–82). This stress on action is carried over into his religious works.

48. Cohen, *Religion of Reason Out of the Sources of Judaism*, 13; *RdV*, 15.

49. Seeskin, *Autonomy and Jewish Philosophy*, 159.

50. Cohen, *Religion of Reason Out of the Sources of Judaism*, 14–23; *RdV*, 17–27. Ketil Bonaunet, in his book *Hermann Cohen's Philosophy of Religion* (Bern: Peter Lang, 2004), errs in his interpretation of Cohen precisely in taking Cohen at his word on this point. As we will see, while Cohen claims religion only fulfills this supplementary function, Andrea Poma is quite correct in pointing out that in reality the *Eigenart* status of religion means much more than its supplementary status. Poma writes, "For Cohen the peculiarity (Eigenart) of religion consists in placing the principle of foundation in God, i.e., reconsidering the content of ethics, above all, and more generally, that of the whole system, in the perspective of correlation with God" ("Correlation in Hermann Cohen's Philosophy of Religion: A Method and More than a Method," 75). That is, by means of this shift to theocentrism, Cohen's religious thought radically reconfigures his vision of the human being, and needless to say, while his position in the *Religion of Reason Out of the Sources of Judaism* may be compatible with the *Ethik des reinen Willens* (in the way that a supererogatory ethic is still compatible with a more universal societal ethic) it is by no means identical or merely supplementary to it, despite what Cohen occasionally says.

51. On the nature of the construction of the inherently teleological ethical human Self in Cohen's ethics, see Cohen, *Ethik des reinen Willens*, 77, 79, 187–189, 233, 245.

52. Cohen, *Religion of Reason Out of the Sources of Judaism*, 138; *RdV*, 159.

53. Ibid., 11; *RdV*, 13.

54. See David Novak, "Hermann Cohen on State and Nation: A Contemporary Review," 270; we will discuss this topic further below.

55. Cohen even had the title changed from the first edition of this work, which

due to a printer's error read, with the definite article, *The Religion of Reason Out of the Sources of Judaism.* Subsequent editions have the more ambiguous title, *Religion of Reason Out of the Sources of Judaism.* On this point, see Schwarzschild's "The Title of Hermann Cohen's 'Religion of Reason Out of the Sources of Judaism,'" reprinted in Cohen, *Religion of Reason Out of the Sources of Judaism,* 7-8.

56. One of the most prominent contemporary Cohen interpreters, Kenneth Seeskin, holds this position; see his *Jewish Philosophy in a Secular Age,* 3; and "How to Read *Religion of Reason,*" his introductory essay to the English translation of Cohen's *Religion of Reason Out of the Sources of Judaism,* 29. Bonaunet also maintains this reading, in *Hermann Cohen's Kantian Philosophy of Religion.* While I disagree with this position, a confrontation with the work of such a noted scholar as Seeskin—with whose interpretation of Cohen I find myself largely in agreement—cannot be addressed here.

57. Cohen, *Religion of Reason Out of the Sources of Judaism,* 8; *RdV,* 10.

58. Poma, "Religion of Reason and Judaism in Hermann Cohen," 125.

59. Cohen, *Religion of Reason Out of the Sources of Judaism,* 50; *RdV,* 58.

60. Cohen, *Religion of Reason Out of the Sources of Judaism,* 122, 268; *RdV,* 141, 163. We will discuss this issue further in chapter 8.

61. See Poma, "Religion of Reason and Judaism in Hermann Cohen," 128.

62. Here I am using 'philosophy' in an explicitly Habermasian sense, as a sort of mediator between different traditions.

63. Thus, I firmly disagree with the entire approach of Bonaunet, who in *Hermann Cohen's Kantian Philosophy of Religion,* 9-26, attempts to utilize Cohen's thought as a form of 'post-metaphysical' philosophy of religion which is compatible with Habermas's demands upon religion in regard to the epistemic conditions of modernity. Bonaunet's conception of Cohen focuses almost entirely on his thought concerning the individual, either through repentance or through the relation to the Other, while he all but ignores the social dimension of Cohen's thought, in which these individual elements are embedded. This social dimension, as we will see, is in keeping with the discursive structure of the elective-monotheistic worldview.

64. In *Ethik des reinen Willens,* Cohen is very critical of Kant's use of the postulates of God and immortality, claiming that Kant sacrifices scientific rigor when he makes these theological notions essential to his ethics. Cohen claims that Kant's position is not so much pure ethics as "Ethico-Theology" (228). Cohen ties this criticism into his larger critique of Kant's notion of freedom and the noumenal self, which he argues is metaphysical in nature and, as a result, forces Kant to compromise his transcendental-critical philosophy in numerous ways. See *Ethik des reinen Willens,* 317-322, 338-343.

65. See Poma, "Authentic and Historical Theodicy in Kant and Cohen," *Yearning for Form and Other Essays on Hermann Cohen's Thought,* 50.

66. See Poma, "Correlation in Hermann Cohen's Philosophy of Religion: A Method and More Than a Method," *Yearning for Form and Other Essays on Hermann Cohen's Thought,* 75; and *The Critical Philosophy of Hermann Cohen,* 157-168.

67. See Poma, "Correlation in Hermann Cohen's Philosophy of Religion," 77.

68. It is important to point out the level of hermeneutical sophistication at which Cohen works. As Zank reveals in *The Idea of Atonement in the Philosophy of Hermann Cohen,* before Cohen founded the Marburg school of Neo-Kantianism, he not only received rabbinical training but also graduated from Berlin University, where, like Wilhelm Dilthey, he studied with August Boeckh, a pioneer in the

contemporary form of hermeneutics that is now paradigmatic in the humanities (218–219).

69. However, rabbinic notions of interpretation have clearly influenced Cohen's notion of reason. This can be seen in the infinite, ongoing nature of reason as a perpetual, interpretive enterprise, which is similar to that of rabbinic understandings of the study of revealed texts. On this point see, Almut Sh. Bruckstein's "On Jewish Hermeneutics: Maimonides and Bachya as Vectors in Cohen's Philosophy of Origin," *Hermann Cohen's Philosophy of Religion*, 36, 41, 43. Nevertheless, despite the important similarities between rabbinic methods of exegesis and Cohenian reason, there remain considerable methodological differences in that ultimately, for Cohen, critical reason is privileged over any dogmatic claims to an authoritative status as divine revelation.

70. Cohen, *Religion of Reason Out of the Sources of Judaism*, 3–5; *RdV*, 3–6.

71. Ibid., 3; *RdV*, 4.

72. Ibid., 24; *RdV*, 28.

73. Ibid., 8; *RdV*, 9.

74. Ibid., 24; *RdV*, 28.

75. Again, Strauss is correct on one level in suggesting that Cohen's appropriation of Judaism is rooted in an acceptance or 'internalization' of the Enlightenment critique of such notions as revelation, creation, and so on. However, Strauss dismisses his project outright because he believes any synthesis between "Enlightenment and Orthodoxy" is a contradiction in terms (*Philosophy and Law*, 24). To be sure, Cohen's approach is distinctly modern, and as a result the literal meaning of such terms as 'creation' and 'revelation' are transfigured into a modern idiom. However, in contrast to such modern thinkers as Hick and Habermas, that Cohen preserves the discursive structure of the monotheistic worldview intact should be evidence that such a 'synthesis' cannot simply be dismissed. What Strauss fails to recognize is that Cohen's so-called 'internalization' of creation, revelation, etc. is really no internalization at all but a translation of these concepts into the 'metaphysics of practical reason,' where they become tasks to be externalized. For an excellent account of the relevance and challenge of Strauss for contemporary Jewish thought, see Leora Batnitzky, *Leo Strauss and Emmanuel Levinas: Philosophy and the Politics of Revelation* (Cambridge: Cambridge University Press, 2006).

76. Cohen, *Religion of Reason Out of the Sources of Judaism*, 88; *RdV*, 102–103.

77. Cohen's language in *Religion of Reason Out of the Sources of Judaism* is more evocative of the messianic vision of the Hebrew prophets than is his more formalistic notion of the cosmopolitan confederation of nations from the *Ethik des reinen Willens*, but whether there are substantial differences between them is difficult to discern. It is beyond the scope of this project to consider the potential differences or similarities.

78. For example, Cohen chides his Christian contemporaries for their fascination with the biographies of the prophets themselves (*Ethik des reinen Willens*, 55). In particular, Cohen is distressed by his contemporaries' preoccupation with the accounts of the prophets' encounters with the divine, their becoming inhabited or possessed by the 'word of the Lord.' Cohen argues that the authors of these books are merely using the "device" of revelation, and in fact, the literal level of revelation which garners such attention from his contemporaries is, in fact, merely "a mythological concept." Cohen argues that if these books are read with sufficient rigor, the mythic and anthropomorphic device of revelation soon "shatters itself insofar as the reason of human beings is unified and reconciled [with the reason of] God."

79. Cohen, *Religion of Reason Out of the Sources of Judaism*, 88; *RdV*, 103.

80. With the important and famous caveat, which Cohen makes in the introduction: "even if I am referred to the literary sources of the prophets for the concept of religion, those sources remain mute and blind if I do not approach them with a concept, which I myself lay out as a foundation in order to be instructed by them and not simply guided by their authority" (Ibid., 4; *RdV*, 4–5).

81. Ibid., 89; *RdV*, 104.

82. See Poma, "The Holy Spirit Out of the Sources of Judaism and Kantianism," *Yearning for Form and Other Essays on Hermann Cohen's Thought*, 302.

83. Cohen, *Religion of Reason Out of the Sources of Judaism*, 96; *RdV*, 111.

84. Cohen, "Religion und Sittlichkeit," 134.

85. Ibid., 133.

86. Seeskin explains: "As God is our creator, in Cohen's opinion, we, as it were, are God's discoverer. This does not mean that God is contingent but that given Cohen's idealism, the only way we can understand God is as a being in relation" (*Autonomy and Jewish Philosophy*, 170).

87. Cohen, *Religion of Reason Out of the Sources of Judaism*, 103; *RdV*, 120.

88. Ibid., 108; *RdV*, 125.

89. Cohen has been critiqued for being an optimist when, politically speaking, there were no grounds for such a view. There is much confusion around his notion of messianism—whether there will be an actual realization of the ideal in history (as he seems to suggest at *Religion of Reason Out of the Sources of Judaism*, 21; *RdV*, 24), or whether it is merely a regulative ideal. However, it is imperative to realize that Cohen's optimism is rooted in his transcendental presuppositions, and not a reflection of his readings of history—which were also flawed. (A matter which immensely wounded his post–World War II legacy, and which haunts him to this day.) I will not venture an answer here, but will say that even if Cohen does think there will be a historical realization of 'totality'—an end to suffering and a realization of the messianic age—it remains in the unforeseeable and very distant future.

90. Cohen, *Religion of Reason Out of the Sources of Judaism*, 105; *RdV*, 121.

91. On Cohen's conception of the self see Schwarzschild, "The Tenability of Herman [sic] Cohen's Construction of the Self," *Journal of the History of Philosophy* (July 1975): 361–384; and Holzhey, "Gott und Seele," 93–103.

8. RATIONAL SUPEREROGATION AND THE SUFFERING SERVANT

1. Assmann, *Die Mosaische Unterscheidung*, 13.

2. Margalit, "The Ring: Or on Religious Pluralism," 156.

3. Zank, *The Idea of Atonement in the Philosophy of Hermann Cohen*, 266.

4. See for example, Jon Levenson, "The Eighth Principle of Judaism and the Literary Simultaneity of Scripture," *The Hebrew Bible, The Old Testament and Historical Criticism* (Louisville: Westminster/John Knox Press, 1985), 62–81; cf. Daniel Boyarin, *Intertextuality and the Reading of Midrash* (Bloomington: Indiana University Press, 1994), 15–16.

5. That is, the idea of God is the *Ursprung* from which Jewish literature springs forth.

6. On the idea of humanity in Cohen, especially its connection to the future, see Gibbs, "Hermann Cohen's Messianism: The History of the Future," 334–335.

7. Cohen, *Religion of Reason Out of the Sources of Judaism*, 115–116; *RdV*, 134.

8. Cohen, *Religion of Reason Out of the Sources of Judaism,* 254; *RdV,* 296–297.

9. It is interesting that even in *Ethik des reinen Willens,* where statehood serves the decisive function of mediating between plurality and totality, Cohen confers special significance on the stateless Jews as teaching humanity about true totality (495). He explains that "the continued existence of the Jews" is significant in "that it prepares the Messianic idea of a united humanity in the confederation of humanity." He continues with the claim that rather than indicating a specific devotedness to a tribe or a particular community, "what is represented" is "the force of a conviction, that is, a form of true totality" (496). As we will see, this is a remarkable adumbration of the role of Judaism in *Religion of Reason Out of the Sources of Judaism.*

10. Cohen often uses terms like 'empiricism,' 'eudaemonism,' 'polytheism,' and 'naturalism' as ciphers for the tendency, particularly strong in (at least his reading of) Romantic idealism as well as positivism, to dissolve the distinction between 'is' and 'ought.'

11. While the difference between Cohen's and Mendelssohn's notions of bearing witness have been discussed in the previous chapter, it is useful to stress here that Cohen's account of bearing witness differs markedly form the standard understanding of this modality of promulgation, which tends to expect to make no inroads with the Other until the *eschaton.* For Cohen, the Jews bear witness to the idea of God which translates into morality and totality, i.e., the ethical transformation of history. Its goal is not to convert people to Judaism in any empirical sense but rather to promulgate morality *in history.* To be sure, such a process is always incomplete, and hence the *eschaton* continues to loom large as a regulative ideal.

12. Cohen, *Religion of Reason Out of the Sources of Judaism,* 52; *RdV,* 61.

13. Ibid., 74; *RdV,* 86.

14. Ibid., 120–121; *RdV,* 139–140.

15. Ibid., 121; *RdV,* 140.

16. Ibid., 243; *RdV,* 284.

17. What redemption means for Cohen is rather complex since he radically rejects all eudaemonism and vigorously criticizes Kant for including happiness as a concern of the 'highest good' in ethics. We will discuss this further below.

18. Cohen, *Ethik des reinen Willens,* 300. The specific role of the relationship between sin and individuality has been thoroughly explored by Zank in *The Idea of Atonement in the Philosophy of Hermann Cohen;* cf. Zank's "'The Individual as I' in Hermann Cohen's Jewish Thought," *The Journal of Jewish Thought and Philosophy* 5 (1996): 281–295; and Bonaunet, *Hermann Cohen's Kantian Philosophy of Religion,* 73–130.

19. Cohen, *Ethik des reinen Willens,* 475.

20. See Cohen, "The Social Ideal as Seen by Plato and by the Prophets," in *Reason and Hope: Selections from the Jewish Writings of Hermann Cohen,* ed. and trans. Eva Jospe (New York: W. W. Norton, 1971), 66–77. For a famous and astute critique of this position see Leo Strauss, "Introductory Essay to Hermann Cohen, Religion of Reason out of the Sources of Judaism," in *Jewish Philosophy and the Crisis of Modernity: Essays and Lectures in Modern Jewish Thought,* ed. Kenneth Hart Green (Albany: State University of New York Press, 1997), 267–284; and "Jerusalem and Athens," in *Jewish Philosophy and the Crisis of Modernity,* 377–405.

21. Cohen, *Ethik des reinen Willens,* 381.

22. Ibid., 546–547.

23. Ibid., 551.

24. Ibid., 376–378. For a profound reading of Cohen's account of sin and atonement through the lens of his philosophical system, with a particular emphasis on his logic and philosophy of science, see Zank, *The Idea of Atonement in the Philosophy of Hermann Cohen*, 230–264.

25. Cohen, *Religion of Reason Out of the Sources of Judaism*, 414; *RdV*, 480.

26. Cohen, *Ethics of Maimonides*, 113; *CEM*, 261.

27. Ibid., 114; *CEM*, 261.

28. Cohen, *Religion of Reason Out of the Sources of Judaism*, 211, 432; *RdV*, 246, 501.

29. Ibid., 453; *RdV*, 522.

30. As with Mendelssohn, Cohen was living and working as a Jew in Germany, and in the later nineteenth and early twentieth centuries virulent antisemitism was rife. I will treat Cohen's polemical account of Christianity as a merely heuristic device, and therefore exclude its political implications for society at large. These concerns, as important as they are, are extrinsic to the focus of this work. For an excellent account of Cohen's philosophical engagement with his antisemitic environment see Zank, *The Idea of Atonement in the Philosophy of Hermann Cohen*, 77–161. Cohen's critique also stems from genuine philosophical concerns, and is not merely a political act. Whether fairly or not, like Mendelssohn before him, Cohen thinks that many of the errors and problems that plague key philosophers in the West, including Kant, are a result of errors that stem from their Christian presuppositions. On this point see Zank, *The Idea of Atonement in the Philosophy of Hermann Cohen*, 271.

31. It should be noted that Cohen tended to be far more sympathetic to modern Protestantism than to Catholicism or medieval Christianity. Often his critiques of Christianity are aimed at the latter two rather than the former, which he tended to view as closer to Judaism. But Cohen's approval of modern Protestantism is not without a polemical edge: To the degree that modern Protestantism fully realizes its own rationality, it will come to resemble Judaism more and more.

32. Cohen, "Religion und Sittlichkeit," 134.

33. I use the masculine pronoun for God here purposefully, to highlight the anthropomorphic nature of mythic ways of thinking.

34. Ludwig Feuerbach, *The Essence of Christianity*, trans. George Eliot (Amherst, N.Y.: Prometheus, 1989) 251.

35. Of course, for Feuerbach, all monotheists are mythic-monotheists.

36. Feuerbach, *The Essence of Christianity*, 260.

37. Cohen, "Religion und Sittlichkeit," 139.

38. Ibid., 136.

39. Ibid., 136.

40. Ibid., 137; cf. *Ethik des reinen Willens*, 46, 47, 49, 53, 55–56, 61, 62, 453–455.

41. Cohen, *Ethik des reinen Willens*, 455.

42. Ibid., 47.

43. Cohen is a profound commentator on Ezekiel, whom he puts on par with Socrates in terms of discovering the concept of the individual, when he argues that the child should not suffer for the sins of the father (Cohen, *Religion of Reason Out of the Sources of Judaism*, 20; *RdV*, 23). For a detailed discussion of Cohen's account of Ezekiel, see Zank, *The Idea of Atonement in the Philosophy of Hermann Cohen*, 118–134.

44. Cohen, *Ethik des reinen Willens*, 303.

45. Ibid., 287.

46. Ibid., 317–322.

47. Ibid., 319. For a nuanced account of the discrepancy between Kant and Cohen on law and religion, see Robert Gibbs, "Jurisprudence is the Organon of Ethics: Kant and Cohen on Ethics, Law, and Religion," in *Hermann Cohen's Critical Idealism*, 193–230.

48. Cohen, "Religion und Sittlichkeit," 142.

49. Cohen, *Ethik des reinen Willens*, 49.

50. Ibid., 288.

51. Cohen, "Religion und Sittlichkeit," 139.

52. Cohen, *Ethik des reinen Willen*, 47.

53. Cohen, *Religion of Reason Out of the Sources of Judaism*, 239; *RdV*, 280.

54. Cohen, "Religion und Sittlichkeit," 134.

55. See Holzhey, "Gott und Seele," 88–93.

56. Notice here that Cohen differs from Mendelssohn and Kant. The other thinkers of the religion of reason trajectory still maintain a notion of there being a zero-sum game between God and human beings, such that if one side is elevated in dignity or value, the other side must be diminished. However, as Seeskin points out, in terms of the issue of autonomy, "Cohen's achievement rests on his ability to discuss the problem of autonomy in a way that rejects the idea that God and man are locked in a test of wills where one party's gain is the other's loss. Rather than a way of establishing independence from God, human autonomy . . . is the spiritual glue that binds man and God together" (Seeskin, *Autonomy and Jewish Philosophy*, 179). Seeskin's point here can be extended beyond autonomy to refer to the general relationship between the human being and God in general, in that Cohen removes any sort of antagonism between the two parties, although he preserves their difference.

57. At this point in our discussion it becomes necessary to use the term Other a bit more expansively. One's status as an insider, a Jew, is established primarily on the basis of knowledge which (as we will see) in turn sustains one in adversity, i.e., the Jew's suffering is redemptive. A person who suffers without it having a positive religious significance is the Other regardless of her ostensible religion, since her suffering is indicative that she lacks the knowledge and thus the peace of the Jew (meant normatively, not descriptively). This should become clearer as we proceed.

58. Cohen, *Religion of Reason Out of the Sources of Judaism*, 132–133; *RdV*, 153–155.

59. By 'immediacy' I do not mean to suggest some sort of Levinasian encounter with the face, but rather, that the Other ceases to be an object of indifference and her suffering can be recognized for what it is—an offensive blight which indicates the failure of culture and one's involvement in culture.

60. Cohen, "Religion und Sittlichkeit," 142–144.

61. Cohen, *Religion of Reason Out of the Sources of Judaism*, 214–215, 264; *RdV*, 250–251, 308–309.

62. See Hartwig Wiedebach's "Hermann Cohens Theorie des Mitleids," in *Hermann Cohen's Philosophy of Religion*, 235–236.

63. Cohen, *Religion of Reason Out of the Sources of Judaism*, 135; *RdV*, 156.

64. Ibid., 135–137, 184–185; *RdV*, 156–158, 216.

65. For a discussion of how affects can play a role in a rationalist ethics without compromising autonomy, see Cohen, *Ethik des reinen Willens*, 199.

66. Cohen, *Religion of Reason Out of the Sources of Judaism,* 138, 141; *RdV,* 160, 164.

67. Ibid., 147–148; *RdV,* 171.

68. Ibid., 148; *RdV,* 171. I have slightly emended the translation.

69. Cohen, *Ethik des reinen Willens,* 303.

70. Cohen, *Religion of Reason Out of the Sources of Judaism,* 190; *RdV,* 222.

71. For an in-depth discussion of the role of *t'shuvah* in Cohen's thought, see Zank, *The Idea of Atonement in the Philosophy of Hermann Cohen,* especially 134–151. However, the entire book can be seen as a prolonged meditation upon this theme, since Zank, quite correctly in my opinion, sees atonement as the center of gravity of Cohen's philosophy of religion.

72. Cohen, *Religion of Reason Out of the Sources of Judaism,* 193; *RdV,* 225.

73. Ibid., 194; *RdV,* 226.

74. Ibid., 194; *RdV,* 226.

75. Ibid., 264; *RdV,* 308.

76. Ibid., 204; *RdV,* 238.

77. To be sure, Cohen approves of Kant's effort to free Christianity of these fetters in *Religion within the Limits of Reason Alone.*

78. Ibid., 253–254; *RdV,* 295–297. Another major reason why Cohen's thought has fallen out of favor with contemporary Jews is that he was an ardent anti-Zionist. The mission of the Jews, he believed, was to stand apart from the nations, and Zionism, in his view, was the attempt to become like all the other nations.

79. Ibid., 149; *RdV,* 173.

80. For an excellent treatment of the notion of the suffering servant motif in *Religion of Reason Out of the Sources of Judaism,* through the lens of the notion of the tragic hero in Cohen's *Ästhetik des reinen Gefühl,* see Wiedebach's "Hermann Cohens Theorie des Mitleids," 231–244.

81. Cohen, *Religion of Reason Out of the Sources of Judaism,* 149; *RdV,* 173.

82. Ibid., 286; *RdV,* 333. Wendell Dietrich makes an important point that is well worth considering at present: "The motifs of Jewish suffering and martyrdom as stated by late nineteenth century German Jews may well have for us a jarring and disturbing resonance. Historians of thought are well advised to heed Peter Gay's advice: it is dangerous to read everything in the nineteenth century from the perspective of our knowledge of Germany in the 1930's and 1940's. Cohen should be permitted to stand for what he stands for, no more and no less. In his time, a variety of historical options were still open for the development of the German nation and the situation of the Jews in Germany" ("The Function of the Idea of Messianic Mankind in Hermann Cohen's Later Thought," *Journal for the American Academy of Religion* 48, no. 2 [June 1980]: 256 n. 6).

83. Cohen, *Religion of Reason Out of the Sources of Judaism,* 264; *RdV,* 304.

84. Ibid., 225; *RdV,* 262.

85. Ibid., 225; *RdV,* 263.

86. Ibid., 227; *RdV,* 265.

87. Ibid., 227; *RdV,* 265.

88. Ibid., 234; *RdV,* 274.

89. Ibid., 234–235; *RdV,* 274.

90. Poma, "Authentic and Historical Theodicy in Kant and Cohen," *Yearning for Form and other Essays on the Thought of Hermann Cohen,* 52. For critiques of Cohen's anti-eudaemonist theodicy, see Poma, "Suffering and Non-Eschatological Messianism in Hermann Cohen," in *Hermann Cohen's Critical Idealism,* 413–428;

Susan Neiman, "Commentary: Cohen and Kant," in *The Jewish Political Tradition: Volume One: Authority,* ed. Michael Walzer, Menachem Lorberbaum, and Noam J. Zohar (New Haven, Conn.: Yale University Press, 2000), 92–96.

91. Cohen, *Religion of Reason Out of the Sources of Judaism,* 286; RdV, 333. I have slightly altered Kaplan's translation here and included the German from which I derive my alterations.

92. Cohen, *Religion of Reason Out of the Sources of Judaism,* 286; RdV, 333–334. Interestingly, Cohen writes, "It is truly an unparalleled irony of history that the story of Jesus Christ's life, sealed by his death, should have become the source of the main difference between Christianity and Judaism. The history of this passion is an imitation of the messianic imagination of Deutero-Isaiah, while the latter, as is now commonly agreed, anticipated the history of the 'remnant of Israel.' And hence, according to this original poetic image, the historical Christ is actually the history of Israel" (*Religion of Reason Out of the Sources of Judaism,* 439–440; RdV, 508).

93. Ibid., 286; RdV, 333.

94. Ibid., 283; RdV, 330.

95. Ibid., 266; RdV, 310.

96. Ibid., 265; RdV, 309–310.

97. Charles Taylor, "Notes on the Sources of Violence: Perennial and Modern," *Beyond Violence: Religious Sources of Social Transformation in Judaism, Christianity, and Islam,* ed. James L. Heeft, S.M. (New York: Fordham University Press, 2004), 15–42.

98. Taylor, "Notes on the Sources of Violence," 39. As a paradigmatic example of this paradoxical violence, Taylor cites Robespierre's desire to create a "republic without a death penalty" while this only "somehow energizes a program of escalating butchery" (39).

99. Cohen, *Religion of Reason Out of the Sources of Judaism,* 357; RdV, 415.

100. It is important to note that Assmann's work is not itself without critics. For a thorough and highly insightful critique of Assmann's methodology which problematizes the means by which he formulates the relationship of monotheism, intolerance, and violence, see Peter Schäfer's recent article, "Geschichte und Gedächtnisgeschichte: Jan Assmanns 'Mosaische Unterscheidung,'" in *Memoria— Wege jüdischen Erinnerns. Festschrift für Michael Brocke zum 65. Geburtstag,* ed. Birgit E. Klein and Christiane E. Müller (Berlin: Metropol, 2005), 19–39.

101. Assmann, *Die Mosaische Unterscheidung,* 35.

102. Though he does not cite Assmann, Jonathon Kirsch makes a great deal of this point in regard to the emergence of Christianity in the Roman empire. Kirsch, *God Against the Gods: The History of the War Between Monotheism and Polytheism* (New York: Viking Compass, 2004), 119–146.

103. Cohen, *Religion of Reason Out of the Sources of Judaism,* 253; RdV, 295.

104. Ibid., 258; RdV, 301.

105. Ibid., 260; RdV, 303.

106. Ibid., 268; RdV, 313.

Conclusion

1. I am again bracketing developments in contemporary Islamic thought, mainly due to my lack of knowledge in this regard.

2. David Novak, *The Election of Israel: The Idea of the Chosen People* (Cambridge: Cambridge University Press, 1995), 9.

3. Ibid., 8.

4. Ibid., 9.

5. Kenneth Seeskin, *Searching for a Distant God: The Legacy of Maimonides* (New York: Oxford University Press, 2000), 192 n. 52.

6. Novak, *The Jewish Social Contract*, 20.

7. Novak's thought is extraordinarily resilient, given that while it theologically privileges Judaism, it does so in a decentered way that allows for other theological communities to privilege their own respective traditions. Novak works to elaborate the modern political sensibilities necessary for theological communities (or at least traditionalist Jewish ones) to thrive in a democracy without compromising their beliefs and practices. In this sense, he is an important interlocutor for Habermas, although to my knowledge there has been no critical work done in this vein.

8. Habermas, *Religion and Rationality*, 150.

WORKS CITED

Adams, Nicholas. *Habermas and Theology*. Cambridge: Cambridge University Press, 2006.

Adelmann, Dieter. "Ursprüngliche Differenz: Zwischen Einzigkeit und Einheit im Denken von Hermann Cohen." *Archivio di Filosofia* 71 (2003): 19–40.

Altmann, Alexander. *Moses Mendelssohn: A Biographical Study*. London: Vallentine Mitchell, 1973.

———. "Moses Mendelssohn's Concept of Judaism Reexamined." In *Von der mittelalterlichen zur modernen Aufklärung: Studien zur jüdischen Geistesgeschichte*. Tübingen: J. C. B. Mohr (Paul Siebeck), 1987. 234–248.

Anderson-Gold, Sharon. "God and Community: An Inquiry into the Religious Implications of the Highest Good." In *Kant's Philosophy of Religion Reconsidered*, ed. Philip J. Rossi and Michael Wreen. Bloomington: Indiana University Press, 1991. 113–131.

———. *Unnecessary Evil: History and Moral Progress in the Philosophy of Immanuel Kant*. Albany: State University of New York Press, 2001.

Anscombe, G. E. M. "Modern Moral Philosophy." In *Ethics, Religion and Politics: Collected Philosophical Papers*, vol. 3. Oxford: Blackwell, 1981. 26–43.

Arkush, Allan. *Moses Mendelssohn and the Enlightenment*. Albany: State University of New York Press, 1994.

Assmann, Jan. *Die Mosaische Unterscheidung: oder der Preis des Monotheismus*. Munich: Carl Hanser Verlag, 2003.

———. *Moses the Egyptian: The Memory of Egypt in Western Monotheism*. Cambridge, Mass.: Harvard University Press, 1997.

Audi, Robert, and Nicholas Wolterstorff. *Religion and the Public Sphere*. New York: Rowman and Littlefield, 1997.

Bamberger, Fritz. "Mendelssohn's Concept of Judaism." In *Studies in Jewish Thought: An Anthology of German Jewish Scholarship*, ed. and trans. Alfred Jospe. Detroit: Wayne State Press, 1981. 343–360.

Batnitzky, Leora. *Leo Strauss and Emmanuel Levinas: Philosophy and the Politics of Revelation*. Cambridge: Cambridge University Press, 2006.

Beck, Lewis White. *A Commentary on Kant's Critique of Practical Reason*. Chicago: University of Chicago Press, 1960.

Bonaunet, Ketil. *Hermann Cohen's Philosophy of Religion*. Bern: Peter Lang, 2004.

Borradori, Giovanna. *Philosophy in a Time of Terror: Dialogues with Jürgen Habermas and Jacques Derrida*. Chicago: University of Chicago Press, 2003.

Boyarin, Daniel. *Intertextuality and the Reading of Midrash*. Bloomington: Indiana University Press, 1994.

Bruckstein, Almut Sh. "On Jewish Hermeneutics: Maimonides and Bachya as Vectors in Cohen's Philosophy of Origin." In *Hermann Cohen's Philosophy of Religion*, ed. Stéphane Moses and Hartwig Wiedebach. Hildesheim: Georg Olms Verlag, 1997. 35–50.

Buell, Denise. *Why This New Race: Ethnic Reasoning in Early Christianity*. New York: Columbia University Press, 2005.

Byrne, Peter. "John Hick's Philosophy of Religions." *Scottish Journal of Theology* 35 (1982): 289–301.

Cassirer, Ernst. *The Philosophy of the Enlightenment.* Trans. Fritz C. A. Koelln and James P. Pettegrove. Princeton, N.J.: Princeton University Press, 1951.

Cohen, Hermann. "Charakteristik der Ethik Maimunis." In *Hermann Cohens Jüdische Schriften,* vol. 3. New York: Arno Press, 1980. 221–289.

———. *Ethics of Maimonides.* Trans. Almut Sh. Bruckstein. Madison: University of Wisconsin Press, 2002.

———. *Ethik des reinen Willens.* In *Werke,* vol. 7. Repr. of 2d ed. (1907). Hildesheim: Georg Olms Verlag, 1981.

———. *Logik der reinen Erkenntnis.* In *Werke,* vol. 7. Repr. of 2d ed. (1914). Hildesheim: Georg Olms Verlag, 1981.

———. *Religion der Vernunft aus den Quellen des Judentums,* 2d ed. Frankfurt: M. Kaufmann, 1929.

———. *Religion of Reason Out of the Sources of Judaism,* 2d ed. Trans. Simon Kaplan. Atlanta: Scholars Press, 1995.

———. "Religion und Sittlichkeit." In *Hermann Cohens Jüdische Schriften,* vol. 3. New York: Arno Press, 1980. 98–168.

———. "The Social Ideal as Seen by Plato and by the Prophets." In *Reason and Hope: Selections from the Jewish Writings of Hermann Cohen,* ed. and trans. Eva Jospe. New York: W. W. Norton, 1971. 66–77.

Connolly, William E. *Pluralism.* Durham: Duke University Press, 2005.

D'Costa, Gavin, ed. *Christian Uniqueness Reconsidered: The Myth of a Pluralistic Theology of Religions.* Maryknoll, N.Y.: Orbis Books, 1990.

Dietrich, Wendell S. "The Function of the Idea of Messianic Mankind in Hermann Cohen's Later Thought." *Journal of the American Academy of Religion* 48 (June 1980): 245–258.

Eisen, Arnold. "Divine Legislation as 'Ceremonial Script': Mendelssohn on the Commandments." *AJS Review: The Journal of the Association for Jewish Studies* 15 (Fall 1990): 239–267.

Erlin, Matt. "Reluctant Modernism: Moses Mendelssohn's Philosophy of History." *Journal of the History of Ideas* 63 (January 2002): 83–104.

Fackenheim, Emil. "Kant and Judaism." *Commentary* (December 1963): 460–467.

———. "Kant and Radical Evil." In *The God Within: Kant, Schelling, and Historicity,* ed. John Burbidge. Toronto: University of Toronto Press, 1996. 20–33.

———. *To Mend The World.* Bloomington: Indiana University Press, 1982.

Feuerbach, Ludwig. *The Essence of Christianity.* Trans. George Eliot. Amherst, N.Y.: Prometheus, 1989.

Firestone, Chris L., and Stephen R. Palmquist, eds. *Kant and the New Philosophy of Religion.* Bloomington: Indiana University Press, 2006.

Fotion, Nick, and Gerard Elfstrom. *Toleration.* Tuscaloosa: University of Alabama Press, 1992.

Foucault, Michel. "What Is Enlightenment." In *Foucault Reader,* ed. Paul Rabinow. New York: Pantheon, 1984. 32–50.

Gibbs, Robert. "Hermann Cohen's Messianism: The History of the Future." In *"Religion der Vernunft aus den Quellen des Judentums": Tradition und Ursprüngsdenken in Hermann Cohens Spätwerk,* ed. Helmut Holzhey, Gabriel Motzkin, and Hartwig Wiedebach. Hildesheim: Georg Olms Verlag, 2000. 331–349.

———. "Jurisprudence is the Organon of Ethics: Kant and Cohen on Ethics, Law, and Religion." In *Hermann Cohen's Critical Idealism,* ed. Reinier Munk. Dordrecht: Springer, 2005. 193–230.

———. "Preface." *Journal of Jewish Thought and Philosophy* (2006): iii–vii.

Goetschel, Willi. *Spinoza's Modernity: Mendelssohn, Lessing, Heine.* Madison: University of Wisconsin Press, 2004.

Goodman, Lenn. *The God of Abraham.* New York, Oxford: Oxford University Press, 1996.

Gottlieb, Michah. "Mendelssohn's Metaphysical Defense of Religious Pluralism." *The Journal of Religion* 86 (2006): 205–225.

Griffiths, Paul, and Delma Lewis. "On Grading Religions, Seeking Truth, and Being Nice to People—A Reply to Professor Hick." *Religious Studies* 19 (1983): 75–80.

Guyer, Paul. *Kant on Freedom, Law and Happiness.* New York: Cambridge University Press, 2000.

Guttmann, Julius. "Mendelssohn's *Jerusalem* and Spinoza's *Theologico-Political Treatise.*" In *Studies in Jewish Thought: An Anthology of German Jewish Scholarship,* ed. and trans. Alfred Jospe. Detroit: Wayne State Press, 1981. 373–377.

Habermas, Jürgen. "A Conversation About God and the World: Interview with Eduardo Mendieta." In *Religion and Rationality: Essays on Reason, God and Modernity,* ed. Eduardo Mendieta. Cambridge, Mass.: Massachusetts Institute of Technology Press, 2002. 147–168.

———. "Faith and Knowledge." In *The Future of Human Nature.* Cambridge: Polity, 2003. 101–115.

———. "A Genealogical Analysis of the Cognitive Content of Morality." In *The Inclusion of the Other,* ed. Ciaran Cronin and Pablo De Greiff. Cambridge, Mass.: Massachusetts Institute of Technology Press, 1996. 33–46.

———. "On the Relation Between the Secular State and Religion." In *The Frankfurt School on Religion,* ed. Eduardo Mendieta, trans. Matthias Fritsch. New York: Routledge, 2005. 339–350.

———. *The Philosophical Discourses of Modernity: Twelve Lectures.* Trans. Frederick G. Lawrence. Cambridge, Mass.: Massachusetts Institute of Technology Press, 1990.

———. "Religion and the Public Sphere." *European Journal of Philosophy* 14, no. 1 (2006): 1–25.

———. *Religion and Rationality: Essays on Reason, God and Modernity.* Ed. Eduardo Mendieta. Cambridge, Mass.: Massachusetts Institute of Technology Press, 2002.

———. "Themes in Postmetaphysical Thinking." In *Postmetaphysical Thinking: Philosophical Essays,* trans. William Mark Hohengarten. Cambridge, Mass.: Massachusetts Institute of Technology Press, 1992. 28–53.

———. *Theory of Communicative Action, Volume 1: Reason and the Rationalization of Society.* Trans. Thomas McCarthy. Boston: Beacon Press, 1984.

———. *Theory of Communicative Action, Volume 2: Lifeworld and System: A Critique of Functionalist Reason.* Trans. Thomas McCarthy. Boston: Beacon Press, 1989.

———. "Transcendence from Within, Transcendence in this World." In *Religion and Rationality: Essays on Reason, God and Modernity,* ed. Eduardo Mendieta. Cambridge, Mass.: Massachusetts Institute of Technology Press, 2002. 67–94.

Halbertal, Moshe, and Avishai Margalit. *Idolatry.* Trans. Naomi Goldblum. Cambridge, Mass.: Harvard University Press, 1992.

Heschel, Susannah. *Abraham Geiger and the Jewish Jesus.* Chicago: University of Chicago Press, 1998.

Hess, Jonathan M. *Germans, Jews and the Claims of Modernity.* New Haven: Yale University Press, 2002.

Heyd, David, ed. *Toleration: An Elusive Virtue.* Princeton, N.J.: Princeton University Press, 1996.

Hick, John. *God Has Many Names.* Philadelphia: Westminster Press, 1980.

———. *Problems of Religious Pluralism.* New York: St. Martin's Press, 1985.

Holzhey, Helmut. "Cohen and the Marburg School in Context." In *Hermann Cohen's Critical Idealism,* ed. Reinier Munk. Dordrecht: Springer, 2005. 3–40.

———. "Ethik als Lehre vom Menschen: Eine Einführung in Hermann Cohens *Ethik des Reinen Willens.*" *Journal of Jewish Thought and Philosophy* 13 (2006): 17–36.

———. "Gott und Seele: zum Verhältnis von Metaphysikkritik und Religionsphilosophie bei Hermann Cohen." In *Hermann Cohen's Philosophy of Religion,* ed. Stéphane Moses and Hartwig Wiedebach. Hildesheim: Georg Olms Verlag, 1997. 85–104.

Jaffee, Martin S. "One God, One Revelation, One People: On the Symbolic Structure of Elective Monotheism." *Journal of the American Academy of Religion* 69, no. 4 (December 2001): 753–775.

Kajon, Irene. "Critical Idealism in Hermann Cohen's Writings on Judaism." In *Hermann Cohen's Critical Idealism,* ed. Reinier Munk. Dordrecht: Springer, 2005. 371–394.

Kant, Immanuel. *Ak. = Kants gesammelte Schriften.* Ed. Preussischen Akademie der Wissenschaften. Berlin: Walter de Gruyter, 1902–.

———. "An Answer to the Question: What Is Enlightenment?" *Perpetual Peace and Other Essays.* Ed. and trans. Ted Humphreys. Indianapolis: Hackett, 1983. 41–49.

———. "Beantwortung der Frage: Was ist Aufklärung?" In *Ak.,* vol. 8.

———. *Critique of Judgment.* Trans. Werner S. Pluhar. Indianapolis: Hackett, 1987.

———. *Critique of Pure Reason.* Trans. Norman Kemp Smith. Boston: Macmillan, 1929.

———. *Critique of Practical Reason.* Trans. Werner S. Pluhar. Indianapolis: Hackett, 2002.

———. *Foundations of the Metaphysics of Morals. Second Edition, Revised.* Trans. Lewis White Beck. New Jersey: Prentice-Hall, 1997.

———. *Grundlegung zur Metaphysik der Sitten.* In *Ak.,* vol. 4.

———. "Idea for a Universal History with a Cosmopolitan Intent." In *Perpetual Peace and Other Essays,* trans. Ted Humphrey. Indianapolis: Hackett, 1983. 29–40.

———. "Idee zu einer allgemeinen Geschichte in weltbürgerlicher Absicht." In *Ak.,* vol. 8.

———. *Kritik der praktischen Vernunft.* In *Ak.,* vol. 5.

———. *Kritik der reinen Vernunft.* In *Ak.,* vols. 3–4. In keeping with standard practice, the 1781 and 1787 editions are cited as 'A' and 'B.'

———. *Kritik der Urteilskraft.* In *Ak.,* vol. 5.

———. "On the Common Saying: That May be Correct in Theory, but it is of no use in Practice." In *Immanuel Kant: Practical Philosophy*, trans. and ed. Mary J. Gregor. Cambridge: Cambridge University Press, 1996. 278–309.

———. *Die Religion innerhalb der Grenzen der bloßen Vernunft*. In *Ak.*, vol. 6.

———. *Religion Within the Limits of Reason Alone*. Trans. Theodore M. Greene and Hoyte H. Hudson. London: Harper Torchbooks, 1960.

———. "Über den Gemeinspruch: Das mag in der Theorie richtig sein, taugt aber nicht für die Praxis." In *Ak.*, vol. 8.

———. "Zum ewigen Frieden: Ein philosophischer Entwurf." In *Ak.*, vol. 8.

Kavka, Martin. *Jewish Messianism and the History of Philosophy*. New York: Cambridge University Press, 2004.

Kelley, George Armstrong. "The Structure of Legality in Kant." *The Journal of Politics* 31 (May 1969): 513–527.

Kepnes, Steven D. "Moses Mendelssohn's Philosophy of Jewish Liturgy: A Post-Liberal Assessment." *Modern Theology* (April 2004): 186–212.

Kirsch, Jonathan. *God Against the Gods: The History of the War Between Monotheism and Polytheism*. New York: Viking Compass Press, 2004.

Köhnke, Klaus. *The Rise of Neo-Kantianism: German Academic Philosophy between Idealism and Positivism*. Trans. R. J. Hollingdale. New York: Cambridge University Press, 1991.

Korn, Eugene. "Gentiles, the World to Come, and Judaism: The Odyssey of a Rabbinic Text." *Modern Judaism* 14 (Oct. 1994): 265–287.

Leibniz, G. W. *Theodicy: Essays on the Goodness of God, the Freedom of Man, and the Origin of Evil*. Ed. Austin Farrer, trans. E. M. Haggard. New Haven: Yale University Press, 1952.

Levenson, Jon. "The Eighth Principle of Judaism and the Literary Simultaneity of Scripture." In *The Hebrew Bible, The Old Testament and Historical Criticism*. Louisville: Westminster/John Knox Press, 1985. 62–81.

Librett, Jeffrey S. *The Rhetoric of Cultural Dialogue: Jews and Germans from Moses Mendelssohn to Richard Wagner and Beyond*. Stanford, Calif.: Stanford University Press, 2000.

Locke, John. "A Letter Concerning Toleration." In *Two Treatises of Government and A Letter Concerning Toleration*, ed. Ian Shapiro. New Haven: Yale University Press, 2003. 211–256.

MacIntyre, Alisdair. *After Virtue. Second Edition*. Notre Dame: University Notre Dame Press, 1984.

Maimonides, Moses. *Guide to the Perplexed*, 2 vols. Trans. Schlomo Pines. Chicago: University of Chicago Press, 1963.

———. *Mishneh Torah*. "Hilkhot Sefer Shofetim 8:11." In *A Maimonides Reader*, trans. Isadore Twersky. Springfield, N.J.: Behrman House, 1972.

Margalit, Avishai. "The Ring: or on Religious Pluralism." In *Toleration: An Elusive Virtue*, ed. David Heyd. Princeton, N.J.: Princeton University Press, 1996. 147–157.

Meeker, Kevin, and Philip L. Quinn, eds. *The Philosophical Challenge of Religious Diversity*. New York: Oxford University Press, 2000.

Mendelssohn, Moses. "Gegenbetrachtungen über Bonnets Palingenesie." In *Moses Mendelssohn: Gesammelte Schriften Jubiläumsausgabe*, vol. 7. Berlin: Friedrich Frommann Verlag (Günther Holzboog), 1971. 67–107.

———. "Jerusalem: oder über religiöse Macht und Judentum." In *Moses Mendelssohn: Gesammelte Schriften Jubiläumsausgabe*, vol. 8. Berlin: Friedrich Fromann Verlag (Günther Holzboog), 1983. 99–204.

------. *Jerusalem: Or on Religious Power and Judaism.* Trans. Allan Arkush. Hanover, N.H.: Brandeis University Press, 1983.

------. *Moses Mendelssohn: Selections from His Writings.* Ed. and trans. Eva Jospe. New York: Viking Press, 1975.

------. "Phaedon: oder über Unsterblichkeit der Seele in drey Gesprächen." In *Moses Mendelssohn: Gesammelte Schriften Jubiläumsausgabe,* vol. 3.1. Berlin: Friedrich Fromann Verlag (Günther Holzboog), 1971. 7–128.

------. *Phaedon: or the Death of Socrates.* Trans. Charles Cullen. Bristol: Thoemmes Continuum, 2004.

------. "Sache Gottes: oder die gerettete Vorsehung." In *Moses Mendelssohn: Gesammelte Schriften Jubiläumsausgabe,* vol. 3.2. Berlin: Friedrich Frommann Verlag (Günther Holzboog), 1971. 221–260.

Mendus, Susan. *Toleration and the Limits of Liberalism.* Atlantic Highlands, N.J.: Humanities Press, 1989.

Meyer, William J. "Private Faith or Public Religion? An Assessment of Habermas's Changing View of Religion." *Journal of Religion* 75 (1995): 371–391.

------. "Review of *Postmetaphysical Thinking: Philosophical Essays,* by Jürgen Habermas." *Journal of Religion* 73, no. 4 (October 1993): 646–647.

Michalson, Gordon E., Jr. "God and Kant's Ethical Commonwealth." *The Thomist* 65 (2001): 67–92.

------. *Kant and the Problem of God.* Oxford: Blackwell, 1999.

------. "Moral Regeneration and Divine Aid in Kant." *Religious Studies* (September 1989): 259–270.

Milgrom, Jacob. "Priestly ('P') Source." *The Anchor Bible Dictionary,* vol. 5. New York: Doubleday, 1992. 454–460.

Morgan, Michael. "History and Modern Jewish Thought: Spinoza and Mendelssohn on the Ritual Law." *Judaism* 30 (1981): 467–479.

------. "Mendelssohn's Defense of Reason in Jerusalem." *Judaism* 38 (Fall 1989): 449–459.

Mulholland, Leslie A. "Freedom and Providence in Kant's Account of Religion: The Problem of Expiation." In *Kant's Philosophy of Religion Reconsidered,* ed. Philip J. Rossi and Michael Wreen. Bloomington: Indiana University Press, 1991. 77–102.

Munk, Reinier. "Alterität im Denken Hermann Cohens." In *Sinn, Geltung, Wert: Neukantianische Motive in der modernen Kulturphilosophie.* Ed. Christian Krijnen and Ernst Wolfgang Orth. Würzburg: Königshausen und Neumann, 1998. 109–121.

------, ed. *Hermann Cohen's Critical Idealism.* Dordrecht: Springer, 2005.

------. "On the Idea of God in Cohen's *Ethik.*" *Journal of Jewish Thought and Philosophy* 13 (2006): 105–114.

------. "The Self and the Other in Cohen's Ethics and Works on Religion." In *Hermann Cohen's Philosophy of Religion,* ed. Stéphane Moses and Hartwig Wiedebach. Hildesheim: Georg Olms Verlag, 1997. 161–181.

Neiman, Susan. "Commentary: Cohen and Kant." In *Authority,* vol. 2 of *The Jewish Political Tradition,* ed. Michael Walzer, Menachem Lorberbaum, and Noam J. Zohar. New Haven: Yale University Press, 2000. 92–96.

Netland, George A. "Professor Hick on Religious Pluralism." *Religious Studies* 22 (1986): 249–261.

Newman, Jay. *Foundations of Religious Tolerance.* Toronto: University of Toronto Press, 1989.

Novak, David. *The Election of Israel: The Idea of the Chosen People.* Cambridge: Cambridge University Press, 1995.

———. "Hermann Cohen on State and Nation: A Contemporary Review." In *Hermann Cohen's Critical Idealism,* ed. Reinier Munk. Dordrecht: Springer, 2005. 259–282.

———. *The Image of the Non-Jew in Judaism: An Historical and Constructive Study of the Noahide Laws.* New York: Edwin Mellon Press, 1984.

———. *The Jewish Social Contract: An Essay in Political Theology.* Princeton, N.J.: Princeton University Press, 2005.

O'Neill, Onora. *Constructions of Reason: Explorations of Kant's Practical Philosophy.* New York: Cambridge University Press: 1989.

———. "Vindicating Reason." In *The Cambridge Companion to Kant,* ed. Paul Guyer. Cambridge: Cambridge University Press, 1992. 280–309.

Palmquist, Stephen. "Does Kant Reduce Religion to Morality?" *Kant-Studien* 83 (1992): 129–148.

———. "'The Kingdom of God is at Hand!' (Did Kant Really Say That?)." *History of Philosophy Quarterly* 11 (October 1994): 421–437.

Poma, Andrea. "Authentic and Historical Theodicy in Kant and Cohen." In *Yearning For Form and Other Essays on Hermann Cohen's Thought.* Dordrecht: Springer, 2006. 43–60.

———. "Autonomy of the Law." In *Yearning For Form and Other Essays on Hermann Cohen's Thought.* Dordrecht: Springer, 2006. 261–272.

———. "Correlation in Hermann Cohen's Philosophy of Religion: A Method and More Than a Method." In *Yearning For Form and Other Essays on Hermann Cohen's Thought.* Dordrecht: Springer, 2006. 61–86.

———. *The Critical Philosophy of Hermann Cohen.* Trans. John Denton. Albany: State University of New York Press, 1997.

———. "The Existence of the Ideal in Hermann Cohen's Ethics." In *Yearning For Form and Other Essays on Hermann Cohen's Thought.* Dordrecht: Springer, 2006. 273–294.

———. "The Holy Spirit out of the Sources of Judaism and Kantianism." In *Yearning for Form and Other Essays on Hermann Cohen's Thought.* Dordrecht: Springer, 2006. 295–312.

———. "Plato's Idea of the Good in its Different Interpretations by Cohen and Natorp." In *Yearning For Form and Other Essays on Hermann Cohen's Thought.* Dordrecht: Springer, 2006. 21–42.

———. "Religion as a Fact of Culture and the System of Philosophy." In *Yearning For Form and Other Essays on Hermann Cohen's Thought.* Dordrecht: Springer, 2006. 169–203.

———. "Religion of Reason and Judaism in Hermann Cohen." In *Yearning for Form and Other Essays on Hermann Cohen's Thought.* Dordrecht: Springer, 2006. 111–128.

———. "Suffering and Non-Eschatological Messianism in Hermann Cohen." In *Hermann Cohen's Critical Idealism,* ed. Reinier Munk. Dordrecht: Springer, 2005. 413–428.

———. *Yearning for Form and Other Essays on Hermann Cohen's Thought.* Dordrecht: Springer, 2006.

Quinn, Philip L. "Kantian Philosophical Ecclesiology." *Faith and Philosophy* 17, no. 4 (October 2000): 512–534.

——. "Original Sin, Radical Evil, and Moral Identity." *Faith and Philosophy* 1 (April 1984): 188–202.

——, and Kevin Meeker, eds. *The Philosophical Challenge of Religious Diversity.* New York: Oxford University Press, 2000.

Ratzinger, Joseph Cardinal. *Truth and Tolerance: Christian Belief and World Religions.* Trans. Henry Taylor. San Francisco: Ignatius Press, 2004.

Rosen, Allen D. *Kant's Theory of Justice.* Ithaca: Cornell University Press, 1993.

Rossi, Philip J. "The Final End of All Things: The Highest Good as the Unity of Nature and Freedom." In *Kant's Philosophy of Religion Reconsidered,* ed. Philip J. Rossi and Michael Wreen. Bloomington: Indiana University Press, 1991. 132–164.

——, and Michael Wreen, eds. *Kant's Philosophy of Religion Reconsidered.* Bloomington: Indiana University Press, 1991.

——. *The Social Authority of Reason: Kant's Critique, Radical Evil, and the Destiny of Humankind.* Albany: State University of New York Press, 2005.

Rotenstreich, Nathan. "On Mendelssohn's Political Philosophy." In *Essays in Jewish Philosophy in the Modern Era,* ed. Reiner Munk. Amsterdam: J. C. Gieben, 1994. 70–85.

Rothberg, Donald Jay. "Rationality and Religion in Habermas' Recent Work: Some Remarks Between Critical Theory and the Phenomenology of Religion." *Philosophy and Social Criticism* 11 (Summer 1986): 221–244.

Rousseau, Jean-Jacques. "On the Social Contract." In *Rousseau: The Social Contract and Other Later Political Writings,* ed. Victor Gourevitch. Cambridge: Cambridge University Press, 1997. 39–152.

Runzo, Joseph. "Kant on Reason and Justified Belief in God." In *Kant's Philosophy of Religion Reconsidered,* ed. Philip J. Rossi and Michael Wreen. Bloomington: Indiana University Press, 1991. 22–39.

Savage, Denis. "Kant's Rejection of Divine Revelation and His Theory of Radical Evil." In *Kant's Philosophy of Religion Reconsidered,* ed. Philip J. Rossi and Michael Wreen. Bloomington: Indiana University Press, 1991. 54–76.

Scanlon, Thomas. "The Difficulty of Tolerance." In *Toleration: An Elusive Virtue,* ed. David Heyd. Princeton, N.J.: Princeton University Press, 1996. 226–240.

Schäfer, Peter. "Geschichte und Gedächtnisgeschichte: Jan Assmanns 'Mosaische Unterscheidung.'" In *Memoria—Wege jüdischen Erinnerns. Festschrift für Michael Brocke zum 65. Geburtstag,* ed. Birgit E. Klein and Christiane E. Müller. Berlin: Metropol, 2005. 19–39.

Schmid, Peter A. *Ethik als Hermeneutik. Systematische Untersuchung zu Hermann Cohens Recht- und Tugendlehre.* Würzburg: Königshausen & Neumann, 1995.

Schneewind, J. B. "Bayle, Locke, and the Concept of Toleration." In *Philosophy, Religion, and the Question of Intolerance,* ed. Mehdi Amin Razavi and David Ambuel. Albany: State University of New York Press, 1997. 3–15.

——. *The Invention of Autonomy: A History of Modern Moral Philosophy.* New York: Cambridge University Press, 1998.

Schwartz, Regina. *The Curse of Cain: The Violent Legacy of Monotheism.* Chicago: University of Chicago Press, 1997.

Schwarzschild, Steven S. "Do Noachites Have to Believe in Revelation? (A Passage in Dispute between Maimonides, Spinoza, Mendelssohn and Hermann Cohen): A Contribution to a Jewish View of Natural Law." In *The Pursuit of the Ideal: Jewish Writings of Steven Schwarzschild,* ed. Menachem Kellner. Albany: State University of New York Press, 1990. 29–59.

———. "The Tenability of Herman [sic] Cohen's Construction of the Self." *Journal of the History of Philosophy* (July 1975): 361–384.

———. "The Title of Hermann Cohen's Religion of Reason Out of the Sources of Judaism." Reprinted in Hermann Cohen, *Religion of Reason Out of the Sources of Judaism,* 2d ed. Atlanta: Scholars Press, 1995. 7–20.

Seeskin, Kenneth. *Autonomy in Jewish Philosophy.* Cambridge: Cambridge University Press, 2001.

———. *Jewish Philosophy in a Secular Age.* Albany: State University of New York Press, 1990.

———. *Searching for a Distant God: The Legacy of Maimonides.* New York: Oxford University Press, 2000.

Seligman, Adam B. *Modest Claims: Dialogues and Essays on Tolerance and Tradition.* Notre Dame: University of Notre Dame Press, 2004.

Smith, Wilfred Cantwell. "Idolatry." In *The Myth of Christian Uniqueness: Toward a Pluralistic Theology of Religions,* ed. John Hick and Paul F. Knitter. Eugene, Ore.: Wipf and Stock, 1987. 53–68.

Sorkin, David. *Moses Mendelssohn and the Religious Enlightenment.* Berkeley: University of California Press, 1996.

———. "Moses Mendelssohn's Biblical Exegesis." In *Moses Mendelssohn im Spannungsfeld der Aufklärung,* ed. Michael Albrecht and Eva J. Engel. Stuttgart-Bad Cannstatt: Frommann-Holzboog, 2000. 243–276.

Stout, Jeffrey. *Democracy and Tradition.* Princeton, N.J.: Princeton University Press, 2004.

Strauss, Leo. "Introductory Essay to Hermann Cohen, Religion of Reason out of the Sources of Judaism." In *Jewish Philosophy and the Crisis of Modernity: Essays and Lectures in Modern Jewish Thought,* ed. Kenneth Hart Green. Albany: State University of New York Press, 1997. 267–284.

———. "Jerusalem and Athens." In *Jewish Philosophy and the Crisis of Modernity: Essays and Lectures in Modern Jewish Thought,* ed. Kenneth Hart Green. Albany: State University of New York Press, 1997. 377–405.

———. "Progress or Return." In *Jewish Philosophy and the Crisis of Modernity: Essays and Lectures in Modern Jewish Thought,* ed. Kenneth Hart Green. Albany: State University of New York Press, 1997. 87–136.

Sutcliffe, Adam. *Judaism and Enlightenment.* Cambridge: Cambridge University Press, 2003.

Taylor, Charles. "Notes on the Sources of Violence: Perennial and Modern." In *Beyond Violence: Religious Sources of Social Transformation in Judaism, Christianity, and Islam,* ed. James L. Heeft. New York: Fordham University Press, 2004. 15–42.

Twersky, Isadore, ed. *A Maimonides Reader.* Springfield, N.J.: Behrman House, 1972.

Twiss, Sumner B. "The Philosophy of Religious Pluralism: A Critical Appraisal of Hick and His Critics." In *The Philosophical Challenge of Religious Diversity,* ed. Philip L. Quinn and Kevin Meeker. New York: Oxford University Press, 2000. 67–99.

Ward, Keith. "Truth and Diversity of Religions." In *The Philosophical Challenge of Religious Diversity,* ed. Philip L. Quinn and Kevin Meeker. New York: Oxford University Press, 2000. 109–125.

Werbick, Jürgen. "Absolutistischer Eingottglaube?—Befreiende Vielfalt des Polytheismus?" In *Ist Der Glaube Feind Der Freiheit? Die Neue Debatte Um Den Monotheismus,* ed. Thomas Söding. Freiburg: Herder, 2003. 143–175.

Wiedebach, Hartwig. "Hermann Cohens Theorie des Mitleids." In *Hermann Cohen's Philosophy of Religion,* ed. Stéphane Moses and Hartwig Wiedebach. Hildesheim: Georg Olms Verlag, 1997. 231–244.

———. "Physiology of the Pure Will: Concepts of Moral Energy in Hermann Cohen's Ethics." In *Hermann Cohen's Ethics,* ed. Robert Gibbs. Leiden: Brill, 2006. 85–104.

Wiehl, Reiner. "Identity and Correlation in Cohen's System." In *Hermann Cohen's Critical Idealism,* ed. Reinier Munk. Dordrecht: Springer, 2005. 67–96.

Williams, Howard. *Kant's Political Philosophy.* New York: St. Martin's Press, 1983.

Wood, Allen W. "Kant's Deism." In *Kant's Philosophy of Religion Reconsidered,* ed. Philip J. Rossi and Michael Wreen. Bloomington: Indiana University Press, 1991. 1–21.

———. *Kant's Ethical Thought.* Cambridge: Cambridge University Press, 1999.

———. *Kant's Moral Religion.* Ithaca: Cornell University Press, 1970.

Wong, David B. *Moral Relativity.* Berkeley: University of California Press, 1984.

Wreen, Michael, and Philip J. Rossi, eds. *Kant's Philosophy of Religion Reconsidered.* Bloomington: Indiana University Press, 1991.

Wyschogrod, Edith. "The Moral Self: Levinas and Hermann Cohen." In *Crossover Queries: Dwelling with Negatives, Embodying Philosophy's Others.* New York: Fordham University Press, 2006. 405–422.

Yovel, Yirmiahu. *Kant and the Philosophy of History.* Princeton, N.J.: Princeton University Press, 1980.

Zagorin, Perez. *How the Idea of Religious Tolerance Came to the West.* Princeton, N.J.: Princeton University Press, 2003.

Zank, Michael. *The Idea of Atonement in the Philosophy of Hermann Cohen.* Providence, R.I.: Brown Judaic Studies, 2000.

———. "'The Individual as I' in Hermann Cohen's Jewish Thought." *The Journal of Jewish Thought and Philosophy* 5 (1996): 281–296.

Zenger, Erich. "Was ist der Preis des Monotheismus?" Republished in Jan Assmann, *Die Mosaische Unterscheidung: oder der Preis des Monotheismus.* Munich: Carl Hanser Verlag, 2003. 209–220.

INDEX

ROBERT ERLEWINE is Assistant
Professor in the Department of
Religious Studies at
Illinois Wesleyan University.

Milton Keynes UK
Ingram Content Group UK Ltd.
UKHW011828160823
426985UK00003B/93